PRAISE FOR

THE WEIGHT OF SILENCE

'Occasionally something unexpected happens in the international world of publishing and this is it . . . A force of nature, [Therese] explodes in print . . . It is bold, brave and visually stimulating . . . What she has done and how she has done it is what good and great writing is all about. Yee-ha!' ***The Australian***

'Five stars . . . One of the most compelling childhood memoirs I have ever read . . . It's an unforgettable book that will remind you of many childhood stories that have never been told.' ***Good Reading Magazine***

'A heartfelt, funny and deeply moving memoir about flawed families, unconditional love and growing up too fast but turning out okay anyway.' ***Canberra Times***

'What can you say about a book that articulates a girl's deepest fears after a lifetime of silence? Therese displays the rare and fragile qualities of creativity, intuition and charm . . . She presents her skill as a poet with gentle insights and truisms. This is a book for anyone who has lost themselves or is still looking.' ***Sun Herald***

'A beautifully written chameleon of a book . . . It will perform its way into your heart and mind, then quietly turn itself inside out and reveal its secrets before rushing headlong into the final pages that will leave you holding your breath. A courageous debut.' ***Manly Daily***

'This memoir is a bouquet of dark humour laced with heartbreak and the kind of suburban detail to which we can all relate. Therese has crafted a coming of age reminiscence populated by wonderful characters and suffused with such unblinking honesty . . . A highly worthwhile read from a sharp new Australian voice.' ***Madison Magazine***

'What a book! An extraordinary achievement for a first time Australian author . . . It's a real page turner and difficult to put down. I was just blown away.' ***First Tuesday Book Club***

ALSO BY CATHERINE THERESE

The Weight of Silence

Things She Would have said Herself

CATHERINE THERESE

Published in Australia and New Zealand in 2023
by Hachette Australia
(an imprint of Hachette Australia Pty Limited)
Gadigal Country, Level 17, 207 Kent Street, Sydney, NSW 2000
www.hachette.com.au

Hachette Australia acknowledges and pays our respects to the past, present and future Traditional Owners and Custodians of Country throughout Australia and recognises the continuation of cultural, spiritual and educational practices of Aboriginal and Torres Strait Islander peoples. Our head office is located on the lands of the Gadigal people of the Eora Nation.

Copyright © Catherine Therese 2023

This book is copyright. Apart from any fair dealing for the purposes of private study, research, criticism or review permitted under the *Copyright Act 1968*, no part may be stored or reproduced by any process without prior written permission. Enquiries should be made to the publisher.

A catalogue record for this book is available from the National Library of Australia

ISBN: 978 0 7336 4889 2 (paperback)

Cover design by Christabella Designs
Front cover illustration by Elisa Talentino
Typeset in 12/20 pt Simoncini Garamond by Bookhouse, Sydney
Printed and bound in Australia by McPherson's Printing Group

The paper this book is printed on is certified against the Forest Stewardship Council® Standards. McPherson's Printing Group holds FSC® chain of custody certification SA-COC-005379. FSC® promotes environmentally responsible, socially beneficial and economically viable management of the world's forests.

For Dad,
for everything
all at once, always – and in all ways,
for my beautiful Mum,
my deepest bow
and love
X

What would happen if one woman told the truth of her life?
The world would split open.

MURIEL RUKEYSER

Gracelessly

According to the rules at Leslie Bird's convent school, long hair had to be worn up and away from the face, in case a visage laid bare confessed un-Catholic thoughts. Stray hairs were pinned. Plaits, tails – pony or pig, secured with elastics and ribbon – exposed not only Leslie's doughy little face but her unsightly nape, so a matronly shoulder-length style, upturned collars and polo neck jumpers – a lifetime's penance – was ordained early. Which was difficult for an earnest good girl without a saint's name.

Christened Grace Leslie Maloney, Leslie surrendered her Grace to a classmate in the second grade with the same first and last names. Beautiful and petite with glossy black braids, Grace Anne Maloney appeared more deserving of the title. Ostensibly Leslie's mother agreed with the teacher's suggestion that it would make life easier in the classroom and playground, but her acquiescence was more deeply motivated by the realisation that her second daughter had not been born lovely. On the contrary, her given names said quickly, Graceleslie, seemed to have sealed her fate.

Leslie's father wasn't bothered. He called her Tadpole, for swimming was Leslie's favourite thing in all the world. Darting, diving, floating, stroking; swinging from branches on the banks of the Macquarie River, disappearing underwater, breaking Bathurst's record for holding her breath – one minute, seven seconds. Leslie rode her pushbike to the river, up and out of her seat, with the wind in her hair, practising her times tables and Tarzan calls until her fingers left the handlebars to fidget with her curls to camouflage her neck and spare others' feelings; callous strangers who might be turned off their swim, taunt her, or, worse, whack the fist-sized haemangioma on her neck that resembled the cane toads introduced to the Top End of Queensland the same year of her birth.

When word of the ridicule reached her father, he drove to the river and instructed nine-year-old Leslie – having, it turns out, her last ever swim, hair river-slicked, neck exposed and glistening – to cover herself up quick smart. 'And busy yourself elsewhere.' Leslie's mother suggested that the library was as good a place as any, and, coincidentally, the only public place other than church that she trusted her daughter wouldn't be sullied. So, when all the other kids in town were off squealing and splashing, little Leslie lost and found herself among books.

Sometimes reading and understanding them. Sometimes not. Sometimes just hiding behind their covers as words swirled about her, louder than her own thoughts.

As she grew, books became friends, foes, portals and props. Something for Leslie Bird to hold on to, after shame set upon her so early.

~

From the very first glance, Wallace interpreted Leslie's hair-twirling and downcast eyes as coy and come hither, quite irresistible alongside her bosoms, bookishness and halo of auburn hair. As far as Leslie Bird knew during the long years of marriage in which she always, without exception, stood either behind or beside her husband, Wallace might have only seen what she kept hidden once, in 1959 while courting at Luna Park, when Elvis's 'All Shook Up' sent them toppling up and over the Turkey Trot, tumbling into one another.

'Goodness,' Leslie gushed as a blast of warm air and Wallace, sturdier than she expected, ruffled her skirt, before gravity deposited them both in front of thc hall of funny mirrors, erect.

So taken with the sight of herself, flushed and elongated, with her waist cinched; Leslie fluffed up her hair – exposing her nape.

Wallace gasped.

Two Can Play This Game

DECEMBER 2013

Seeping

AFTERNOON, 20 DECEMBER 2013

There they are, Leslie and Wallace Bird, egg and sperm who spawned five-and-a-half offspring, sitting, waiting in Concord Hospital; Leslie tutting at Christmas bunting draped above triage; clutching the lapels of her navy cable-knit cardigan, left shoulder raised slightly accommodating a bulge beneath her blouse: the portable coagulation device that monitors her blood clotting. A small inconvenience, she's become quite fond of as an appendage, its heft as reassuring as a child on her hip . . . once upon a time.

Reaching into her right pocket, she rubs a small bottle of graphite powder that has a long thin nozzle. Rubbing relieves Leslie Bird. And stops her screaming, *Xmas isn't even a word, you blasphemous fools,* as she sits next to Wallace, whose own blood is leaking, slowly seeping down the back of his trousers as his left hand rummages, trying to unstitch the darning Leslie's inflicted on his pant pockets.

Despite the opposing nature of their blood's behaviour, husband and wife have at least one thing in common – both like to keep their desires close at hand.

Wallace sighs then mumbles something Leslie's learned to ignore, so as not to encourage his ramblings. In the past it was wheat prices, wages or rehearsals for looming confrontations that set him off, but today – and every damn day since retiring from fifty-three years of baking bread – it's right-wing talkback radio and infomercials recycled at a pitch favoured by the hard of hearing and barmaids calling last drinks. Today, ten years after Wallace Bird's last dozen, seventy-nine and senile in an emergency department with the middle finger of his right hand arthritically erect, giving all the world the flip, it's an infomercial he's mumbling: '. . . Olympic divers use it as a towel. Look at that. Completely dry . . . ShamWow.'

Leslie scans the room, as you do when you're sitting alongside a loose cannon, but no one seems to be taking much notice of Wallace's shenanigans, apart from a bottle blonde and her son seated a little way along, and an old bloke sitting opposite who glances up briefly from a sailing magazine he's flicking through. Beside him is a tiny little woman. Sick. Seriously, by the looks of things. Brown bread – almost dead. *Toast*, Wallace would say. Wallace thinks everyone, including and most importantly himself, is a goner whenever they have so much as a sniffle.

She could be seventy or a hundred. Maybe younger? The old bloke's wife. A thin-haired smoker. You can tell by the concertinaed lips, the way he ignores her and the show of scalp, Leslie thinks, fluffing up her own thick curls. But then again maybe not? Leslie has a friend, Pat, about the same age, who smokes like a chimney and has hair so sparse it's hard pressed to hold a bobby pin, and she looks ten years younger.

('Piffle. She looks twenty years younger than you, Les,' Martha had said when Leslie shared her observation. 'It's the sex. Women who never marry or have children still want it and look younger. And skinnier.')

Martha is Leslie's older sister. An exception to her own assumptions. Single. Never sought it or got it. Big. And barren.

('Such an awful word, *barren*, isn't it?' Leslie mused. 'Makes you think of deserts – desert-ed. I wonder if it's Latin?'

Martha nodded. 'It comes from *desertum* – a thing abandoned.'

'Now, now, that's enough of that. Don't go getting all down on yourself.' Leslie chided. 'In our day women too selfish to have children were just called spinsters.')

The tiny sick woman has transparent skin, heart med hued and bruised. Coffin ready. Leslie notes the considerable savings of a child-sized casket and how women over fifty go one of two ways, Kathy Bates or Joan Didion. Bloated like dugongs or whittled.

Personally, Leslie prays for the latter. No. Hopes not prays. One rung back on the kid yourself ladder.

The thought of pallbearers straining beneath her heft had caused her, years before, to shift from butter to margarine; sugar to sweetener; no cheese, if you please; no, thank you, no white bread and jam; except on Sundays in summer after she'd read metabolism sped up through sweating. Still, the way she was going she'd be craned to the altar. (Pews would have to be moved, she told herself as she stood in the Woolies dairy aisle before her old friend, Farmers Thickened Cream.)

The tiny woman's husband is also little, but not emaciated like her. He's roughly shaven. Practical-looking. A taxi driver or pool attendant, someone who knows the ropes; lanes and people.

'They reckon she could be forty by the time she conceives,' the wife tells the husband, pointing to something in the tabloid she's reading. 'See? There's hope for Becky yet!'

The husband doesn't ask who she's speaking about, but the tiny woman answers, as if he has, 'Albert's wife. Charlotte. No. Not Charlotte. Charlene. Olympic swimmer. Short hair. South African. Had her passport confiscated a week before their wedding. Remember how Zoloft-ed she looked at the church in Monte Carlo? She'd just found out Albert had fathered another child. I was sure she'd walk out on him. Or deck him. Broad shoulders, that girl.'

'Albert who?' the husband asks, turning another page of *Offshore Sailing*.

'Such a shame he didn't get his mother's looks,' the tiny woman continues. 'He seemed to, when he was little, before the curse struck. Remember when Stephanie joined the circus and married the elephant trainer who left her for Miss Topless Belgium? And how Caroline's handsome husband died in the speedboat accident? Fool. What did he expect? Princess Grace drove off the cliff and then they all followed. Poor Stephanie – three bastards, her father's messy mouth and nightmares. She was in the car with Grace, you know. Fractured her neck and couldn't go to her own mother's funeral. Imagine that.'

'Imagine,' the husband says, shaking his head and raising his eyebrows at Leslie, who looks around for the nosy parker he seems to be acknowledging before making a show of reaching into her handbag for her library book.

'Remember when Becky had her thumb taped to her pinkie in first grade, so she couldn't hold her pencil? Says here Albert's wife is left-handed. Conceived naturally. I'm going to subscribe to this.' The tiny woman says, 'I wonder what it's called . . .' She flips back to the front cover only to find it's missing. Torn off and folded into Leslie's handbag earlier, after Leslie found a ten-dollar coupon for Puzzle Club on the inside cover. Crosswords are Leslie's armour against dementia. Sudoku too. Puzzle Club delivers door to door.

Leslie leans forwards and says, '*Hello*.'

The tiny woman flinches, looks up at Leslie and responds warily, 'Hello.'

'No, no. Not hello to you.' Leslie laughs. '*Hello* is the name of your magazine. British, I believe. Not that I ever read the tabloids; you see them occasionally at the supermarket checkout, hairdressers and whatnot . . . but I'm more of book person, you see.' Leslie holds up her novel. 'I very rarely go anywhere without one.'

'Suit yourself,' the tiny woman says.

The husband blurts, 'I thought Becky didn't want a baby.'

'Most women don't,' the wife responds, 'until their kids move out of home. What do you think they're going to do?'

'Get a divorce?'

'Not the Grimaldis, you idiot. The doctors. What are they going to do to me today?'

The husband doesn't answer, but carefully dog-ears the page he's on.

Leslie gasps then opens up her book – to the same page she's been on for the past few weeks.

'You're coming in with me, though, aren't you?' the tiny woman asks her husband. When the nurse arrives and escorts her away, the back of her head glows – *bare as a rockmelon*, Leslie thinks, *why wouldn't you wear a hat*?

The husband calls back, 'I'll wait here,' then rolls his magazine into a baton and gently taps it against his thigh, up-nodding in Wallace's direction.

'Becky's the daughter,' Leslie whispers to Wallace, who appears oblivious, sitting with his left hip hitched, leaning as far from her as possible, keeping his options and butt cheeks open.

Too old for another haemorrhoid operation, Wallace Bird has reached a position of inflamed compromise. Moral camouflage. 'Gillard's bloke – what's his name? He'd be proud of me,' he says to Leslie, who shudders at the mere mention of the former prime minister, just as Wallace's bowel spasms and he squeezes his buttocks, as something solid escapes into the nappy that Leslie insisted he wear and he'd begrudgingly agreed to, on the proviso that she wouldn't say a word to the doctors about – well, anything. 'Not a word you hear,' he'd said and Leslie had nodded. 'Not my business what you've been up to or taking.'

Fed up with waiting, Wallace looks at his watch, swivels it around his wrist.

'Tim,' Leslie says, folding her arms across her chest.

'What?' Wallace yells.

'Not what – who. Gillard's boyfriend. The hairdresser telling men to get their prostates checked by little Asian doctors. You'd think he'd fix up her colour.' Leslie glances towards the blonde.

Sitting with his back to Leslie, in his spit-shiny shoes, Wallace wonders if people realise they're husband and wife or just assume he's a dutiful son taking his mother to the hospital. *I'm still a bit of alright*, he thinks to himself, on a good day; he still hears his mother's bias when he looks in the mirror. Not that he doesn't love the old woman beside him ('the most wonderful woman in the world', as he often refers to Leslie in company, ever grateful that her rage has simmered to silence); he just gets surprised – *Jeeeesus Christ* – that this hefty old Bird is his bride. For they looked nothing alike, Leslie now and then; not even related.

The change of life (or *wife*, Wallace joked) besieged Leslie at fifty, settling first upon her vision, so that whenever she looked in the mirror what she saw was so blurry she could easily imagine herself fading away, like the last little row of letters on an eye chart. *C or is it E or G, gosh, I don't know*, Leslie had thought, squinting, who could be bothered? Why they made the letters so tiny was beyond her. A conspiracy, she suspected, like menopause. When she realised the word read pause-o-men backwards, she decided they were out to get her. 'Men. Latin, optometrists,' she'd roar at anyone who asked for an explanation. But no one did.

It wasn't so much that Leslie Bird felt herself fading away as she aged, more that she was disappearing altogether. Not quite dead, but might as well be. Her skin and bones, with minds of their own, rearranging themselves to spite her, as if she'd been born squinting and scowling, bouffant in bifocals and cardigan, no matter the weather. All that had transpired in her life was being etched, year upon year, to reveal this final portrait. Some might say handsome, others terrifying – including Wallace, who wished he could thaw the earlier version of Leslie, frozen in his mind. The green-eyed, auburn-haired beauty he'd said 'I do' to when he was the handsome lad who'd wooed her at the cinema on a double date with Cary Grant and Deborah Kerr in *An Affair to Remember*, with a box of Roses (chocolates, not flowers), twisting the red-and-gold wrapper from her favourite oozy caramel into a ring that he slid upon her finger. When he asked her to do him the honour, right after Deborah Kerr said, 'Anything can happen, don't you think?', Leslie, a sucker for soft centres, said yes.

She – *that* Leslie – was so damn lovely.

Wallace leans towards her and murmurs, 'You can't live without it, ShamWow! Order now and get a second one free.'

Leslie shushes him. Too distracted to read, she puts her book away and grabs a magazine from a pile on her left.

A nurse at reception looks up from her monitor. Looks down again. Answers the phone. 'Emergency?'

'You'll be saying "wow" every time,' Wallace mutters.

The old fella waiting for his wife stands up and moves seats.

Leslie grips on to hers and says, 'See!'

The boy and blonde seated further along grip their seats too; every time Wallace 'wows' and leans, they're rocked forwards and backwards and the boy giggles. Unbeknown to Wallace, their seats are connected at the base to his. And the wistful-looking blonde is recalling her own late father's slow retreat from reality; explaining the vagaries of dementia to the boy. How someone can seem perfectly normal – 'better than normal, they can be brilliant and tender one minute, then batshit crazy the next'. She tells the boy to ignore the old man's rude finger.

Wallace's old rheumy eyes are fixed on them and he's grinning unintentionally; since his last set of ill-fitting dentures made him look like a braying donkey. 'Stop staring,' Leslie would normally say. 'Be quiet. And for goodness sake leave yourself alone.' But not today. Wallace can please himself, for his gawking at a bottle blonde is the least of Leslie Bird's concerns, having left two perfectly good forequarter chops defrosting on the sink at home to follow dopey Dr Olmos's orders to take her seeping husband to hospital: '*immediately!*'

Surveying the rest of the rabble in emergency, Leslie nibbles her little finger, up and down like a corncob, wondering where all the neat and tidy people take their ailments and how much longer they'll have to wait for Wallace to see someone. Letting out a heavy sigh, she rolls her eyes towards the boy and his brassy mother, thinking how much nicer she'd look with less peroxide and cleavage and more eyebrows. Bosoms and brows being just two things on a long list of Leslie's bugbears, growing longer with her years – from dole bludgers and bleeding hearts to left-handers, voters, single mothers, the centre-parted; anyone tattooed not Anglo-Saxon, Catholic, conservative, wavy or short-haired. Boat people, young people and old people also made the list. And don't get Leslie Bird started on her conspiracy theories, or what she saw reported on *Today Tonight*, without a beta blocker or ten close at hand.

Sick of waiting a second longer, she retrieves a biro from her handbag and flips through the magazine, tutting and circling décolletages on almost every page, remembering the day she'd learned that the lovely French word meant *without a collar*, and how she'd called Caroline (her daughter not Princess Grace's) to tell her and all Caroline had to say was: 'So?' *So disappointing.* Leslie shakes her head at the memory then sits up abruptly, looks at the clock on the wall, and elbows Wallace and asks him a little too loudly, 'What do you think's taking her so long?'

'Might have croaked. She didn't look long for it.'

'Not Brown Bread – your daughter. Caroline! Don't tell me you've forgotten she drove us here after all that trouble you got us into – and went off to park – what – over an hour ago?' Leslie fumes. She can just imagine Caroline dawdling in the car park, flirting with strangers.

Wallace smirks. 'No, I didn't forget, but it sounds like you did.' He lowers his voice to a whisper. 'You might want to keep it down a bit, love. Don't want to go making a scene.'

What Leslie wants is to kill him. Not *kill him* kill him. Just kill him so he shuts up.

Gripping her biro and magazine she draws arrows from the circled bosoms and writes, *Can you believe it?* and *Disgusting* in the margins – without dotting the i's, having learned her lesson. Yes indeed. Leslie Bird has learned how a tiny dot can inadvertently become a pen stabbing the page, revealing a rage you've spent seventy odd years concealing. How it's always the tiniest of things that expose you – a door ajar, a word underlined, a Bic tip making confetti of Kim Kardashian's bosoms; though Leslie was almost certain she'd been cleared as a suspect in the defacing of her daughter Bernadette's *Who* magazine's Most Beautiful cover. How 'beautiful' could be used to describe such a blousy antonym as a Kardashian was still beyond her. Beautiful was a word Leslie Bird cherished. Bestowed sparingly. Mary Tyler Moore. Pam Ayres. Women with thick hair, high morals and necklines. Like herself.

Having hidden the *Who* beneath other trash on Bernadette's coffee table, she'd wagered it would go unnoticed, just like her opinions, but the paper spots of the reality star clung stubbornly to her navy woollen skirt, giving rise to accusations of vandalism that Leslie carefully brushed aside, exclaiming it wouldn't be the first time she had left her youngest's house feeling a little dotty – before pausing for effect and glancing at her daughter's three daughters, whom she couldn't call grand or look at without feeling duped by their father, Amir. The memory incited a rage that tightened her jowls, making Leslie Bird feel unsure of who she hated more: Amir, Wallace, Julia Gillard or – 'Caroline! Look, there she is!' Leslie tears up at the sight of her middle daughter. Her transport and translator. 'Did you manage to get a park? Your father was worried sick. Weren't you?' Leslie flicks Wallace's pocket with the magazine. 'Worried his chops would go off and about that – that floosy over there, weren't you, Wal? Couldn't keep his eyes off her.' Leslie motions with her head towards the blonde.

Caroline takes a deep breath, shrugs apologetically at the blonde and sits down, as Leslie launches into her Grace Kelly, Brown Bread and Becky story, a nurse calls out, 'Mr Bird?'

'Oh, that would be right.' Leslie sighs.

Caroline stands up and offers her father her arm.

'Becky couldn't have a baby,' Leslie continues, pressing her tongue into the side of her cheek. 'Couldn't or wouldn't? I've said to your father some women just aren't cut out to be mothers.'

'Is that right?' Caroline scoffs, as Wallace hauls himself up and shakes out his long legs.

Leaning heavily on Caroline they squelch away for his prostate exam, leaving Leslie to stew about them looking like twins from the waist down, and how no one ever cares one iota about anything she has to say.

With the excuse of needing to stretch, she stands up, walks a few steps, then sits herself back down further along the row, until she's right beside the blonde, who turns and asks her, ever so kindly, how her day is going.

'Oh, hello there!' Leslie says, acting surprised, before asking her what she made of the tiny woman.

Half an hour passes before Caroline returns, alone, and Leslie asks accusingly, 'Where's your father?'

Caroline throws her handbag to the floor. Creaks her neck. 'He's in the toilet, getting himself sorted after he –'

Leslie cuts her off. 'I was just telling Sharon . . . this is Sharon,' she introduces her new best friend. 'I was just telling Sharon . . . now what was I telling you? No, don't tell me! I know. I was saying how desperately I need to get my colour done too! Oh and we were talking about the Grimaldis, weren't we!' Leslie taps Sharon's leg.

'Actually, you were telling me how proud you are of your daughter. How lucky you are having a doctor for a daughter,' Sharon says, smiling at Caroline. 'I can't imagine how thrilling that must be.'

'Neither can she.' Caroline glares at Leslie, incredulous her mother is perpetuating this myth about her older sister Shelley – here – in a hospital, of all places. 'Seriously, Mum?'

Leslie hums, then tilts her head to the side. 'People said they were arguing right before she died.'

'Who?' Caroline and Sharon ask in unison.

'Grace and Stephanie.' Leslie shakes her head. 'Stephanie wanted to marry a racing car driver – the actor's son – what's his name? You know the one. And Grace wouldn't have it. The poor thing was probably just trying to talk sense into her when they went off the cliff.

'Belmondo – that's it!' Leslie Bird exclaims, looking pleased with herself.

Tapping

MID-MORNING, 20 DECEMBER 2013

Wallace Bird has been shitting himself for most of his life. Long before Nu-Lax and nappies there was Senokot and beer, and before that a long line of brutal bastards, from the Christian Brothers at school to his father at home, to his uncle, who scared more shit out of Wallace in death than in life, after jumping from a church tower and splattering himself all over Wallace's primary schoolyard, bequeathing him both nightmares and callused hands – from the wood he took to cutting at ten, for his widowed aunty and cousins, left to shiver through Grenfell's winters.

Then there was Dr Needs, who yanked out all of Wallace's teeth at fifteen – without anaesthetic. *As you do – did – in the name of preventative dentistry.* And Father Frank, whom words fail to approximate, because some things are best left unsaid – aren't they? – to stop them being made real again and again. And then there was Sammy O'Sullivan's mother Merle, the old biddy, who could turn your bowels to water with a mere glance. And perhaps most terrifying of all, Wallace's beloved bride, Leslie Bird.

~

'If you were living in America, you could buy three pints. Blood's brokered, less regulated than poultry or pretzels,' Dr Olmos declares, circling numbers on Wallace's blood counts. 'But not here, folks. Here it's first in, best dressed, so you'd better get yourselves to hospital to find out the cause of this deficit. Any questions, Mr Bird? . . . Mr Bird?'

Leslie covers her mouth to stifle a snigger as she watches the rangy doctor, with his toffy coif, squint and tap at his computer and address her husband as if he were a normal person. A person who might answer a question. A person not hiding the source of his blood loss.

'Mr Bird?'

Wallace stares at the floor, thinking of stars and stripes. Of red, white and blue. Deficits. Profits. The opening riff of Glenn Miller's 'In the Mood'.

'Wallace!' Leslie elbows him.

'What?' Wallace startles.

'The doctor wants to know if you have any questions,' Leslie speaks in a slow, loud voice – the same voice she'd once used potty training their children – rolling her eyes at Dr Olmos, pinching her left earlobe, she mouths the word *deaf*. Then waits for an acknowledgement. A nod, a wink, an eyebrow lift to indicate the doctor knows what she has to put up with – *What we're dealing with here, 'folks'*, she wants to say to him. But there is nothing, nada, not a single twitch as he waits for Wallace. *As if he has all the time in the world, not a house to clean or dinner to prepare. Of course,* Leslie thinks, *another stupid man*, as Wallace finally blusters forth.

'I'll give you a question, doc – have you ever been to America?'

The doctor nods. 'Yes, yes I have. And you?'

'Nah . . . Always wanted to go – to say thanks, you know – but the missus won't fly. Will you, love?'

'What a load of rubbish,' Leslie snaps. 'It's not that I won't, it's that I *can't*. Not after what happened when –'

'Any other questions, Mr Bird?' Dr Olmos interrupts.

Wallace shrugs. 'Now that you mention it, doc, why do me feet burn at night? I can't sleep because me feet burn.'

'Your feet burn, Mr Bird?'

'Huh?' Wallace looks confused.

'Your feet burn, Mr Bird.'

'What are you, a fortune-teller?' Wallace looks at Doctor Olmos in awe.

Doctor Olmos presses on the bridge of his glasses and rubs the length of his nose repeatedly, as one might a magic lamp – praying for patience?

'Let's see, Mr Bird. Do your feet tingle? Do you have pins and needles?'

'I'll say they do!' Wallace turns to Leslie. 'The man's a genius.'

'Do they only burn when you're in bed or when you're sitting? Would you like to tell me more?'

'Would I what!' Wallace wants to buy this man a beer.

'Tell me about the pain, Mr Bird.'

Oh, the pain, Leslie thinks, *I'll tell you who's the pain.*

Folding her arms, pushing back against her seat, readying for Wallace's sob story, she begins tapping her feet, pedalling out the organ chords of 'Holy, Holy, Holy Lord' completely unaware of the transaction about to take place between doctor and patient.

'Tell me how they ache, Mr Bird?'

There it is *ache*. Kerching!

More than its meaning, the little word's sonorous vowel sound seems to restore Wallace's hearing and awaken memories that have hibernated in his amygdala, during the long winter of his marriage. Wide-eyed, he blinks, ready to take on the world – in the same way Leslie would, if she heard the word repulsive. He sits himself upright and speaks directly.

'Oh, they ache alright, doc. They ache all night, from me head to me toes. They ache to Billy-o. When I was a young fella, me mother'd toss another dog on the bed, keepin' the home fires burnin', I guess, with the old man off gallivantin' God knows where. I couldn't get to sleep and then I wake up in agony – don't I, love?'

Leslie ignores him. 'Go on tell him,' Wallace implores her. 'Tell the doc how ya – how I – you know – wake up me bride with me moaning.'

Feigning indifference after the doctor's slight, Leslie thinks, *Two can play this game* and taps her feet even faster, racking her brain for the name of a movie, that starred Jim Carrey, whom she normally couldn't bear, but thought was brilliant in. Drawing a blank, she shrugs and glances out of the window, to a troupe of swaying gums; clears her throat and deadpans, 'It's not your moaning. It's your snoring that wakes me – Wallace.'

Something passes between them when Leslie calls Wallace – Wallace. Something old. New. Borrowed. Black. The way she says it. She never says it. She says *my husband*, *him*, *you*, *your*. She bandies the imperative and Wallace gets the gist, except for a few years of confusion after the last of the kids left home, when Leslie said something like 'Get off,' and Wallace looked around and said, 'Me?' And genuinely meant it.

It took time to recalibrate from a household of six to two.

Two people rarely apart, most days barely speaking. Leslie nudging Wallace with an elbow or look, and when she does need to address him – say, if she's in the bathroom and the phone's ringing and he refuses to answer it, because answering the phone is women's business; wives, daughters, assistants – she might be forced to call out, 'Answer that, will you, Wal?'

Though she despised diminutives, for as long as Leslie had known Wallace, she'd shortened his name to Wal, as lengthening it seemed to summon his simple mother, who'd fawned and proclaimed him in public as Wallace Albert Bird, until he married, when she took to calling him Bertie, her pet name for him in private and reminding Leslie that Bertie meant noble and bright and that she would always be the first woman in Wallace's life. 'So don't go getting any big ideas about replacing me,' went the smothering that gave him the deluded impression of his own worth and left Leslie living with a numbskull, arousing in her a fierce determination that spared rods and cloying love would never ruin her own children. The ingrates.

'Your feet, Mr Bird?' the doctor prompts, but Wallace is now decades away, his thoughts having drifted back to America – the big brass brother and soundtrack of his 1940s childhood. Swanky and doughboys they called the soldiers for their *yes, sir, no, ma'am* manners and uniform, but to a teenage apprentice baker, in Grenfell, New South Wales, (only child of an adoring mother and absent father) in love with the freckles on the nose of his best friend's sister, Yanks would always be the ones you could count on. Pause for gratitude, awe and sorrow.

'Wallace!' Leslie raises her voice, reaching out to prod him.

'Ah, forget it.' Wallace waves his arms, almost striking her. 'They're my flamin' feet and they burn to bejesus.' But as he says it, he looks down at his shoes and feels his toes curl inside them – in retreat – he offers faintly. 'But I guess they're not really burning, are they, doc?'

'Probably not,' the doctor agrees.

Leslie smiles. *Dumb and Dumber*, that was the name of the film, and her favourite scene was when the imbeciles got stuck licking a pole together.

'Most likely it's your circulation, Mr Bird – not enough blood getting to your feet.'

Wallace, only hearing, 'Get to your feet,' stands up as straight as his hip replacement will allow, then licks his fingertips and grooms his eyebrows, feeling as woozy as any old bloke missing half his blood, hearing and marbles, swaying beside his secret keeper of half a century; certifications from this and that university looking down on him from the walls of the surgery as one of the incessant voices inside of his head – Jed Clampett, the old fella from *The Beverley Hillbillies* – snipes, 'A nice young feller, but if brains was lard, he wouldn't grease too big a pan,' making Wallace Bird feel a complete and utter idiot. A has-been. Never was. Or will be. A man standing to attention when he should be sitting.

Leslie watches him, thinking, *Who are you? You strange, strange man.*

As the doctor continues his assessment, she turns her gaze to the carpet and spots a bit of it bunched up beneath a leg of his desk and begins wriggling about in her seat, to see if she can smooth it out; when the words of a poet, scrawled inside a Mother's Day card, suddenly return to her, 'I know her so well she's a complete and utter mystery to me.' *No.* Leslie shrugs. She didn't understand them anymore now than when her eldest, Shelley, had dispensed them last year; over a lunch of steaming ramen, so pungent it had reminded Leslie of a gummy sock she'd once found tangled in her sixteen-year-old son Michael's sheets, the last time she ever changed them.

The quote seemed cruel then. And even crueller now to Leslie, who wondered who the 'I', the 'her' and the 'she', were, that Shelley had scribbled about. And all those questions rolled into statements with no punctuation, not to mention her horrid penmanship?

'Slant,' Shelley had termed it. Not the excuse for handwriting, but the way of telling someone something. 'Tell it slant,' she'd said, as she swivelled her chopsticks from pork to pointing at Leslie, whose hip joints ached deeply from perching on a grey plastic crate, having her gabardine-ed bottom fossil-ed, while a French bulldog pulling on its lead licked at her bunion; soaked in stock that had slopped from her blue and white bowl, when she'd spat back a fleshy dumpling that had detonated boiling water, scorching her tongue and blistering the roof of her mouth for the next week.

Tell it slant – my foot! Leslie Bird thought, as she set to straightening out the last wrinkle of the doctor's carpet. *I hate dogs, the inner city. Asian food. Aside from curried prawns and spring rolls, especially the Ho-Mai frozen variety, and find it the height of hypocrisy that a daughter of mine could quote poetry, sounding as if she possesses an understanding of the world and not consider, for a single second, sentencing her poor old mother to a stinking ordeal in a hell hole of a suburb, when I'd rather have been sitting at home with a knife and fork, white bread and folk. Wallace even!*

It surprised Leslie Bird, just how much she missed him. Then and now. Her eyes welled up.

Sit down, you big silly fool, she wants to say to him, when Dr Olmos walks out from behind his desk to coax Wallace back onto his chair.

'Please take a seat, Mr Bird.'

'Thanks. Gee. Thanks a lot, doc. Gosh.'

Wallace is terribly moved by the doctor's helping hand. By his overwhelming kindness. More than kindness. Fondness. The man understands him. Ache and pain. *Jeez, he might even like me* Wallace thinks. When the doctor turns his back for a moment, he says to Leslie, 'Did you see him reach out to me, Les, and help me sit back down? Clearly didn't want me to leave.'

'Clearly,' Leslie says, shaking her head.

The doctor resumes his inquiries. 'Now, Mrs Bird?'

'Yes, doctor?' Leslie blushes beneath his gaze.

'Do *you* have a question?'

'Do I have a question?'

Leslie daren't speak the truth, feeling it isn't her place or appropriate – appropriateness being an attitude she holds dear, as a lone practitioner in an inappropriate world. And then there is the whole business of being an accessory to Wallace's acts or omissions. And, if she's honest, all that talk of haemoglobin, America, platelets and ranges made Wallace sound less husband, more experiment, to Leslie, so it was difficult to know what to say in response to such international numerical matters. And what with Wallace staying silent on the matter of his missing blood, shrugging when Dr Olmos had asked after his stools, stomach and diet; what he'd been up to or taking, even after Leslie gave Wallace her raised eyebrows, 'speak up you idiot' look, which he failed to respond to; claiming later, when she demonstrated it again, not to have noticed it – and how if he had, he might have thought she were constipated.

That her husband of fifty-odd years did not understand the intimate gestures or value the charades of marriage only cemented Leslie Bird's sense of being utterly alone in it. Alone and yet always with him, retirement binding them at the arthritic hips in a three-legged race to the grave – via the hospital, where the doctor insisted, they go – immediately!

'Oh no, doctor, I haven't got a single question.' Leslie taps her feet. 'But do you know if there's parking at the hospital? Do they take Medicare? Will they know to expect us? *What should we say when we get there? Is there a cafeteria? Does it have egg and lettuce sandwiches?* What are the opening hours?' *Tap, tap.*

For all her righteous bearing, Leslie Bird's heel-and-toe tapping is less of a sign of her frustrations and more an echo of what remained in her body after three decades of church organ playing, before being replaced by a 'convert', no less, with a guitar, drum kit and PowerPoint presentation. With the rest of her thickened, given up and over to age, something beautiful and girly lingered in Leslie Bird's elegant ankles, pivoting in third position, to music that once soared from beneath her pedals, up into the organ pipes and out in ecclesial ecstasy. When her left foot struck a low C, and an apocalyptic grumble stirred the least devout heavenwards, Leslie had felt herself to be a conduit; the lead rider, pedalling the congregation towards the pearly gates, pounding at St Peter's portico, before soundlessly lowering the keyboard lid and returning to her pew, to study fellow parishioners' fat bottoms and crowns from over the tops of her cat's-eye glasses. She mouths 'Peace be with you,' and means you; you the peloton, this community she's accompanied, inspected and not spoken a single word to for thirty years. Leslie's toe-tapping is an act of self-soothing. Not that she's aware.

~

At some time down the track, say, when proclivities are reminisced, she may look indignantly at Caroline – it's always Caroline stirring things up – and say, 'What foot-tapping? Excuse me. I do not.'

Leslie loathed others reminiscing, which intruded on her ownership of the past. Her feet, who did or said what – the 'facts', as she recalled them – were her business and not to be tampered with. Busybodies. They bothered her as much as Wallace's Lana and squeaky doorjambs, for which she carried in her pocket at all times a bottle of graphite powder to secretly squeeze into locks and hinges, all the while oblivious that her own shrill emissions and greasing obsession were fodder for the family. On the contrary, Leslie Bird saw herself as discreetly easing tensions, in modest servitude of serenity. 'After all, a creaking door is enough to drive you spare.'

The Lubricator, her brood branded her behind her back.

Leslie's third-born (she would argue her fourth) Michael, forty-five, a sentimental loafer with menopausal hips, sleep apnoea and a chihuahua named Trevor, officiated an Instagram site named @SHELLBEBACK that featured a profile picture of Leslie's freshly set head atop Arnold Schwarzenegger's bulky body. It had 349 followers and counting, a broad church that included her local priest, Father Carmelo, chaser of skirts and conversions, who'd once motioned Leslie into the presbytery moments before mass on the pretext of discussing the day's selection of hymns, only to speak instead of his favourite work of art, Bernini's sculpture of St Theresa. 'Do you know it?' Leslie didn't, but nodded. 'Yes, of course, Father.' 'It's orgasm, don't you agree? The open mouth, closed eyes, arrow plunging, pure ecstasy?' he said, thrusting a well-thumbed art history tome and Mediterranean hips towards Leslie's lap. Leslie fled.

So, there was him on the list of Instagram followers, and Caroline, Bernadette, Shelley, Lana and their families and Wallace's best friend Bob Savage. Five Borneo wildlife volunteers, three social workers from St George Hospital, two physios from Windsor Uniting Care, Martha, the entire staff of Ryde City Library and Bird Bakehouse, including Ron (Wallace's hirsute retired Richmond store manager) whom Leslie despised for his chest-length beard and prepositions, which he had a habit of placing at the end of a sentence. 'What are you doing that for?' he would query apprentices and Leslie, popping in and out to do the bakery's books, would explode, 'It's not *what*, Ron – it's *why* – with no *for* on the end. You can simply ask "Why are you doing that?"' 'To shit you – no end – that's what for,' Ron grumbled. Poor Ron was now in rehab following a stroke that left him with only the slightest movement in his right pinkie, which his physios strengthened by holding his phone, encouraging him to like Instagram posts, until he could finally poke one on his own. In no time Ron became @shellbeback's number one liker, just ahead of Leslie's brood, their partners, and her grandchildren; who made Leslie feel feted, following her about snapping pictures. 'I wonder if this is how Lady Diana felt?' she asked Wallace once, when posing as if she wasn't – knitting, darning, turning the bed down, ironing, wiping up.

Unbeknownst to Leslie the photographs were forwarded to their favourite Uncle Michael, who would copy, paste and post to the site, so they could all hashtag Arnold Schwarzenegger's infamous lines, #gettothechopper #itsshowtime. Prized, of course, were photos of Leslie actually caught lubricating hinges, guarding her pocket, unscrewing, recapping, closing a door; #hastalavistababy. The post that scored the most likes – 247 and counting – was a picture of Leslie bending over with her big firm Mrs Doubtfire bottom in the air and a look of horror on her powdery face, as she's caught squeezing graphite into a doorjamb, tube in hand, cap in teeth. It was captioned #tohellwityou.

One day when he was nimble enough Ron would make it his screen saver. He was not alone. Leslie's rear spread far and wide, eventually appearing on the screens of even her most trusted allies, Martha and Jo-Dee Lane, Leslie's hairdresser, to whom Leslie extended uncustomary benevolence in exchange for the secret business they shared at Jo-Dee's salon basin.

There, stripped of her glasses and dignity; dripping wet, the angry fist-sized haemangioma at the base of Leslie Bird's neck was revealed, lumpen and warty, untouched since childhood, when her sister Martha carefully brushed her locks to avoid rupturing the blood vessels that multiplied despite courses of cortisone that left Leslie with a permanent sense of cushioning, anxiety and an amphibian attached to her person for all but an hour and a half every six weeks for the past fifteen years, when Jo-Dee's simple, kind presence allayed her distress. And for that Leslie Bird was grateful. Very grateful. Willing even to overlook the dopey girl's dubious lifestyle, partner Alex, open-toed sandals, hyphen and double e.

~

Leslie continues tapping her feet in time with Doctor Olmos's typing, the two of them back-up percussion to Wallace's internal heckles. *The world's only living brain donor* – tap, tap – *first-class drongo* – tap – *bloody galah.*

Wallace glares at Leslie as if it were all her fault. All of it. In fact, these days he finds it hard to think of anyone who doesn't contribute to his constant feeling of failure.

Amir and Viktor, his sons-in-laws had been on his side, before they buggered off, during what Leslie describes as the Birds' very own anni horribilis – the years between 2009 and the present – when the family imploded and grief blurred time.

Oh, and there was Doug, dutiful Doug, Wallace's right-hand man, head baker of forty years and captain of their darts team, whose cat-loathing missus, Nelly, had him so under the thumb that Doug favoured hiding out in his shed, hammering away at his fingers with a mallet, in the hope of winding up back in hospital where he'd be fussed over, given three square meals a day, for crying out loud. Doug declared, 'No nagging or bashings.' Even the tea ladies had a manner of making Doug feel a certain way, he thought Wallace, with his own share of misery, would understand. It wasn't self-sabotage but preservation that landed him instead in the funny farm, walking about with his fingers aloft, like antennae. Until one day he skipped out on a group activity and a search party was dispatched to look for Doug and a polypropylene rug that went missing at the same time. The rug was later located rolled up on the back verandah – with Doug inside, seeping into the pile – dead from a bullet by his own hand. Tucked inside his top pocket were the title deeds of his house, transferred in full to a local cat shelter, Moggie's Rescue.

'Guess he had the last Meow,' Wallace said to Bob (Bullseye) Savage, who not only had had Wallace's back but inherited Doug's captaincy of their darts team, SAWTI (Sexy and We Throw It), at the local pub. It was Bob who suggested Wallace start calling his two sons-in-laws Amir and Viktor, instead of The Muslim and The Kraut, and invite them to flesh out their team numbers after Doug's death hit them both hard. And in no time the four of them were competing, speaking the same language – clickety-clack, black eye, diddling, yes boss, no boss – over schooners, scorching pies and claims by Wallace that he and Bob had mixed marriages too.

'Not that I'm a poofter or nothin', I'm sure you blokes have plenty of squabbles with me daughters over what to put in the lunchbox and the like; but I reckon the real "mixed" marriage is living with a sheila full time.'

'Too right,' Bob, the snowy-bearded bard, agreed with Wallace.

Savage by name, lamb by nature, more likely to resuscitate than hurt a fly, Bob Savage was known to carry water bowls and sleeping bags beneath the tarp on his ute to comfort strays. He ran the local service station and turned his hand to anything mechanical, motorbikes, tractors, hair straighteners, and fixing things, including himself. A legend in spare parts, dressing up as Santa Claus in the heat of summer, working the bowsers, selling raffle tickets, lending his lap to the Children's Hospital to hear wish lists and hold back tears, until 7-Eleven bought out the garage and he hung up his white overalls and was replaced by a Sunil who asked too many questions with a Californian accent, which shit Wallace no end.

'They study sitcoms for idioms, words to woo us into their two-for-one offers, bread and milk, lattes and Krispy Kremes – they've even installed a slushy machine,' Bob said.

Bob told Wallace over a beer that he ought to volunteer for something, to keep himself from 'atrophying', just as he'd done, joining motoring associations and Rotary, and even flying to a Toastmasters conference on the Gold Coast, returning with a new gait and a business card that read:

Bob Savage
A Real Good Bloke and Facilitator

The card wasn't Bob's only souvenir. He also brought back a pair of sunburnt ears which propagated the melanoma that would cause a traffic jam in Newport at his funeral; in a send-off that would have made the big man proud. Attended by such luminaries as the glamorous local member, pigeon-breasted Bronwyn Bishop, Toastmasters impromptu hall of famer Mandy Weir, and Matt Roach, the boss of Bob's adoring daughter, who gave the funniest and most moving eulogy anyone had ever heard or ever will again, as pictures of her and her mother wearing tit slogan t-shirts, sitting on the back of a ute at the Bathurst 500, flashed up behind Bob's coffin.

Wallace had struggled with Bob's popularity and big words – sitcom, idiom, facilitator. The way Bob had pronounced 'a-trophy-ing' took Wallace back sixty years to Grenfell, standing beside his best friend Sammy O'Sullivan, holding St Joseph's under-13's footy shield.

Wallace looked up the meaning of Bob's atrophying – wither, deteriorate, degenerate – so he could drop it later in conversation, but didn't, couldn't, having become its definition. Bob had been so loved by all, that Wallace had felt his own light fade in the vicinity of his wattage and vocabulary, and so let their friendship dim, ignoring Bob's calls, including the articulate messages and sympathy he'd left on the answering machine that Toby, Caroline's husband, had installed, after shit hit the fan with Amir and Viktor, not long before Bob's own death. After which, Wallace took to staying home with the dictionary feeling sorry for himself, yelling, 'A man doesn't need no pity from no one,' at Leslie, the TV, the Foxtel remote and the phone when it rang out, beeped and announced their accidental greeting:

'Way you go, Wal. Say something.'

'What?'

'I don't know. It's your contraption.'

'What the hell? Hello . . .'

'Tell it you're not here.'

'But I am . . . Jesus Christ . . .'

The phone rang day and night after word spread of the Birds' message duel, but the only messages left were anonymous giggles and requests for miracles. 'I've got five loaves and fishes and was wondering if . . .' questions and orders from their jostling middle-aged children, 'Are you there? Mum. Dad. Mum. Are you there? Jesus. Pick uuuuup.'

Wallace wondered if there was one person still on his side. If Toby buying the answering machine might mean that at least he thought he was still a bit of alright in the head and still had friends who might call and was here for a few years yet?

He said it before and he'll say it again of his only remaining son-in-law: 'I know he knows I'm a dickhead, but he's never let on.'

Wallace Bird
Dickhead and Bloody Grateful

So much like my own bumbling parents, Dr Olmos thinks of his elderly patients, grateful for their inability to comprehend, respond and formulate questions; he finishes collating Wallace's medical history to give to his secretary so she can prepare a report for them to take to the hospital, as Leslie continues tapping her feet and Wallace mumbles about the US of A and Brave Bertie, then burps his stupid dentures back and forth, a grotesque habit he'd acquired during their settling-in phase, when his pale lips struggled to enclose them. Tilting his chin upwards, he rubs his throat and swallows over a great big lump in it – *Glenn Miller missing in action* – and hisses at Leslie, 'What are you gawking at?'

'No idea.' Leslie shakes her head. 'None at all.'

'Okay, folks, you're all set to go. And when you get to the hospital, don't forget to go in through emergency so you'll be seen sooner.' Dr Olmos opens the door for them and points towards reception.

Wallace hobbles out in front, leaving Leslie with a view of a claret stain blooming on the back of his trousers. *Like a Rorschach ink blot test,* she thinks, followed by, *What a mess. And Australia bleeding into Indonesia.*

Then: *Breadcrumbs.*

If she crumbed the forequarter chops she'd left defrosting in the kitchen at home, Wallace would be none the wiser if they were on the nose tomorrow.

She adds breadcrumbs to her mental shopping list. Then Preen.

~

Too upset to drive, Wallace throws Leslie his keys. Begrudgingly she catches them and agrees to take the wheel on one condition: that he lift himself up and onto the towel she's furiously placing beneath him on to her seat. Having to travel with towels in the first place enrages Leslie Bird, for it's nothing, she thinks, but Wallace's stupidity that makes them a necessity and him increasingly dependent.

She takes a deep breath, inserts the key in the ignition and pleads with him to perch as lightly as possible. He nods as she drives slowly forwards, clutching his seatbelt, then begins gesturing wildly, bellowing directions, 'Not here. Here!' and making demented declarations about the 'good sort' back at reception being more than a secretary if charged with report writing; thereby, elevating himself to a subject worthy of respect before belching so loudly that his teeth eject making Leslie swerve and Wallace lurch and grab the wheel and blast the horn at the bloke behind them blowing his, when the boom gate rises and falls on the Camry's bonnet before Leslie reverses as Wallace commands her to 'Move the fucking thing' and reinsert the parking ticket which spat out and vanished, between Leslie's whispered petitions for her husband's profanity and the door jammed against the ticket machine.

Failing to find it, Leslie freezes.

'What are you waiting for?' Wallace screams. 'Pretzels?'

Leslie looks at him. Really looks at him. Takes off her seatbelt. Gets out of the car. And walks away.

Anni Horribilis

2009–2013

Fuck Love

'Are you okay there, Lesy? Neck comfy? Water warm enough?'

Leslie Bird nods, as she never feels kindlier towards the world than when her neck's aching, jammed up against the salon basin, while having her comfort questioned by Jo-Dee Lane, her hairdresser, who speaks to Leslie as if she isn't a disfigured frump but something else. Someone else. A woman without her eyes shut tight and an ugly secret. Someone whose opinion might even be valued, so much so that, more than once, Leslie Bird found herself too choked up to answer and feigned nodding off and waking up, just as her temples were dabbed and her head gently wrapped in a warm black towel that Jo-Dee Lane carefully folded origami-style around Leslie's face and neck to conceal what is never mentioned.

In fact, the cane toad squatting on Leslie Bird's neck is all but forgotten when she huddles inside the bonnet dryer, gazing at herself at a safe distance from the mirror. Her big old face framed by black and her eyebrows, the age-defying auburn eaves rising above her vanishing lips, deepening jowls and marionette lines. What an awful, awful word, Leslie thinks: *marionette.* What could be worse than being called a puppet? And yet that is exactly what she feels like, bombarded day and night by PC rubbish and her thankless children telling her what not to say and do. Leslie opens and closes her mouth. *Puppet.* Shudders. Squints at her reflection, thinking, *I look just like my aunt Louise. And my uncle Earl. Oh dear. Or an astronaut? A nun? I could have been one. Should have been one. Well, Wallace took care of that.* Leslie gathers the towel in closer around her face and makes the sign of the cross then sees herself as a Muslim and shouts, 'Goodness!'

Jo-Dee rushes over to see if she is okay. Lifts the bonnet dryer.

Leslie waves her away. Pulls the towel off and looks in the mirror – this time she sees an old woman who may have just been swimming and towelled her hair. *Oh my*, she thinks, *it must be sixty-seven years since I've swum.* She pats her chest with one hand while holding the other in the air, taking a moment to recompose, before swallowing and asking, 'How is he?'

Jo-Dee looks confused. 'He who?'

'Alex!' Leslie tuts. 'Your boyfriend.' No matter what people say, Leslie Bird is determined to enforce the correct gender.

'She's okay,' Jo-Dee says, inspecting Leslie's colour, rubbing at her regrowth. 'Still sore. But more herself every day. Amazing breasts! You should see them. Let's get you rinsed now, Lesy.'

'Yes, let's.' Bewildered, Leslie stands up, walks the few steps to the basin and plonks herself down.

'Can you move back a bit, Lesy? Sit up a little higher? Sorry, darling, but I don't want to get you wet. Just tilt your head back a little more. That's it.'

'That's it alright.' Leslie tries not to moan as the edge of the basin presses into her vertebra and Jo-Dee prattles on about her partner Alex's life as an editor at a posh publishing house and his/her own underpants during recent traumatic reassignment surgery.

Amid pondering prepositions and the disposal of certain body parts – whether they are grafted to a recipient or transplanted like her grandmother's aspidistras, crudely cut and re-potted, Leslie doesn't like to ask – as Jo-Dee massages her haemangioma-ed terrain, she also wonders why people no longer say husband, wife, boyfriend or girlfriend. If it's easier to leave a partner than a spouse or friend? Perhaps partner paired with divorce, is a get out of gaol free card, the old titles too full of obligation for the average bed hopper? Leslie Bird supposes that Jo-Dee may be on to something though, endorsing Alex's suggestion that art critics are snipers taking pot shots from the arts pages and that short listings are related to the length of one's temper and fringe, since three of Alex's brooding star authors became Jo-Dee's clients, requesting their bangs be trimmed back almost to the hairline in a style that makes Leslie shudder and think of fools, nude emperors, cracked mirrors and bloody foreheads. Twitchy dumb kids; her own – Michael, ten, dawdling from his bedroom clutching a pair of scissors in his porky fingers, claiming not to know who'd hacked off his hair and half an eyebrow. Even after she guided (not grabbed) him by the neck and pushed (not shoved) him towards the bathroom vanity.

'What are you insinuating? That I'd harm my own flesh and blood? It was an accident!' she'd repeated at the hospital to the parade of stethoscope-ed busybodies hell bent on interrogating her. 'The boy simply tripped and hit his head while I was trying, as any responsible parent would, to show him the consequences of his actions.' *Look what you've done to my mirror!* Even with blood dripping and the doctor stitching, Michael refused to accept that he was at fault. All he could do was shrug, and so it seemed did Leslie, right there and then giving up on her sloppy jalopy son, predicting he would never amount to anything more than a fool in emergency. A lie person. Not that she'd ever say so. Or use the word 'liar' – or 'hate', for that matter.

'I've always loved a short fringe myself, so neat and tidy,' Leslie hears herself say to Jo-Dee, the exact opposite of what she's thinking about Alex's authors. More often than not these days, when lost for words, she hears herself saying 'poor thing' about everyone and everything, not least Jo-Dee's Alex. In addition, and at complete odds with her disdain for swearing and acronyms, she also catches herself thinking, *WTF?* Some days it's all that loops through her mind, as if life for Leslie Bird has become this one awful unanswerable question.

The first time she'd heard it – through Bernadette – she thought her daughter had said WWF and asked her if she remembered her brother wearing a red-and-yellow bandana and cheering on Hulk Hogan and the other man . . . what was his name?

'Andre the Giant? WTF, Mum?' Bernadette had said.

And when Leslie asked what it meant she felt the rush of confusion, humiliation and revulsion her children evoked.

As Jo-Dee jabbers on at the basin, Leslie makes a mental list to jot down later and consider: *father/son lying gene, Miles Franklin, LGBTI.* Listing while listening helps Leslie to endure the graphic description of Alex's hideous-sounding surgery; the estrogen injections, penile inversion, the endless dilations of the new 'vagy', as Jo-Dee calls the vagina, making Leslie cringe, cross her legs and think of folding socks and breakfast spreads in her mother's dank kitchen; where yeast once rose beneath lace doilies weighted with the same cheap tiny blue stones as the many rings on the fingers working conditioner into her scalp.

'The thing is to keep it expanding,' Jo-Dee Lane says, pressing deeply into Leslie's pressure points, 'or it might collapse or lose its length.'

Vagymite. Vagy-might-not? Leslie thinks to herself, then says, 'Seriously? Oh dear. Oh no. Really? Dear oh dear. I mean. I can't believe . . . How did the . . . ? No. Is there a . . . ? Does it . . . ? Do they . . . ? Where do you . . . ? Is that right? Oh . . . I see.'

'We chose him for his depth,' Jo-Dee says of the plastic surgeon.

'And rightly so,' Leslie declares. 'Wisdom and experience are essential in a doctor.'

Jo-Dee explodes with laughter. Turns off the taps and explains that by depth she'd meant eight centimetres. 'He's known for his deep vagies, Lesy – you're such a scream.'

A scream indeed; Leslie Bird is howling inside, wincing as Jo-Dee describes Alex's forehead feminisation – the off-cut brow bone brought home from Thailand, clearing customs to sit in a saucer on Jo-Dee's kitchen counter until their cleaner mistook it for brisket and fed it to their pooch Pronto.

'Hey, you should visit some time, Lesy,' Jo-Dee suggests. 'Alex would love to meet you. And Pronto, of course. He's a little yappy, but he means well.'

'Don't we all.' Leslie smiles politely.

'Come for afternoon tea and you can see our new place in Camperdown. Who knows, it might even be a distraction?'

Leslie nods, thinking, *Not on your life.*

~

Smack bang at the traffic lights just above the kebab shop, went the invitation. *Take the stairs next to Curvaceous Brides – you can't miss it*, Jo-Dee had written, seemingly proud of the chaotic location, oblivious to the mass of drivers, pedestrians, lewd late-night drunks, fat fiancés, bored bridesmaids, the stench of roasting doner and – the cause of nocturnal eyepatches, earplugs and Alex's facial tic – the garish neon flashing outside their bedroom window, blinking as if it were a sign of something else . . . or someone else?

The Fuck Love man, maybe, loitering nearby, when Leslie Bird arrives for her first visit (after Martha insisted it would take her mind off her Bernadette miseries). She's not only all sorts of anxious and angry with herself for being unable to decline Jo-Dee's invitation (after all the trouble the silly girl had gone to paying for a fancy card and stamp); she's also completely exhausted after waking at dawn, trying to decide whether to take an early bus or chance delays, run late and arrive flustered? Leslie has a preference for early arrivals, giving herself time to get her bearings, catch her breath and find a nice quiet spot in which to read her book, if need be, and she had decided to do just that when she ran into Fuck Love.

Thirty-something, older or younger; Leslie can't tell. Or look past his vulgar attire. Made in China, she thinks. His eyes are old, cold, hardened. Had seen things she would never understand, not from the blatant glances she's stealing standing near him on the footpath nursing her warm foggy Tupperware of freshly baked date slice. Nor from the Louis Theroux documentaries she'd watched furtively as Wallace, who never slept, dozed, which was just as well as he wouldn't have tolerated their candour. Not because Wallace was removed or immune from real life, but because he desperately wanted his 'bride' to be. He wanted Leslie untainted. In the dark. Turning the bed down. Tucking him in. Washing up. In the kitchen. Setting the table at 5 pm. A knife and fork laid out – as good as the hands on a clock. Wallace Bird would prefer his bride standing anywhere but near a dead-eyed man on Parramatta Road wearing a *Fuck Love* t shirt, skinny jeans, shaven head and a tattooed face. The three teardrops beneath his left eye are prison issue, Leslie concludes, via paperclips and pen ink. She'd seen them etched and explained on Theroux's show and marvelled at Louis's ability to coax his subjects into the spotlight, where they blazed unknowingly beneath the audience's gaze.

~

Not unlike Leslie's good self, many moons ago, sitting puffed up with pride, smoothing down her skirt in Sister Joan's office, after accepting an invitation for afternoon tea with her daughter's principal. 'Why would I, goodness, of all people, be singled out for high tea?' Leslie had asked nine parents of Caroline's teammates by the sidelines of the netball courts, feigning modesty. And only the orange quarter lady had taken the bait, speculating that perhaps Leslie Bird would be offered presidency of the P&F. As for the others, the shruggers and non-committers, they were probably full of envy. Leslie thought, having read once that, of all the seven deadly sins, envy was the only one that destroyed both the giver and receiver, and she avowed not to be destroyed. No, rather, she would pray for the sinners after the final quarter, especially the wing defence's mother, team manager Mrs Madigan, who was referred to in the Bird household as Kerchief for her inflated sense of authority and uniform of short white netball skirt and polo shirt with upturned collar, a navy neckerchief and regulation briefs, which shocked every time the wind fluttered her pleats or she flashed down the sideline shouting, 'Out. Jump. Pass. Over a third.'

Kerchief could barely hide her disbelief when Leslie suggested that her invitation to the principal's office 'might not be all about me, you know, it may be about my Caroline' – who was poised at that very moment to shoot from the outer rim of the goal circle; Leslie held her breath, counting out three seconds, flinching at the defenders leaping and clawing at her girl, before exhaling. 'I was thinking we might be nominated for school captain.' 'Or at the very least chapel prefect.' Kerchief smirked, as Leslie shouted, 'Obstruction,' when Caroline's shot for goal failed, giving the opposition the throw-in.

No amount of rebounds could save Leslie Bird, who was caught offside when Sister Joan, warming a Golden Jubilee teapot in her office, reeled off a record number of school absences – thirty-four with identical infections in Caroline's year alone – after Leslie's second-born was named as the culprit, caught piercing ears in the undercroft using lemonade icy poles and a rusty compass for a dollar a hole! Dollars Caroline saved and spent, unbeknown to Leslie, on booze and pot so rich in head that after sharing a joint at a party she'd lied about attending (Leslie had thought she was meditating at a convent vocational evening) she was prowling about on all fours, purring, thinking herself a cat, vomiting cherry advocaat, witnessed by more than nine parents, including Kerchief Madigan, who were picking up their offspring.

'Milk with your tea, Mrs Bird?' Sister Joan asked as she filled Leslie's cup.

~

Fuck Love – is a paradox, Leslie Bird thinks. Standing there with his emblazoned swear words and menacing ink, hands gently pushing an elderly lady in a wheelchair, parking her directly in front of Jo-Dee and Alex's stairwell. Leslie had spotted the unlikely duo after alighting the bus. Hung back. Waited. Looked at her watch. Curious. Frightened. She clutches her date slice to her bosoms, thinking old ladies are rolled for less than baked goods and, if push comes to shove, she'll surrender the slice, but never her beloved Tupperware.

'The answer to the Housewife's demand for efficiency and economy . . . the woman's demand for beauty.' Years it had taken

Leslie to acquire a complete set of Tupperware from various parties, ever after making it impossible to scrape out leftovers and not pair containers and hostess.

Series 1 fluted round, used to store raw onion – Linda Burton.

Pantry pairs – Jenny Jones.

Covered cake plate (Leslie's favourite) – Margaret Mary Zeidler.

Leslie remembered laughter, chatter, tears, women's business, games shared, won, lost. The pattern on the A-line dress she wore the day she earned her lettuce spinner. It was green-and-white lattice planted with peonies and climbing roses, and Wallace had winked – 'Ya look blooming beautiful, love' – from where he sat at the dining table, waiting for his dinner, as she'd spun into the kitchen, at five minutes to 5 pm.

With no time to change into a house dress, she'd tied a buttercup yellow-and-white checked apron about her waist and began peeling potatoes, pouring milk, cutting butter, mashing, lightly frying. Flushed with thoughts of friendship, crisp green salad leaves, the garden blooming about her hips, her husband's words and gaze, Leslie Bird moved from sink to stove, calling to the children, with a grace she'd never known. As if she was both Mrs Brady and Alice Nelson, both beauty and utility at once. It's not too much to say that Leslie Bird felt quite lovely and something else; as if she may have discovered a recipe for happiness. Somewhere to go, something to do and something to hope for – frozen poultry. In 1976 a whole turkey was the reward for the Tupperware hostess with the most sales. And though Leslie never claimed the title or fowl, she regarded her collection of orange, green, yellow and brown plastic as priceless trophies.

If Fuck Love even looks like harming her, Leslie's going to dong him over the head with her Modular Mates Series 2 Sweet Keeper. She wondered about the safety of the old woman in the wheelchair too. Having read in the *Daily Telegraph*, seen on *A Current Affair*, pensioners bashed left, right and centre for the fun of it, and home invasions, the perpetrators high on God knew what. 'This ice age is worse than the one that wiped out the dinosaurs,' she'd declared, feeling chuffed at her play on words, until she was put swiftly back in her corner by Shelley reminding her that she was, in fact, a dinosaur.

Since their teens Leslie has felt bullied by all four of her children. A tad less so by Michael than the troika of Shelley, Caroline and Bernadette, but still, like a schoolyard crawler (a 'suck up', they called them these days), she was always creeping after them. Too keen to nod, suggest, fit in and impress. Not so much impress, just at the very least be relevant. Not even relevant, just, well, nothing really; these days Leslie Bird is just grateful to be allowed in the company of the cool kids, who aren't cool at all, but oafish middle-aged pigs who carry on squealing, pointing their fat fingers, as if she doesn't exist. Except when they want something, of course. Caroline attention. Shelley different parents. Bernadette money. Michael – who knows what Michael wants? Whiskers? And Lana; if she has to be included, Leslie would say what Lana mostly wanted was her independence and Wallace. Pigs they may be, but they are *her* pigs, and Leslie knows how pathetic it all sounds and mostly keeps her sadness to herself. What mother ever dares speak the truth – the whole truth – about the motherhood deal? Wallace was too full of himself ever to notice how their children derided her. Sometimes she envied him that oblivion, that singularity, when she, since motherhood, had felt herself divided into six, with herself being the smallest bit. Growing smaller by the years. A fraction of her former self. Death when it came would be purely mathematical. Not by age but by being outnumbered. Watching her brood age beyond puberty, that greatest of all busybodies, had brought Leslie little comfort. She felt as if they were ruining themselves to spite her, and only after her youngest turned forty did she see their wrinkling, fattening, frizzing and receding as a kind of sweet revenge for their cruelty to her. You can live too long, she often thought, not entirely ready to lay down her graphite powder and Tupperware, but leaving would surely be easier when your world has already forgotten you.

If Fuck Love doesn't get you first.

Before Caroline bought Leslie a senior's travel card, she'd schooled her mother repeatedly about not making eye contact with strangers, least of all the tattooed-face variety. 'When you're out and about, practise your feck-off face and keep your voice down.' And Leslie had agreed, but because she rarely went anywhere except the supermarket, church, her hairdresser's, doctors' surgeries and the odd lunch, she forgot and stared at everyone and broadcast her thoughts at the top of her voice – as Caroline experienced first-hand, when she accompanied Leslie on her first foray on public transport in forty-odd years: a round trip from Top Ryde to Macquarie shopping centres, which offered up a smorgasbord of humanity and skirted the university grounds, where a few Muslims and more than a few Asians got on and off, Leslie quietly observed (not shouted, as Caroline reported to the rest of the family).

'I said to her,' Leslie defended herself to Shelley, 'that if people don't want their identities mistaken, they should dress more appropriately and shave off those awful beards. And I don't know what that sister of yours told you to make you rush over here like this, because aside from the little misunderstanding it was a lovely outing. And the main thing is, we made it home alive. And as I said to Caroline and the terrorists, I was only looking, not staring. Not like your father, whose gawking gets us into all sorts of trouble.'

'Turn it up, Les,' Wallace chimed in.

'Seriously, Wal? What about you last Saturday?'

Leslie shook her head slowly, then turned and told Shelley all about the forty-six-dollar bill and a plate of king prawns served up to them at the co-op, after they'd already finished their barramundi and chips and ice-cream sundaes. 'Honestly, your father sat with his back to me throughout the entire meal, fixated on a table full of rowdy men seated behind him – fishermen, it turns out, just back from a long day's trawl. Talk about staring. Your father couldn't take his eyes off them, and when they spoke to him and gestured, he nodded and laughed without a clue as to what they were saying and he was agreeing. *Forty-six dollars* – it could have kept us in corned beef for the rest of the year.'

'I didn't hear you complaining until they slugged us the bill,' Wallace then turned to Shelley. 'You should have seen your mother, peeling and scoffing the prawns like a woman possessed.'

Shelley tutted and asked Leslie how she could possibly accept and devour a kilo of something she had no knowledge of ever ordering, let alone after a gigantic ice-cream sundae. 'I can't believe you did that,' she said, pushing past her mother into the kitchen to fill up her kettle right to the top to make a cup of tea that she'd sip from once then let go cold – infuriating Leslie, who only ever boiled one cup at a time, to save electricity, and drank hers in one gulp.

'What were you thinking, Mum? Why the hell did you eat a whole kilo of prawns?'

'I don't know. Because they were there? And it wasn't a whole kilo; your father and I only had six each.'

Leslie was furious with herself for even attempting to tell a story; a story that would become nothing but fodder for her girls' view of her as greedy and gullible. She could almost hear the conch shells ring out from one daughter's mouth to the others' ears, whilst Wallace got off scot-free. Again. His idiocy was rarely ever mentioned, and when it was, that was her fault too.

'Why didn't you just tell him to turn around and mind his own business? Why wasn't he wearing his hearing aids?'

The barrage from Shelley continued until Wallace got up and left the room, befuddled by Leslie's anger and lack of gratitude after he'd gone out of his way to do her a bloody big favour, by talking up her prawn-peeling prowess and omitting the bit about her wrapping up the leftovers in a paper napkin and taking them home in her handbag, because he knew full well his bride wouldn't be keen on knowing that he'd snooped; but what on earth is a man to do when a pong like that brings you to your knees? Come to think of it, Wallace hadn't seen the prawns since he found them under their bed two nights after the restaurant. 'Hey, where did you end up putting the rest?' he called out to Leslie.

'The rest of what?' Shelley called back, jumping up to refill the jug as Leslie stood firmly in front of the freezer and folded her arms.

~

Fuck Love's grandmother, maybe? Leslie wonders if that's who the old lady in the wheelchair might be. Why else would she be seen with such a specimen? True for both of them, she thinks, the woman's ordinary-looking. Glasses. Sensible shoes. Hair freshly set in unbroken roller waves, as if she'd just left a salon or rolled them herself, lining them up like little cannellini, exposing her chalky scalp. She shows no signs of being an ex-bikie moll or gang matriarch, à la Jacki Weaver. Leslie notices she has her own teeth. And doesn't look ashamed. Simple, perhaps, given the postcode, but not demented. Not like the people Shelley coddles as a Squalor and Hoarding Officer, just around the corner at Royal Prince Alfred Hospital.

'Fancy tainting a prince with that crap?' Wallace had laughed when their eldest do-gooder visited once, all inflated and bilingual after attending a conference; preaching strategies, tool kits, best practice and rating systems in the stupid slow deep voice she adopted whenever she spoke of work or ordered food. *'I'd like a BLT with a side of parmesan and truffle fries.'* Truffle fries? Who on earth does she think she is, Miss High and Mighty? Leslie was thinking, listening to Shelley go on about an embarrassment of no-hopers, when Wallace cleared his throat and said, ‘Nothing a bulldozer wouldn’t fix. And poisoning the pipes would stop ’em breeding.’

‘Excuse me, Dad?’ Shelley feigned disbelief, reverting back to her normal voice. ‘To whom are you referring?’

‘Your hoarders, love – someone oughta slip ‘em a bit of Ratsak.’

‘You’re absolutely disgusting,’ Shelley shouted, then tottered away in her electric blue wedges, the perfect complementary hue to her streaky orange tan, which Leslie was sure she’d seen moving; slipping, sort of, dripping – not like a tap, more as if the tan was oozing up from within. Like the stuff her sister Martha had told her bubbled up from the earth in Rotorua, and smelled like both front and back bottoms.

Was Wallace disgusting? Leslie had wondered. Absolutely, without a doubt – but on this occasion, perhaps it was too strong a word. Perhaps he was just stating the bleeding obvious to no one more deserving of the title than Shelley, their very own Hoarding and Squalor expert. She of the wardrobe full of plastic bags crammed with empty Red Rooster Tropical packs, discarded crumbed bananas; used blue eye-shadow compacts, sanitary pads, *TV Week*s and *Cleo*s, all rotting beneath piles of new clothes with the tags still on. Clothes bought for some slimmer, taller version of herself that never arrived (*shame about that*, Leslie thought), between puberty and when Shelley defected, leaving home and a putrid compost. Lord knows, Leslie had tried to get rid of it, enter the crime scene, double-, triple-bag the evidence of what she saw, first and foremost, as a mighty stain on her parenting. How she, so scrupulously clean and private, could have raised such a slob – nicknamed Smelly by her siblings – was a question that struck so deep in her heart, Leslie thought she might keel over were it not for the rage keeping her upright. Of course, it wasn't her fault, she reasoned; it was Wallace and his filthy flock, throwbacks the lot of them, right back to the sucker sent out from Cork for stealing bread, ironically. Bloody bread. Leslie Bird took a deep breath, thinking she had the answer, without ever truly knowing just how deeply ingrained bread was in the Birds' DNA . . .

That when Wallace's head hit the pillow each night, the very thought of it, delivered him to the swaying sheaths of his childhood. No taller than wheat, its own horizon; 'a world not round but vertical and golden,' swishing, smelling sweetly of newborn heads and his mother's apron, where the sound of a tap on tin, turning a loaf from a pan, chimed with the Sanctus bells he'd once rung by hand, consecrating his old belly full of wine and bread as his thoughts and hands drifted as Leslie lay beside him, reciting the rosary, her own hands clasped in prayer, whilst his kneaded flesh, dreaming of a boy who couldn't grow a seed in his own belly but could tend the earth, bake and nourish others.

Bread was the Birds' offering. Their way of loving. Of rising again.

Nothing but grubs, the lot of them; six generations of Grenfell bakers following each other blindly, like sheep, proving who carried the grubby gene. Grubby is all relative, Leslie thought, and made sure to instruct her brood to distinguish themselves from the Dirty Birds, another family who lived in Ryde with most unfortunately the same surname.

The Dirty Birds lived a few blocks away on an otherwise lovely street that Leslie had to traverse to get to mass, so there was no escaping their filthy front yard, where sofas, car chassis, whitegoods, plastic chairs, steel drums, mattresses, tree stumps, a pair of rubber boots, an egg beater and a dead dog, among other things, marinated. I kid you not; a large decapitated black and tan Alsatian, decomposed amid the debris. How it got there, who it belonged to, where its head was, no one knew. Leslie blamed the riffraff living in flats up on Epping Road. *What else are they going to do with their dead dogs but hurl them at us?* Thinking the authorities ought to be informed, she called the council eleven times, but nothing was done, despite her being on a first-name basis with the switchboard operator, who recognised Leslie's tone and put her straight through to Garbage Disposal – not the mayor, whom Leslie had requested. She visited the chambers twice. Would have gone more but parking was difficult. Nose to kerb, and whose business was it anyway telling her which way to angle the Camry? Then it rained almost all of April, dampening the Alsatian's pelt, filling its cavities until it bloated above the steaming heap of rotting garbage, so that it flailed like one of those inflatable men outside of car yards. Leslie tried hard not to look at the carcass, but couldn't help it. And tried even harder to work it into conversation, 'Nice day today,' she'd say, 'but not if you're a headless Alsatian.' But no one welcomed the subject. They called her, 'Gross. Perverted. Macabre. Obsessed.' 'Let it go,' Bernadette said. 'You hate dogs, Mum, so why do you even care?' 'I'll have you know, I've never ever said I hate them.' As she said it, Leslie wondered if it might be a death thing – her not looking away from the carcass? A moral obligation and bound to the Alsatian's fate?

Leslie took thoughts of the Alsatian to mass and prayed to St Jude for his interment and head. The head especially. Who took it, why and where it was now, woke her up at night.

Such utter baloney that she didn't care about dogs. Twice she'd dreamt she'd opened her freezer and found the Alsatian's head beside her prawns.

She even kept a written record of its putrefaction, noting where it was up to – or, rather, down to – every time she drove past.

20 May: Deflated. Fur sparse.

25 August: Skeleton visible. Surprisingly delicate. Not at all what I'd imagined. Do dogs have elbows?

On 21 October, twenty-nine weeks after her first note, Leslie logged her final observation: a long black tuft of tail hair that had blown onto a low branch of the walnut tree that spanned and shaded the Dirty Birds' yard and flapped there at half-mast until the following June.

God only knew what else was buried there and stewing, as the stench emitted was so hideous you had to drive with the windows up and cover your nose when passing by. And even then you might catch a taste of it at the back of your throat. Once after a particularly nasty fight, Wallace said, 'Let's go for a ride, the change of scenery will do us good, Les.' And he was right. There was something healing about sitting side by side, moving in the same direction, Leslie thought . . . until Wallace pulled over outside the Dirty Birds', set the windows to automatic, lowered and locked them. Turned the engine off and waited until she gagged and eventually apologised.

So, when Leslie Bird found herself in the position of shielding Wallace from Shelley's disgusting waste, she reasoned, with all that business behind her, that it was just another sacrifice she was willing to make in this world for salvation in the next, and so she focused in on the task at hand, in much the same way she'd endured her children's endless measles, mumps, asthma, ear infections, eczema, nightmares, nagging, vomiting, tantrums, teething, tonsils, bed-wetting and bickering; before the years turned truth into fiction, their childhoods into the most wonderful time of Leslie's life. First they had to be survived. Which Leslie did by knitting, darning, stitching; teaching herself to eyeball a quarter-inch seam allowance on her Singer's throat plate when sewing patchwork quilts early in the morning or late in the evening, whenever the children were finally asleep, she focused on nothing but the next stitch, so that when her flock went to bed each night it wasn't only their mother's love and labour that comforted them, but her sanity.

Sort of.

Wallace had no idea, of course, what Leslie was piecing together either back then or when she set about clearing out Shelley's wardrobe – stowing the plastic bags in boxes in the garage, transferring them into and out of the boot of her cars, shifting them on shopping days and the like, to prevent Wallace ever getting a whiff of his daughter's deficit, which seemed to Leslie to cast a shadow over all women's private business.

Long before councils bestowed wheelie bins, the Birds had one medium aluminium garbage can that couldn't possibly cope with what needed to be disposed, so Leslie vigilantly watched the weather forecasts, wind direction in particular, praying a strong southerly might collide with Wallace needing an early night. It was months before the perfect conditions arrived, when she woke one night, in the early hours to Wallace's snoring and the wind howling. She nudged him several times in the ribs and toed him on the calf, and when he failed to respond she climbed out of bed and crept on tippy toes by torch light downstairs to the garage and hauled the bags up, one by one, outside to her beloved incinerator, where she emptied the bags into roaring flames until a plume of smoke trailed from their backyard like a new Pope was in Rome, only in Ryde it signified smelly Shelley had moved out! At the ripe old age of twenty-eight, she'd relocated west, to become a high-heeled social worker in St Marys. 'Until the Tongans and Sudanese moved in and preferred dealing with one of their own,' Wallace told people, when explaining how Shelley was moved on to Royal Prince Alfred and gained herself a new title and an honorary doctorate from the University of Sydney after her induction into the Hoarding Hall of Fame for Services to Squalor in New South Wales! Her most notable achievement being her cunning and discretion when relocating the lush heir of a media magnate from his maggot-infested waterfront home and fleecing him of a million-dollar donation to the hospital in exchange for a couple of small concessions. Namely the publication of his manifesto, *The Secrets to My Success* (a replica of AA's twelve-step program, give or take a word or two), an office with a fully stocked bar and view of the university chapel, and a gold plaque inscribed with his new title: Professor of Nothingness.

On her induction into the Hall of Fame, Shelley spoke of the importance of developing extraordinary empathy and listening skills. 'Not just for hearing,' she said, pausing and narrowing her right eye at the audience with all the sincerity of Bill Clinton denying Monica Lewinsky, 'but for listening deeply, to *really* hear.'

It seemed to Leslie the kinder Shelley became to strangers, the crueller she was towards her parents; speaking to them as if the hostile world she worked in was somehow their fault. Scoffing when they confessed, they didn't know what 'quantity easing' meant, tottering about in her ridiculous heels, fluttering her false eyelashes, which were not made of human hair, according to Caroline, an expert on all things related to her big sister, but of mink: 'from these poor little things kept in cages no bigger than an open newspaper before their fur's collected and recycled into lashes'.

'Well, they must be heavy,' Leslie said, shaking her head, 'because she walks around most of the time with her eyes closed. Have you noticed that when you're trying to talk to her, she looks at you all superior and bored, fluttering them like you've said something stupid when you haven't said a word? I don't know where to look. It's like talking to someone with a walleye. Do you talk to the good eye or the other one?'

'Neither. We always talk side by side.'

'Why do you think she bothers with them when they make her look so silly?'

'Who knows?' Caroline shrugs.

'Well, I'd still like to know where to look when I talk to her.'

'Okay, I'll google it. What should we ask?' Caroline takes out her phone.

'Ask where to look at your daughter when she resembles Tammy Faye Bakker. Before not after.'

'Before Reverend Jim?'

'No – death.'

'Okay, wait . . . nope, looks like there's nothing here. Seems like you're the only person in history who's ever googled that question.'

Leslie was chuffed. Not only to be acknowledged as an original thinker, but this was the longest conversation she'd had with Caroline since the nasty business between her and Bernadette had erupted, when Caroline called her sister menstrually retarded for claiming she could control her cycle through yoga poses she'd learned after moving to the Blue Mountains, abandoning her daughters. 'Why can't you just stay home and look after them and bleed like the rest of us?' Caroline had pleaded and Bernadette volleyed, 'Why don't you mind your own business and take care of the kids you've never had because you're too fucking selfish?'

'Mark my words, the family's over,' Wallace declared to Leslie. And for a while – a good while – it seemed it was.

'Wait, there's something here on LazyEyeEtiquette.com,' Caroline said, clicking on the link. 'It says, "Always look at the bridge of the nose".'

'Okay, thanks.' Leslie sighed. She was at her wits' end with Shelley's stupid lashes and not seeing her eldest's eyes for years. Not to worry. She wasn't even sure if she wanted to anymore. People grow apart. Not that Shelley ever owned up to having false teeth, tan, fingernails or eyelashes, no, the poor dear was half mink, half porcelain. Fragile. So fragile in fact that her left eye closed completely from too much eyelash glue and her right winked and wept in sympathy, at a dinner one night with her mother, when it was just the two of them; so where else was Leslie supposed to look? She'd made a mighty effort throughout the meal not to stare, to act engaged and to listen, despite not caring one iota for Shelley's subjects, nor going out at night. There was just something so awful about all these people ha-ha-ha-ing, at ease eating and paying a fortune for what they could very well fix for themselves at home if they weren't such lazy gadabouts. Leslie Bird thought she might explode if she ignored Shelley's eyes for a second longer. So, she inquired about the big globs of glue and Shelley not only insisted that there was nothing wrong with her eyes, but hissed, 'There's nothing wrong with me, Mum; the problem is you. You've got far too much time on your hands spying on everyone.'

~

Fuck Love moves around in front of the old lady and squats down on his haunches so they are face to face. *So she can read his t-shirt now too*, Leslie realises. *What if those awful words and tattooed tears are the last thing she sees? Good Lord. Why isn't she flinching?*

On the contrary, the old lady looks relaxed. Leslie ponders again if they might be related and if this is the old duck's penance for being such a soft touch when Fuck Love was growing up. Maybe she was one of those pushover grannies left in charge of ratbag grandkids? Boys especially; Leslie has seen them running amok in her own neighbourhood when fathers are absent and mothers worked. Seen these old types turn a cataracted eye, busying themselves with daytime TV, shandies and pokies on the weekend. The types who think having their hair set will distract you from their failings. Leslie watches as Fuck Love places both hands on the old lady's knees. Her date slice trembles as she clutches her Tupperware and handbag and prays it isn't a mugging or worse she is witnessing as Fuck Love leans in, right next to the old lady's head as she mumbles something.

'Go again?' he shouts at her.

The old lady sits up a little straighter and enunciates slowly and loudly, 'Tell Mrs Parker to take a picture – it lasts longer.'

Fuck Love laughs and kisses her on the top of the head before turning to Leslie and saying, 'How about it, Mrs P?' before unlocking the brakes and pushing off.

Who on earth would want a picture of that? And who's Mrs Parker? How bizarre. Must be on drugs, Leslie thinks, feeling shaken but somewhat relieved that the ordeal is over as she climbs the stairs and steadies herself on the landing with a few deep breaths before arriving at Jo-Dee Lane's door, which is ajar.

She knocks and calls out, 'Hello – it's only me.' A dog yaps and a strange voice – like someone pretending to be someone else: the wolf from 'Little Red Riding Hood' – calls out, 'Shut up, Pronto. Come in, Only Me.'

Great, a wise guy, Leslie thinks as she walks down a tiny hallway, into a cramped, clammy, low-ceilinged space adorned with fraying silk wall hangings, ostensibly Japanese, and piles of books: Bellows, Banville, Updike, Woolf, Cunningham; books everywhere, *Caroline's mob*, stacked all over the floor. And there are no chairs that Leslie can see, but a rusted old iron thing jammed outside on a tiny balcony, which is more of an outdoor cupboard than a balcony. There are too many indoor plants for her liking – or anyone's, for that matter, unless of course you're a gnat. Profuse parlour palms and spiky, not soft, maidenhair spill from macramé pot holders in the lounge and bathroom, which she can see right into; a burnished wood vanity, a dripping tap, an overflowing laundry basket and no sign of Jo-Dee, in either the flesh or the décor. *Blimey, Charlie. Where is she?* The place is so crowded Leslie holds on to her slice and handbag. And smelly – phew! It reeks of wet dog, something briny and marzipan. And there – *shoot me now* – sprawled on a sofa among it all, wearing teeny tiny lemon terry-towelling shorts and a crocheted tank top, with enormous pneumatic breasts, peek-a-boo pacifier nipples and the longest bare legs (toned by AFL it turns out) extending over the armrest, lies the wolf (Alex, Leslie presumes), dabbing pawpaw ointment into his/her new hairline and consoling a burly little pug. 'Jo-Dee's just popped out for finger buns,' Alex explains, 'but not to worry, welcome – come in and sit yourself down.'

'Where? On John Updike?' Leslie says. 'No, thank you.'

Staring at the ceiling, not daring to look at Alex – which would be just like looking at an eclipse, Leslie thinks, recalling her primary school playground full of children holding cardboard and mirrors, having been told they'd go blind if they stared directly at the sun, and how she'd tried her hardest to join with them, but couldn't stop herself from peeking.

'Not that it's any of my business,' she says, 'but he could do with a little smothering.'

'Updike?' Alex laughs.

'More like Up-himself.' Leslie bends over and picks up *Rabbit Remembered*. 'I couldn't bear that character of his. Angstrom, isn't it? Harry? What he did to his family. I could have done without it, to be honest, but my daughter Caroline insisted I read it. She's always pushing books on me. Reckoned there was something of her father in him.'

'I couldn't stand him either. The way Harry ogled his daughter-in-law turned my stomach.'

'Oh yes, that too!' Leslie had meant Angstrom dying, but never mind. 'And the arrival of that short-skirted illegitimate, what's her face, on Janice's doorstep, ten years after he died!' Leslie has a head full of steam. 'I wanted to smack him,' she says. 'People ask me why I read these awful men and I tell them it's your enemies you need to understand, not your friends.' Leslie never imagined she'd pass off Caroline's words as her own. But there you go.

Alex nods and eases herself up to sitting, quite taken aback, as Jo-Dee hadn't said a word about Leslie Bird, aside from her being an old fuddy-duddy nosy parker, and probably the most tightly wound and wounded person she'd ever met, who reminded Jo-Dee of her grandmother. With the exception of course of Leslie's haemangioma that terrified Jo-Dee, for as long as Alex had known her; she'd never mentioned that Leslie Bird was a reader! Alex would have picked her as a Mills and Booner. 'Well, look at you!' Alex says, patting the space beside her on the couch.

'No, thank you,' Leslie declines again. 'If Jo-Dee's running late, I should really be on my –'

'She isn't late, you're an hour . . .' Alex decides to let it go. 'I've heard so much about you over the years, Lesy' – Alex pats the couch again, this time with gusto.

'Hmmm. Well . . . look at you,' Leslie deflects, annoyed by the nicking of her name, feeling stranger by the second, rude and heavy, her limbs thickening, persona shrinking in response to this spectacle, the humidity and penetrating gaze from the sofa, which seems to be forcing her up and down an octave and to measure herself as more or less feminine than Alex's big eyes devouring her. *Less for sure. Those bosoms! Heavens. And shapely legs. But then again, the voice? Absent Adam's apple? More. The neck, thick and smooth like the back of a thigh making the head look as if it's attached backwards. Ashamed?* Leslie can't be sure what she's looking at, but the obscene display of flesh makes her feel like fainting, running or staying. Taking a shower or a number, like she does at the deli counter. To order what? Salami? Cabbage leaves?

Now *this* is something you might want to take a picture of. For the first time in her life, Leslie thinks it would be handy to have one of those phones and ditch her library card and borrow books from Alex not just Caroline. How she'd love to sift through his stacks (surely his, as Jo-Dee has never mentioned reading – in fact, Leslie had wondered if she might even be dyslexic). She shoos the pug away from her legs and squeezes out a shallow set of pelvic floor exercises, then tugs at her hair, unfurling strands, patting them into place at her neck, wondering just how much of this 'so much' about her is known, and how long the three of them can remain like this, standing, sitting and snorting.

'You know, since you are here early,' Alex says, 'I wonder if you wouldn't mind helping me with a little something in the bedroom.'

In the bedroom? Early? Hardly. 'Sure!' Leslie exclaims, surprising them both by speaking in an Indian accent, channelling her Punjabi gynaecologist, whose manner and way of changing the subject had eased Leslie's discomfort in the twilight years of her incontinence, an issue that had remained untreated until she found Dr Rishma. After seeing Caroline's holiday snaps from Mumbai; all those bare brown bottoms squatting in squalor at the edge of the airport – Leslie concluded that an Indian obstetrician had seen a lot worse than her old backside and so made an appointment with her.

Unfazed by Leslie's accent, Alex gets up off the couch and announces, 'Just off to the bathroom first, Lesy. Make yourself at home.'

'Oh, I will . . .' Leslie replies, then mumbles '*not*' beneath her breath, before jiggling like a Bollywood extra past the pug and into the kitchen. Leaning over him she growls, 'What are you looking at, fatso? Blow your nose, Winston Churchill. No, no, not Winston – you're Mrs Ellis.' But the dog shows no sign of offence at the comparison to Leslie's feisty fifth-grade teacher, who'd tottered about jauntily on surprisingly great legs, all breathless and busty, top half moving independently of a derriere that threatened to topple her, were it not for some serious step-ins. Pronto just stares at Leslie with his bulging eyes and snorts. Proving her point about dogs being useless.

Why anyone would ever bother with one, she thought; *the same could be said of men.* She recalled one sweltering summer afternoon, back in 1959, trapped inside a celery-coloured Volkswagen Beetle with a flatulent black labrador named Mate and his master, her fiancé (she would never tire of the term *fiancé* – so full of elevating syllables and principles, as opposed to the flat, drab *husband-to-be*). He, Wallace was driving with one hand on the wheel and the other holding a cigarette, seeming delighted that his dear old dog was taking such a keen interest in his beloved on the passenger side of the bench seat, smiling politely, as brides-to-be, non-smokers and dog-fearers tend to do. Huddled against the door, Leslie gazed at the reflection of her engagement ring in the side mirror, turning it this way and that until it caught the light, thinking, *he loves me, he loves me not*, and how easily the hand in the mirror could belong to someone else, such was the distance between how Leslie Bird felt and how she acted. Is it all an act? she'd wondered.

Generally speaking, Leslie Bird avoided mirrors and their truth-telling, but gazing at her glinting digit, was somehow different. Proof perhaps that someone loved her? Small though the stone was, it was hers, and Wallace had asked, and how could she say no? That would have been rude, and Leslie Bird prided herself on not being rude. She was a fiancée, angling her finger, recoiling from old dog emissions and attention.

'Down, boy,' Wallace instructed as Mate ricocheted about the cabin, his tail thumping against the felted ceiling.

'Oh, Wallace, please,' Leslie begged, trying to fend the dog off when it lurched from the back seat. As it nudged then nuzzled at her nape, she lost all composure and screeched, 'He bit me!' She clutched at her haemangioma, crying, 'He could have killed me. Wallace, watch the road!' as Wallace overcorrected the steering and roared laughing.

'There, there, love, calm down. Let's have a look.' Wallace insisted that old Mate wouldn't hurt a fly. 'If anything, he was only mouthin', which is what dogs do when they're playing. He was probably just trying to give you a kiss – and who could blame him?'

Leslie yelped as Wallace puckered up and reached over to lift up her hair. 'NO!' she screamed, so loudly that Wallace stepped on the accelerator, mounted the gutter and crashed directly into the letterbox of a Mr Collins.

Standing by the side of the road with Wallace apologising, Mate panting and the letterbox owner fuming, Leslie thought she might make a run for it. *Leave now. Hock the ring. Don't look back. Start again.* But who was she kidding? She could never have run and let Wallace see her bottom jiggling.

'Have you got a pen, love?' Wallace asked Leslie if she wouldn't mind jotting down Mr Collins's details, which she did, in perfect Pitman, while wondering if her haemangioma, by definition an abnormal collection of blood vessels, might have tricked Mate into thinking that she was on heat or, worse, was some kind of portal? Either way there was no chance she could ever live with this ancient dog – or any, for that matter – after they married. But the dress, the cake, the flowers, were all ordered, the invitations sent. The ship had sailed, so to speak, and Leslie Bird was on it. Listing. Licked. And to top it off, the stupid dog wasn't even Wallace's but some hand-me-down from a mysterious Sammy, whom Wallace refused to talk about without getting silly. *Never mind*, Leslie thought. *I'll take matters into my own hands. Leave Wallace's front gate open so Mate can escape back to his rightful lazy owner, before our big day.*

Leslie Bird could never have imagined the grief that would ensue when her plan succeeded. Or that forever after, Mate would simmer beneath every altercation and that, that moment, back there inside the sweltering VW, with Wallace and his farting frisky old dog, would contain not only their secrets and grievances, but the seeds of their future. No matter how many times they hurtled towards disaster and recovered; the result was essentially the same: I can't know you. And you can't know me. Marriage is proof. Claustrophobic and smelly.

~

Fuck Love would be long gone by now, and the old woman must have dementia, Leslie decides, as she stands in Alex's apartment, waiting to be summoned; chewing her hangnails; wondering why they call it transsexual rather than hypersexual. She turns on the tap in the kitchen to disguise whatever it is Alex is up to in the bathroom and, before she knows it, the sink is overflowing and she is soaked to her elbow, searching for the plug, flicking water at the stupid pug then running wet fingers around the inside of her blouse and the back of her neck, cooling herself down. Goodness. Leslie found it hard to remember feeling as provoked as this. Not since her wedding night, before Wallace revealed his true self, banishing the imposter of their courtship – he of the gentle hand-holding, blushing, pressed handkerchiefs, cheek pecks and shy sideways hugs, Cadbury Snack chocolate-gifting, insisting Leslie have her favourites while he gamely made do with pineapple and orange leftovers. Wallace was so chivalrous that Leslie came to think of him as the perfect gentleman, not unlike the little plastic groom that stood passively beside his bride atop their wedding cake, his tiny shiny black shoes leaving not a trace of himself in the marzipan icing – a sight Leslie marvelled at annually, when she defrosted their top tier on their anniversary.

Years down the track, when the wedding cake was as stale as their marriage, Leslie wondered what became of the little bride and groom that she'd rushed out to buy from Creighton's Bakery the morning after Wallace's proposal. She'd felt giddy when Mr Creighton removed the newlyweds from their display case, where they'd presided over a miniature world of figurines – a little ice skater, a Dalmatian, a baby in a pram and the Lone Ranger – and handed them to Leslie to inspect. She wouldn't make a fuss and ask if they were faulty, she decided, after turning the happy couple upside down and noticing that the bride's skirt disguised the fact that she was only a head and torso. That she had no legs – no legs at all to stand on so was wobbly and obliged to lean against the groom. Like the weak side of the wishbone, Leslie thought, she'd never have wishes granted if they were torn apart. Still – she passed her penny over the countertop, her hand hovering in mid-air until Mr Creighton noticed her finger. 'For crying out loud, Miss Maloney, that's a bobby dazzler. Val Creighton, get yourself in here,' he called to his wife, who shuffled forth from the back room and pushed the condensed white loaf stand to one side, before drying her hands on her apron and taking

Leslie by the elbow to walk her to the window, where she held up Leslie's ring finger to the light, before shaking her head and taking Leslie's face between her hands and kissing her hairline.

From paper to wood to wool, through the years until their silver anniversary, Leslie ran her fingers over the cake's diminishing frosting and cut from it anticlockwise, until one last tiny piece from the centre remained. She offered it to Wallace, thinking surely, he would say, *No. No, you have it, love.* Or, at least. *Let's go halves.* But he didn't; he gobbled it in one go then pushed back from the table and said, with his mouth full, 'I'd better get back to the mowing before it rains.' Leslie waited until she heard the starter motor splutter before slamming her chair against the dining table so hard that the jolly boy money box displayed inside her hope chest swallowed the penny poised at its lips for the past twenty-five years of their marriage.

With God as their witness, Leslie Bird was incredulous the Lord would condone what Wallace had unleashed on their wedding night, mere hours after their vows, all pendulous, glistening and sinister, probing her unwilling private parts in an act that was not something old, borrowed or new, but rather something so revolting, shocking, stolen and pornographic that she had never, ever, truth be known, fully recovered.

Years later, when her son Michael emerged from her person with his own set of arsenal, a miniscule penis all innocent and furled, which looked more flora than fauna to Leslie, as opposed to the big red angry pouch beneath it, she'd pointed at it and asked the doctor if it was normal.

The doctor nodded. 'Completely. It's swollen by your hormones crossing from your placenta.'

My hormones. My placenta. My fault? Leslie could hardly believe it, and yet Wallace had claimed the same thing as he'd so crudely despoiled her on their wedding night. It was the sight of *her.* 'You're just so beautiful,' he said afterwards, patting her on the arm – not caressing or stroking, mind you, but patting, like you might an old acquaintance – before getting out of bed and striding, dangling, to the bathroom, where he remained for way too long, whistling, rustling and flushing, making Leslie wonder why he hadn't just emptied himself in there in the first place. Upon returning to bed and whispering in her ear, 'I love you,' in a voice that yawned over syllables, like that of the hearing impaired, Wallace revealed his next deception: a full set of dentures, which he left on his bedside table, reminding Leslie of Luna Park. With his face sunken in and bearing the first hint of whiskers, which scratched her and reeked of Old Spice, he pressed up against her, as she curled as far away from him as she could, trembling, pondering the dire consequences of her wedding vows. The evolution of man from ape to this – *her* husband, *her* doing, growing heavy by her side, snoring. She had never shared a bed in her life with anyone, let alone slept with a man. Leslie Bird wondered if, in fact, she would ever sleep again, and lay awake for the rest of the night trying to recall the names in the line-up of hunched hairy species processing across her high school science books: *homo sapiens, habilis, erectus.* How could the word 'love' ever be equated with such a violation? There had been no clue, no preparation, just whispers here and there and a pair of paper underpants gifted on her wedding night from her mother with a note pinned to them: *In case you make a mess.* There it was again – *you.*

Leslie expected embarrassment, awkwardness and, of course, intimacy, but had truly hoped, on the odd occasion she'd let herself think of it, ever so fleetingly – amid the flurry of feminine and faith-filled wedding duties, such as hymn and reading selections, seating plans, menus, bridal gowns, bridesmaids, flowers, flower girls, trousseaus – that the fluttering feeling in her tummy she'd felt at times with Wallace was the beginning of something sacred that would deliver them as Mr and Mrs, beyond any of her imaginings. Not this savagery. This utter betrayal. Not just by Wallace, but by the entire congregation. Their friends and family gathered behind them at the altar, most of them knowing her fate and not one of them saying anything but: 'Congratulations!' Sadists, the lot of them, Leslie thought, though there was one guest who couldn't meet her eye in the farewell line at the end of the night: her dear Uncle Joe, who had kept his hands in his pockets and stared at the carpet during 'Auld Lang Syne', then pulled Wallace in close and spoke sternly into his lapels.

Leslie could still not explain this conflation of feelings. Disappointed, disgusted, divided, conquered, duped, deceived, without a single word from Wallace. Not a one. No *Excuse me, please, would you mind, Mrs Bird, if I lumbered on top of you, broke and entered you?*

Decades after that night, she came close to reliving those feelings when reading *On Chesil Beach*, another one of Caroline's must reads, which Wallace later found tucked inside Leslie's bedside table, declared filth and confiscated, though not before she'd underlined:

Her whole being was in revolt

Her composure and essential happiness

Violated

She simply did not want to be entered or penetrated

Sex with Edward (Leslie had crossed out 'Edward' and written 'Wallace') *could not be the summation of her joy, but the price she must pay for it.* (Leslie circled 'it' and wrote 'motherhood!'.)

How she would ever conceive a child enduring this suffering was beyond her.

If only she could, like the mother of Jesus, arrive at that swollen state by magic.

With the recent exception of the author of these words – *miraculously a man* – from her honeymoon forwards, Leslie Bird was frightened of men. She knew what they wanted. What they possessed. What they pretended. Even her own gentle father. A man of such suited dignity and formality that she never once glimpsed more than his forearms, which her mother permitted to be exposed beneath rolled-up shirtsleeves only on Sundays, following mass and after the lunch table was cleared. Even he, in the end, did not escape Leslie's certitude that all men were beasts disguising their intent, dying as he did in a Catholic hospice, all carpet, candles, crucifixes, crisp hospital corners and quiet nuns in habit. A sight so rare these days Leslie suspected they were men in drag, until one of them entered the room to tuck the sheets back up beneath her father's chin and firmly down by his sides after his right leg, in its death throes, bucked the sheets back and exposed his withered limbs, ashen bloodless flesh and the shock of pink between his legs that looked for all the world to Leslie as if he was beginning not ending. *Not you too*, she'd thought, her mind racing to something she'd once heard on late-night radio and written down in her little Book of Facts – that 'testicles were the last organ of the body to decompose'. *Last of all, just bones and those awful things beneath the ground*; Leslie thought of them as landmines littering the world. *So much for Mother Earth.*

~

'I'm ready for you, Leslie,' Alex announces, waving jazz hands at her, leaving the bathroom and heading down a narrow hallway towards the bedroom. The dog barks and runs ahead of Leslie, stopping to shake water from its coat, spraying her. 'Of course, you are, Alex. Do you knit? I love stitching, knitting. Crochet, patchwork,' Leslie babbles back; anything to distract; to delay the inevitable. 'I'm a dab hand at darning too,' she gasps as she enters the bedroom. 'Good gracious! I'll have you know, there isn't a hole I can't mend.'

Alex is sitting splayed off the end of the bed, all daddy-long-legs, shifting loins to the very edge of the bare mattress, prattling about procedures and predicaments.

Why on earth did I come here, Leslie thinks, as the consequences of her morbid curiosity are revealed.

'I think you'll find it's a little dry,' Alex says, angling a hand mirror towards the spot that she feels needs the most help. 'Would you mind taking a little look, Lesy? Jo-Dee's just too tired after work to touch it.'

So there in that tiny room, with Alex nursing her handbag and slice and a panting pop-eyed Pug as her witness, Leslie Bird takes a big deep breath and plants herself squarely between Alex's thighs and parts the hair in front of her; taking extreme care, when sweeping a fringe down over the jagged line of stitches on Alex's freshly hewn forehead.

~

On the bus on the way home, with her Tupperware container empty but her mind full – a veritable kaleidoscope of extraordinary moments that would no doubt have to remain private – it occurred to Leslie Bird that while the flush she felt in her cheeks and abdomen were no doubt signs of shock and excitement, there was an element of flattery too. As Alex had not only requested that she fix her hair, confiding how much she admired Leslie's – its volume in particular – but had issued an invitation for her to return as soon as possible to resume the bookish conversation they began after the hair business, over tea and date slice, before Jo-Dee finally arrived home. It was a conversation that Alex described as 'nothing less than remarkable'. Oh, to be seen and heard for the first time in as long as Leslie Bird could remember, as something other than a ninny or a nobody was indeed flattering, but not a patch on how deeply flattered Leslie Bird felt that Alex had gone to such extraordinary lengths to become a woman himself! *Who wouldn't want to become one, and get rid of that revolting appendage? Bless her,* Leslie thought, wriggling about in her seat, her mind leaping from Jo-Dee's tardiness to Alex to Wallace, who'd be picking her up from Ryde Station any minute. Leslie looks out the window to locate herself, unaware that while she'd been musing the bus had taken a detour.

Thinking she's lost, or has taken the wrong bus or overshot her stop, she panics and moves to the edge of her seat and leans over towards the tweed shoulders of the woman sitting across the aisle from her and says, 'Excuse me, do you know where we are?'

Without flinching or turning to look out of the window or at Leslie, the tweed woman replies, 'We are here.'

Here . . . where? are Leslie's first thoughts. *Idiot*, her second. Then something shifts – within her – like the screen at the end of an automatic car wash, rising to reveal the bright world. Leslie Bird blinks, smiles and says 'Thank you,' thinking, *Yes, we* are *here, aren't we? Alex. Jo-Dee. The tweed woman. The old one in the wheelchair. Even me. And Fuck Love. Bless. We are all here, ever so briefly, just doing our best.*

And then there's Wallace.

Leslie spots him, waiting, parked in a no-stopping zone at the bus stop, oblivious to her driver's horn, admiring himself in the rear-view mirror.

Debt

Nothing upsets Leslie Bird more than losing something.
Nothing.

~

She'd searched high and low. Turned the house upside down. Prayed to Saint Anthony, describing in great detail – the weft, the weave and colour especially.

As if the hue would hasten reclamation, Leslie set about asking Wallace and each of the kids if they'd seen her precious pale green thing.

Against her better nature, she'd even asked Martha, her big sister, but stressed to her that it was mostly moss stitch and made up of six pieces – 'if you count the booties and mittens separately, that is'.

Martha, always dismissive of what she considered Leslie's inane attachments, whether to objects or her kids, pretended to play the violin and changed the subject to fried rice. 'Jasmine or long grain? Boil or absorption?'

Michael moaned. 'You can't be serious, Lesy?' Refusing to be probed, he picked up his phone and took a picture he later posted and captioned, *Mum jumps the shark.* (It garnered 212 likes.)

Wallace, who wasn't listening but was fed up with Leslie's twenty-four-hour, seven-day-a-week rummaging, assumed she was in pursuit of a mate for another odd sock – which she was not – and so told her just to throw the damn thing out, which sent her into a rage that lasted for days, as waste was Leslie Bird's second-biggest bugbear.

Lana, when queried, shrugged and thrust out her bottom lip, making her look dopier than Leslie thought possible. Questioning Lana was just a formality, a case of leaving no stone unturned, as Leslie knew she'd never have loaned her anything. But she couldn't be sure her own girls hadn't.

Shelley, whom it took days to pin down and interrogate – no surprises there, given her habit of ignoring messages from everyone but her eyelash technician – laughed loudly and slapped her hands on the dining table before curling her finger around and around by her ear and pointing at her mother – despite vividly recalling how, many years earlier, her son George had worn Leslie's green things in a PixiFoto shoot in the middle of Broadway Shopping Centre after being ambushed by a $99 offer and gushing compliments. Shelley had made a fool of herself trying to make baby George look less disparaging while propped in a wicker picnic basket amid a garden of plastic sunflowers. Though it wasn't the tacky still life that furrowed George's brow.

Six weeks earlier he'd presented himself, superior and posterior. Tucked up in pike position, his body waited to be born, while his stern little face sat squished between Shelley's thighs, glaring up at her for a full five minutes, while she panted and grunted, as wave after wave of all the conceivable life and death her body contained tore them asunder and George was lifted from her and placed upon her chest, where he foraged silently, deliberating. *You're my mother? Jesus Christ, how disappointing. What do you have to do to get a drink around here?*

Born of her, not to her. George didn't cry once. Crying's for babies.

George had arrived with the demeanour of a thirty-four-year-old defence lawyer biding his time until the bar opened. He does not suffer fools, and suspects his mother is one. More than suspects; he has insider knowledge. She's loving but irrational. He has no desire for either, but has an abundance of the former. Love, that is: self-love. He's the first Bird ever to possess it in a family swamped by self-loathing and shame.

Where on earth he came from baffled Shelley. Beyond sustenance, she's no use to him. Or him to her. His first word was not *Mum* or *Dad*; it contained three syllables: *dinosaur*. One up on two stupid parents. George christened Wallace and Leslie 'Whoppy' and 'Lanny', after getting their names mixed up with Poppy and Granny. And being the only thing he ever confused, that rare show of naivety infused their titles, endearing him all the more to the Birds. By the time he was ten, George advised Shelley not to expect a visit from him when she is old and infirm but to keep her ear out for a nursing home janitor whom he will pay to be his imposter. 'You mean he'll pretend he's you?' Shelley asked, perplexed. 'Exactly,' George said. 'You two should get on famously.' Pleased with the plan, as if he had bequeathed his mother a great gift, he patted her on the head and they both laughed. And Shelley felt herself die a little more inside as she whispered, 'Thank you, Georgie.'

As far as his fleeting father, Mark, was concerned, George inherited his only redeemable feature: a pair of perfectly fluted full lips. Dashing on a man and the feature that sucked Shelley in. That and the dog-eared *Bride to Be* magazines by her bed. When Mark proposed, Shelley said yes to a wedding rather than a marriage. Even Wallace smelled a rat, mumbling to Caroline just before he walked taffeta-ed Shelley down the aisle, 'How long do you reckon this will last?'

If Shelley was sustenance to George, Mark was pout – nothing more. And no one in the family, including Shelley, got to know Mark before he vanished. So over time it seemed perfectly feasible that he never existed at all and that George had arranged his own passage here.

Caroline insisted that George's discerning soul was more attuned to her own and, as such, he should have been born to her. 'He's wasted on you, Shelley. I knew that from the moment I saw him – a good four years before he said, "So what?" to Dad's "Here's a Whoppy!" Do you remember that? How it stopped Dad in his tracks? No one had ever questioned old Wal's way of heralding himself before George. It was genius.'

'It was rude!' Shelley shot back. 'And *yes*, I remember it. I was there. It was me who told you.'

'I just knew George was my ally,' Caroline continued. 'He's not dumb like the rest of you. No offence, of course.'

'Of course.' None – but all taken.

Three weeks after George's PixiFoto shoot, when Shelley returned to Broadway to pick up his portraits, the photo booth was gone, replaced by a sign directing her to the service desk inside Kmart, where she stood in line behind an irate man wrestling an erect beach tent, claiming it had not only refused to collapse but had almost killed him on his drive down from Umina when it smothered both of his kids and his rear vision. When the service assistant said, 'It isn't the EzyShade that's faulty, sir,' he called her a mulleted bitch and stormed off, tossing the tent over the counter, where it landed on her head.

Without blinking, she shrugged it off and said, 'Next? How can I help you?', then took Shelley's receipt and rifled through a drawer before handing her a large envelope of photos and a bill for $399 – 'ninety-nine of which is refundable if you take the lot'. Naturally, Shelley hadn't read the fine print, and she couldn't afford the photos, but she could no more leave them behind than she could baby George – or ignore the service assistant's extraordinary poise.

Kindly Kmart offered a layby scheme, so once a fortnight Shelley lined up at the office at the back of the store, between the shoe department and pool chemicals, jiggling the pram, ignoring George's judgement, and paid them off with money she'd scrimped on housekeeping. 'Of course it's your Nescafe Gold Organic Premium blend' she assured Mark, when he spat out the No Frills shite she'd substituted.

George was on solids by the time she brought the photos home, but rather than gifting them to family and friends, as she'd intended, Shelley neither distributed nor ever looked at them again after noticing that the particularly insipid shade of green George was wearing made his rosacea look hideously red and angry. (A premonition, perhaps, of his cystic acne years ahead, when George will grab his mother by the throat and shove her up against a wall in a Roaccutane rage, leaving a dent in the hallway Shelley still can't pass without thinking of pockmarks or flying beach tents.)

'Are you absolutely sure you haven't seen it?' Leslie probed Shelley one last time.

'Absolutely. Never seen it. Not once.' Shelley shuddered.

~

On the afternoon that Caroline was asked if she'd seen Leslie's green thing, she listened with her eyes closed, pinching the bridge of her nose, making a mental note to add this to the list of evidence of her mother's decline – until Leslie announced that at this stage of the investigation, she'd concluded Bernadette was the prime suspect. Whereupon Caroline sat up, wide-eyed, and urged Leslie to call her. 'Quickly – before it's too late.'

'I already have,' Leslie said, taking off her glasses.

'What did she say?'

'She didn't answer.'

Leslie deflected Caroline's line of questioning, for it was all very well for her to harbour distrust and disdain for her children, but she expected nothing less than for them to all love one another, so that she could maintain the delusion of herself as a wonderful mother. Leslie Bird appreciated nothing more than when a child of hers pretended they didn't remember she'd been a mean mother. And what did they even mean by mean? Leslie tutted. *Toughen up, nincompoops. Call the whambulance.* In her day, what her kids called 'abuse' was simply discipline and responsible parenting, and every single thing she'd done was done for their own good. She wondered why people talked about having favourites, when Leslie Bird felt exactly the same about all of her children: disappointment, love and loathing in equal measure.

'Of course, she didn't answer,' Caroline said. 'Did you leave her a message?'

'No. I hate those things. You know I do. Oh, look at the time. I'd better get the dinner on.' Leslie deflected, knowing what was coming.

'But it's only four o'clock!' Caroline pointed at her watch.

'So it is.' Leslie rolled her eyes.

She couldn't bear to be mocked by her know-all flock, who thought the hours she and Wallace kept were geriatric. On the contrary, Leslie maintained eating early benefited their digestion and incontinence, not to mention their back pockets, via the Early Bird and Seniors specials at Ryde RSL and El Rancho, which they visited stealthily to save even more scoffing from the numbskulls who christened common sense 'fasting diets' or some other rubbish that sold books at Christmas, without realising they're endorsing not only their parents' sensible lifestyle, but generations of pre- and post-war Aussies waiting for the ice man to top up their chests, eating bread and dripping, skinny and happy, not an obese fad faster in sight.

'It just makes sense to get dinner out of the way,' Leslie sighed. 'So you can get cleaned up and off to bed. Done with each other, the day and the dread.'

'Well, I guess you can just ask Dette tomorrow,' Caroline said, ignoring Leslie's 'dread', knowing it meant nothing but death ahead on her mother's to-do-list. 'Isn't she coming over while Amir's at the house? She asked if she could hang at ours, but Toby said until they sort their shit out, and love the girls more than they hate each other, he doesn't want her around. He says he's had a gutful.'

Oh, boohoo for Toby, Leslie thinks. *Grow up and raise children of your own, you selfish brat. What on earth would you know about love?* As far as she knew, Caroline's husband had never even cared for a dog. He'd had a parrot that died when he was seventeen and told Leslie that he could never go through that pain again, when she'd broached the subject of the children they'd never had. The way he talked about that bloomin' bird – whispering with his head bowed while Caroline leaned in, nodding, rubbing him on the back – made Leslie feel uneasy, as if she'd never loved anyone or anything as much as Toby had loved that damn bird, and that his choosing never to love again was somehow a noble gesture. Whereas her love was like a leaky tap. Something to be fixed. Better still, stopped. It put her in mind of things that she'd read about devolution – dumb people breeding and smart ones abstaining, slow simmers, stale eggs, Lana, wombs for rent and that acronym DINKS. *Then why get married and abbreviate everything?* Leslie wondered what any of this said about Caroline's marriage or fertility.

She'd tried to think it through, but got confused. There was no greater mystery to Leslie Bird, aside from Sydney real estate, than her own adult children. When they were little, she knew who they were. Both suburbs and children. They were who she said they were. Michael, for example, was sweet and thick. Balmain a dump full of wharfies. But now? A sensitive artist and a boho enclave? *Oh, please, give me strength.*

'Each to their own, Les,' Wallace said. 'At least Caroline has a nice place and car. If you can call their old joint and a fancy car with a reversing camera left day and night on the streets as a temptation for thieves and wildlife "nice". I'd call it stupid.'

Leslie agreed. 'And aren't the giant fig trees lovely, buckling the footpaths, tripping up old parents when someone draws the short straw and actually takes you over there for a visit, as you've got no chance of parking there on your own, even with your disabled sticker. Who in their right mind would spend millions to live in suburbs with no visitor parking only to be keyed and covered in bat poo?'

'Or wee-d on,' Wallace added, still reeling from the time when Shelley and Mark were renting in Surry Hills, and a disgruntled Rabbitohs fan unzipped himself and peed straight through their front window grille onto the floorboards. Another bugbear. 'What ever happened to carpet and lino?' Wallace asked.

Leslie shook her head. 'Floorboards were what you had if you couldn't afford coverings.'

'Too right.'

Caroline's garden, though tidy, wasn't to their taste either. Toby's topiaries and hedges struck another queasy chord, along with his thing for shredding documents, Dyson vacuum cleaners and cutting cakes according to the Frobenius-König theorem. *Pretentious, that's what they are, and if Toby's had a gutful of Bernadette and Amir, then what in God's name have I had?* Leslie wondered. *A whole body full – five times over? More.*

'Of course, Bernadette's coming over tomorrow,' she replied to Caroline, wanting to scream, *How can I stop her, or any of you for that matter, what with your father inviting people willy-nilly, greedy for company, oblivious to anything going on around him. There's no way now or ever again to erect a 'No Vacancy' sign out the front.* No vacancy in her heart, was what Leslie meant; no room for one more single ache. But she didn't dare say a word, knowing it would come out all wrong, like it did with Bernadette.

Bloody Bernadette.

Always oversized, but now so ridiculously large she looked down on everyone. Not just in the way a bully inflates themselves, but as if she'd been scornfully stretched in all directions by the arrival of each child. 'Or has Dutch genes?' Caroline said, citing a giant girlfriend from Rotterdam and the dairy consumed per capita in the Netherlands in the face of her sister's looming; not least over her husband Amir, who was short enough at five foot two to be mistaken for her son. Or sponsor child, as Wallace suggested.

Leslie knows she'll never live down sending Bernadette and her daughters home when they'd stood blubbering on her doorstep, Bernadette broadcasting that she was leaving Amir, while snotty

Lily squealed on her hip and Kamelia and Poppy tugged at her cheesecloth skirt, jangling a cluster of brass bells on her waistband and awful memories for Leslie, of being engulfed once by an angry mob of protestors, when she and Wallace were separated in the city. He'd crossed the road, she'd hesitated and the protestors surged up behind her, banging tambourines, blowing whistles and shouting, 'No more something or other'? *Circuses, was it?* Leslie couldn't make out what they wanted only that they wanted it now. When the lights changed, Wallace watched aghast, as the protestors rushed towards him, with their banners hovering directly above Leslie's head; effectively framing her. It took Leslie more than a moment to catch her breath and ask Wallace what on earth all it was about.

It took Wallace more than a moment to answer, 'No more female circumcision.'

Leslie had never been winded before, but wondered now if she was? And if her initial hesitancy was causal in finding herself in the middle of something so unspeakably awful, through no fault or desire of her own?

Bernadette had looked strange to Leslie, out there on the verandah with her girls. Not just upset. Crazy. Unkempt. The stuff people do to themselves to look nice clearly wasn't being done, and Leslie wondered who in their right mind would go out visiting when their hairdryer had broken, leaving them half curly, half straight? And so enormous, flaunting flesh a husband had rejected. Wearing a stupid fluorescent pink Fitbit on her wrist that kept count, presumably, of her steps from the couch to the fridge.

Leslie had stood cowering, holding the door pulled to behind her, wanting to scream, *I told you so, you fool, now pull yourself together, tuck yourself in, discipline those brats and fix up your hair.* But she didn't do that; she merely asked them to keep their voices down to save Wallace and every other busybody getting wind of the drama. She quietly suggested to Bernadette that she go back to her husband – 'where you belong' – just as her own mother had done when Leslie had tried to leave Wallace both before and after they were married and Old Agnes had volleyed: 'That's your lot. You've made your bed, now lie in it.' Making Leslie feel as if she'd bid and won the worst imaginable, unbearably heavy load that she'd had to carry around for the rest of her life. Alone.

Leslie swore to her mother that she'd never ask for help again. So, when she did, Agnes looked her up and down from behind a locked flyscreen and simply said, 'No, thanks. Goodbye.' Then slammed the door . . . in Leslie's face.

Leslie tried to set the record straight. She hadn't slammed the door on Bernadette and her granddaughters, as was widely wrongly reported, no sirree. It was the opposite to slamming. Leslie Bird made absolutely sure that none of the tiny little hands reaching out for her got jammed, by pushing them away one by one before she gently latched the door and stood on the other side with her head in her hands, until they left.

How on earth she could be blamed for what Bernadette got up to in the past year was beyond her. Just like the fools who blamed Brisbane's deadly floods on climate change. Leslie shuddered to think what might happen when Bernadette visited tomorrow.

Unable to get to sleep, Leslie Bird calmed her nerves by getting out of bed and creeping upstairs to wander about her brood's bedrooms, performing one last search, just in case she'd missed it – like the glasses on the end of her nose. She worked methodically. Turning things upside down. Inside out. Straightening up and sorting out, this from that, having no success, but thinking as she went how amazing it was that one could accumulate so much stuff. Sitting for a moment to catch her breath on the end of Bernadette's narrow bed, Leslie wondered where the years had gone – and how they'd grown so pear-shaped?

When she'd finished tidying – save for the wedding dresses wrapped in bedsheets hanging in Shelley's wardrobe; two ThighMasters, a sewing machine and an Ab King Pro in Caroline's; and Wallace's winter clothes folded in Michael's bureau – the bedrooms looked largely untouched. Preserved. Just the way she liked her chokos and children's childhoods.

Wallace was wide awake when she climbed back into bed. Rolling onto his side, he hoisted his thigh over her, pinning her in a position you'd think would have rendered her breathless, if she hadn't taught herself to feel nothing. 'What the hell was that racket?' he asked.

'Nothing. Mind your business.'

'Did you find it?'

'Shh. Go back to sleep.'

From beneath her pillow Leslie retrieved her rosary beads and offered up a decade for the return of her precious green knits and a peaceful visit tomorrow – or, at the very least, for Bernadette to be covered up.

~

Bernadette was late. Always late. Not just minutes, *hours* – and never apologised. Weddings, christenings, funerals, you name it, she'd amble in as the pallbearers were straightening their knees, balancing the deceased. Making *you* feel as if you should drop everything – that she was so busy and you were an idiot, who either rushed things or had too much time on your hands. Time to buy the wrong oven gloves or cheese, as Shelley once stood accused, when Bernadette arrived at the very end of her Easter brunch and not only ridiculed her sister for serving gouda at that hour but gathered the brie and camembert up off the board and threw them in the kitchen bin, declaring them, 'Inappropriate and substandard,' before opening the cupboard next to Shelley's sink, pronouncing her glassware smudgy and cheap, then drinking straight from a bottle of sauvignon blanc, getting drunk, calling her eight-year-old nephew George a cry-baby when he called her a fool, then being last to leave.

Bernadette had said she'd be there at twelve, so Leslie made lunch – cold cuts, salad, sliced bread, butter and a bowl of Bernadette's favourite peanut M&Ms – then set the table before pacing back and forth by the front windows, peering through the sheers, without disturbing their folds or dust mites. Straining to hear Bernadette's Mazda approaching over the noise of her heart pounding and Wallace's radio blasting. 'Can you please turn that down or off or something?' She shouted, 'Wear your hearing aids, for goodness sake – I can't hear myself think. Can you possibly imagine how I feel? No, of course not. You've never cared about anyone but yourself.'

'Pardon, love?'

Not that he asked, but when Leslie tried to explain to Wallace a little of her anxiety, how terrified she was of Bernadette and getting blamed for everything yet again, all that came out was: 'Stolen more like it, and by hell or high water I will find it.'

Wallace said, 'That's no good, Lesy. Come here and have a cuddle.'

He was standing beside her, so she couldn't escape his arms. Just had to wait until it was over. Then give him $50 and a shopping list, telling him to make himself scarce. As you might to a ten-year-old.

Once the iceberg wilted, Leslie tucked in. Ate soggy greens, devon and chocolate together, chewing over how much she hated the diminutive Lesy. 'It's a term of endearment,' they all lied. Holding on to the Y. And more often than not it was Little Lesy, which only solidified her decline.

All of the red M&Ms were gone, and she'd cleared the table, frozen the leftovers, washed up and cleaned the kitchen by the time Bernadette thumped on the door at 2.15 pm. Leslie took off her glasses, breathed on the lenses, wiped them with the corner of her blouse and counted to twenty before answering.

'What took you so long, Mother? I've been knocking for hours. I was just about to call the home phone but then thought there was no point, as you're probably too deaf to hear it.'

'Well, hello to you too.'

Bernadette brushed past, presenting a big cheek that Leslie couldn't reach for a kiss that she couldn't bring herself to give. She leaned in and made the sound instead. 'Mwah.'

'What's on your face?'

'Where?' Leslie raised a hand to the corners of her mouth, expecting lettuce. Chocolate?

'There.'

'Where?'

'Lower. On the right side.' Bernadette pointed at her mother. 'It's red. In a line. Looks like lipstick.'

Leslie rubbed, then looked at her fingers. 'No. Nothing. Nothing's coming off.'

'Come here. Let me try.'

Leslie didn't have a choice. Bernadette put down her handbag, grabbed her mother's jaw and scrubbed at her jowls. 'Nup. Still there. Broken capillaries.' She tutted. 'Better get yourself some Preparation H, Little Lesy.' She peered at Leslie's chin. 'And whilst you're at the chemist, show them the creases on your earlobes and get yourself some Nair. Unless, of course, you're doing Movember with Michael?'

'It's only March.'

'How's he going?'

'Who?' Leslie ran a finger across her top lip, then felt both earlobes.

'Michael, your third-born. Remember him? Hospital wardsman, silver frequent flyer, father of a deceased chihuahua named Trevor, amateur painter of paperbark?'

Bernadette loved asking Leslie about her only forgotten son, exposing how little she knew him.

'He's alright, I suppose. I don't know. He doesn't say much. Still on night shift at the hospital, going on and on about all the kids brought in with these new fads.'

'Fads?'

'All those stupid disorders and allergies. You know the ones. Everyone's got some kind of "condition" these days that they blame on their mother.'

'Is he still painting?'

'Hardly. Not since your father kicked him out and killed Trevor.'

'Kicked them both to the kerb, you mean?' Bernadette yelped then laughed in fits and starts.

Leslie joined in and mother and daughter roared uncontrollably, teetering on the edge of hysteria.

'Probably did him a favour,' Leslie gasped through her tears.

'Who, Michael?'

'No, the chihuahua.' Leslie made tiny paws of her hands and curled her lip to expose her front teeth. 'With its epilepsy. I mean it was only a matter of time before he froze permanently.' Leslie convulses. Wets her pants.

Bernadette squeezes her knees together, taking little sips of air, then pulls out a chair.

'Oh dear. Where were we? That's right,' Leslie says, reaching for her earlobes. 'Is it heart-related? Sit down and I'll fix you something.'

Two minutes in, Leslie's damp and disorientated. A crazy lady standing in a casino looking for the toilet, not a matriarch presiding over her own precious kitchen worrying about the link between cardiovascular disease and earlobes.

'No, thanks.' Bernadette stands up and recomposes herself – or, rather, opposes out of habit even the most benign of her mother's suggestions. She moves over to the kitchen bench and starts rifling through her parents' mail. 'So, what's happening? Where's Dad?'

'Shopping. Where else?'

Bernadette thought nothing of opening other people's mail. Nor did she bother concealing the offence, putting a bill back the wrong way around so the cellophane window was blank.

'What about one of these?' Leslie said, handing Bernadette the bowl of M&Ms in exchange for the mail, which she snatched and shuffled back into order and then put in a drawer, while Bernadette poked about the sweets.

Picking out a yellow M&M, she holds it up to the light. 'These are greasy. Where're the red ones?'

'Where's my layette?'

'Your what?'

'You heard me.'

'I did. But I don't know what you mean.'

'Of course you do. I loaned it to you when Kamelia was born.'

Leslie reaches for the bowl and Bernadette lifts it a little higher, so her mother has to stretch and almost topples over.

'Steady on there, Lesy.'

Bernadette plonks the bowl on the bench and barges into the kitchen proper. She opens the pantry door, both to shield herself from Leslie carrying on and to stop herself from picking up a heavy pot and smashing her mother over the head, shutting her up once and for all. She grabs a jar of crunchy peanut butter and unscrews the lid. Plunges her middle finger in, swirls down deep until it's smothered in goop, then walks over to Leslie. Holding it up in front of her mother's flushed face, she licks it slowly, saying 'Still haven't got a clue what you're talking about – Lesyyyyyy.'

'Really? Caroline said you had it.'

'Of course she did.'

'But don't tell her I told you. Here – if you're hungry, let me fix you something.' Leslie ducks behind Bernadette to close the pantry doors. Open doors infuriate her as much as kitchen intruders. 'What about a sandwich?'

'Don't eat bread. Haven't for years. And what makes you think I'm hungry?'

Sucking the last of the peanut butter from under her fingernail, Bernadette goes back for the jar. Stands before the pantry, opening and closing the doors, causing a draught that parts her greasy fringe into cowlicks, reminding Leslie of just how often she had tried and failed to tame them. Lick them. Tamp them, roll them into kiss curls, pin them down.

Bernadette puts her finger to her lips, telling her mother to shoosh. 'Did you hear that, Lesy?'

'What?'

Bernadette leans towards the left hinge and flaps the pantry doors again. 'Oh, nothing. Just thought I heard a squeak.'

Leslie fumes, 'All I'm asking is if you could have a little look for it. Look in the girls' rooms, they might have taken it for their dolls. And please don't talk with your mouth full.'

'Are you serious?'

'Very. The layette was a gift from the Portelli woman in room two thirty-four. Remember her? Of course, you do. She was in the bed next to us. Had the husband . . . what's his name? Stuart, Simon, Steve? That's it Steve. Probably a Stephen, but that doesn't matter. He came into our room in tears, held his wife's hand and stroked it, but he couldn't look her in the eye – frightened, he told her later, that he'd glimpse what she'd suffered birthing their baby, because he felt responsible. Isn't that wonderful? Gosh, I wonder if Stephen's still with us? He doted on the baby, precious little Alicia, but he adored his wife. *My love*, he called her. I can still feel it here.'

Leslie beats a tight fist against her chest, the same as she did with the bells before communion, which she doesn't receive because she hasn't been to confession in decades. 'No need to,' she'd said, cutting Caroline off when she'd asked her mother why she stayed seated while the rest of the congregation lined up for a chew and swig of Christ.

Bernadette scans the kitchen bench until her eyes land on Leslie's knife block – the thought of plunging the carving knife into where a mother's heart should be, where Leslie taps (*Knock knock. Who's there?*), keeps her standing upright, smiling, listening to her mother's drivel.

'It was Mrs Portelli's original design, a knitted bonnet and booties with matching mittens and a matinee jacket, in moss stitch with a lace collar, buttoned at the yoke, the palest shade of mint green, just beautiful. You must still have it. I loaned it to you, as I said, when Kamelia was born, hoping the colour would suit her. You know, we'd never had anyone darker than olive in the family before your little tribe arrived. Your father said Kamelia would look like a bloomin' – I think that was the awful word he used – he said she'd look like a bloomin' –'

'Pretty stalky that you remember the room number and what some other woman's husband said forty-five years ago but not who you gave your beloved knitwear to, because it sure as hell wasn't me.'

Bernadette tosses the empty jar in the bin, employing the harm-minimisation techniques that her counsellor had taught her to use when dealing with the family, her mother and Caroline in particular. Stupid fucking Caroline with her migraines and back spasms from all the stress of choosing between ripping up kauri floorboards or laying travertine. Audi or Lexus? Yoga or Pilates? Should she or shouldn't she give her new Korean cleaner the alarm code? Paint or sketch their father? Invite such and such to her next exhibition? (If only she'd invite Ray Martin, Leslie had said, she might be able to forgive her being a show-off.)

Oh, shut the fuck up and take an Endone. Bernadette thought her counsellor had been almost right when she'd suggested the only way to stop from completely hating her mother and older sister was to decrease exposure. 'And when you can't avoid seeing them – show up, need nothing, then choose,' was the counsellor's advice. 'Needing nothing is the key, as needing love and understanding puts you in deficit.'

That's where she was wrong. Bernadette thought a lot about what she needed from the family. Then chose to take it. It was the least, she reckoned, that the bastards owed her.

With her gaze still fixed on the knife block, Bernadette emphatically denied all knowledge of the knits that were indeed given to her, and accused Leslie of seriously losing her mind, just as hers began dredging up the explicit details of not only receiving the layette, but of her mother's shiny old hands, unclutching, conferring her a bag. The squish of soft things through plastic, the scent of ancient vomit and mothballs that had perfumed the magazine clippings nestled among the palest green three-ply wool – one advertising orthopaedic sandals that claimed to aid weight loss and another titled 'How to Keep Your Husband', the latter eliciting a range of responses, from nervous laughter to disbelief, when she'd shared them with her baby group.

'You know denial is one of the earliest signs of dementia, Mum – you should tell your doctor. Get Caroline to take you. Shit!' Bernadette screamed, as a calendar alert sounded on her phone. She looked at her watch. 'I'm gonna be late for the girls. Shit, shit.' She reached into her handbag, rummaged for car keys, panicked, found them. 'I've got to go. Shit. And I need to bake bread. Can I borrow some flour?'

'Bread?

'Not for me, stupid. The agent said people pay more when a house smells of baked goods. Don't worry. Our neighbours have probably got some. See ya.'

'Before you leave' – Leslie scuttles over, links arms with Bernadette, and steers her towards the front room, where she points to a large pile of bags and boxes and says cheerily, 'I can help you to the car, if you want.'

'For fuck's sake.' Bernadette erupts, pulling her arm free so abruptly that Leslie falls heavily against the doorjamb.

Have you let yourself hate them yet? the counsellor had asked.

'Okay. Don't worry, just leave it.' Leslie moans, rubbing her shoulder. 'Oh dear, what have you done?'

'What have *I* done? Jesus, Mum – what have *you* done?'

'I just thought you might . . .' Leslie clutches at her chest.

'Thought I might what? Need one more fucking thing to do in the middle of divorcing and selling my home? Are you out of your mind?' Bernadette towers over her mother. 'Caroline thinks you are.'

Leslie's hands fly up in surrender. Her shoulder is throbbing as Bernadette loads into the boot of her car all the clothes and crap that Leslie had sorted through and assembled after deciding finally – on the eve of Bernadette's first open for inspection, to clear out her childhood bedroom, to turn it into guest quarters. For guests she'd never have. Not one. Ever.

'I'm thinking peach. Peach for the walls. White for the trim. And some new carpet. Maybe a desk lamp. So the guests can read in bed. People like to . . . never mind what people like to – you just – that'd be right. Off you go, you ungrateful so-and-so!' Leslie shouts at the back of Bernadette's car as her daughter screeches away in the direction of the railway station. She can almost feel her earlobes creasing.

The Smith Family collection bins are located at the very end of the commuter car park. Adjacent to Coles. Beneath the overpass. Beside the toilet block. Bernadette hated the squalid corner, where someone always seemed to be lurking: spitting, wiping a nose on a sleeve or doing up a fly, tripping over the liquidambar pods littering the erupted ground where the charity bins teetered. There were rumours of drug deals behind the toilets and someone sleeping inside the bins. She loathed the thought of opening them, thinking she'd be grabbed. Or, worse, fall in.

When she pulled the car up alongside them, the lids were propped at weird angles. Overfilled. She could see what looked like a stained doona protruding from one and a boogie board from the other. Other people's shit made her sick. She was about to drive off but decided not to – to put the car in park, fuck it, and unload the lot. With the engine running and boot open, she stacked the boxes and bags beside the bins. Some of them toppled over and stuff spilled out – old school exercise books, a pair of blue towelling shorts, a tiny doll with a big yellow head that, when pulled up and away from its body, squealed, '*I'm soooooo silly – I can fit in your pocket.*' Or it said nothing at all until the head was descending, and then it giggled and said, '*Hi,*' or, '*Whoops.*'

The doll had been Dette's favourite for the short time she had it. Not for its babbling, but for the chance to yank its head again and again, in case it might say something else. Caroline had had a brunette version that burped and said, '*Excuse me,*' and, '*Try and find me.*' And something else that no one remembered. The girls pulled them in unison and laughed when one burped and the other said, '*Whoops.*'

Leslie confiscated both dolls after Dette drowned Caroline's in the bath and it slurred like a forty-five record on thirty-three, then stopped speaking altogether.

Caroline and Shelley blindfolded Dette and spun her around in circles at the top of the concrete stairs, and she fell through the balustrading and hit her head. When they couldn't get her to shut up, they called for Michael to help lift up the heavy garage door and then shoved Dette inside, wrapping her bleeding head in a yellow chamois while Caroline covered her sister's mouth with her hand until Dette bit her thumb and Caroline screamed and Leslie came rushing downstairs. Both girls got stitches. Shelley was grounded. Michael beaten. Caroline tried to stop Leslie by jumping on her back while she belted Michael repeatedly, screaming, 'Boys don't hit girls. Don't ever forget that.'

He wouldn't.

The girls cried, more for blameless Michael than themselves, as their brother leaned against the garbage bin with his pants around his ankles, his bottom bearing the brunt of Leslie's fury.

Dette stayed in hospital for three days and had an X-ray that revealed she had a skull fracture. The part of the brain that got squished made her forget how to use the toilet. She had to wear nappies to school and no one wanted to sit next to her. When other kids asked about the terrible smell, her siblings said she had dobber disease.

Dette grew to believe that any tension between herself and her siblings could be sorted out quickly with Chinese burns, pinches, punches, kicks and shoves. 'You use violence to settle conflicts; you never learned to resolve it in other ways,' a counsellor suggested to her once, and Dette thought, *What a dickhead, probably an only child.*

Should I or shouldn't I, Dette was considering picking up the doll from where it had lodged between the charity bin and the tree roots when her phone rang inside her car and a homeless guy wandered over to inspect the stash.

'Go for it,' she said to him, unloading the last of the bags, as the call went to voicemail and Leslie's voice quavered out.

'Hello, Bernadette? It's me: Mum – are you there? You must be. You've just left. In a hurry, mind you. But never mind. Not to worry. Sorry to bother you, darling, I know how busy you are with your baking, but it seems I've made a terrible mistake and sent you off with one too many bags . . .'

'Whoa – who'd have thought she'd apologise?' Bernadette said to the homeless guy leaning against a tree trunk, buttoning up a pair of corduroy trousers that looked a lot like her –

'It seems your father's best winter clothes are in there – his favourite pants from Caroline . . . oh, and that jacket Michael gave him, the one he bought at the service station when he met that lovely Italian fellow who was running late for his flight to Milan with a boot full of Armani he couldn't possibly carry on board. Remember that? How Michael offered to walk to the ATM at Pymble but the Italian insisted not only on driving him, but standing right beside him so no one could see him withdrawing – so dangerous those machines. Michael could only take out his daily limit, thousands less than the stock was worth, but the poor fellow was in such a rush to catch his flight he accepted the eight hundred dollars Michael offered him and then asked if he wouldn't mind walking back up to

the service station, so he could make a quick getaway to the airport. Mary Jackson from church called me saying she'd seen your brother walking along the Pacific Highway with an armful of coats looking like he'd just robbed Lowes! Your father had never worn Armani before. Let alone tan suede with fur! Goodness. Anyway, where were we? That's right: I packed up your father's favourites to take to the dry cleaners, but somehow the bags got mixed up – like me, I guess. So, if you wouldn't mind setting his aside for safekeeping, I'd be ever so grateful. Not to mention your father! I'm happy of course to come over and pick it up. If I can drive, that is. My shoulder's killing me. I took your advice though' – Leslie lets out a long sigh – *'and called Caroline. She said it sounds like a dissociation. I don't know; I guess we'll find out when she takes me to the doctor. Who'll probably order expensive X-rays. Okay, I think that's all. Happy baking. Bye for now . . . Bernadette are you –?'*

As the message cuts out, Bernadette shouts to the homeless guy, 'Knock yourself out,' as she accelerates away. But then she stops. Reverses. Gets out. Grabs the doll. Throws it on the front seat. Drives off again.

In her rear-view mirror, she watches the man rifling through the bags, and for a split-second she imagines chasing him, tackling him to the ground, pulling her father's pants off a leg at a time, as he writhes on the bitumen.

In a year's time, she will tell a stranger in a dress shop that's exactly what happened: that she dacked a hobo wearing her father's cords and idiot brother's stolen fake Armani in a commuter car park. And she'll add in a heckling mob. Do-gooders calling the police. Shouting, 'Hey! Back off! Leave him alone!' She'll stop just short of telling the stranger she was arrested for assault and possession and yet arrested, assaulted and possessed was exactly how she felt leaving Leslie's that day, laden down with a boot full of forty-year-old shit she had to dump before picking up the girls, late again, and baking bread for the slimy real estate agent.

She'd spent a month preparing the house for sale, with three sooky kids under seven and a soon-to-be-ex seething under the same roof. She'd moved back in with them and held a garage sale, arguing with idiots who offered five bucks for her entire record collection. Boz Scaggs. ELO. Peter Frampton. Though she did manage to bury Amir's prized zebra-printed candle collection at the bottom of a box of Supertramp and Bee Gees albums, and watched as the candles disappeared up the street in the back of a ute while Amir searched for them frantically. She doubled over laughing, until tears streamed down her face and she was crying for the first time since the letter arrived from Amir's lawyer requesting a divorce. Arrested, yes: that was exactly how she felt then and now – and fucking amazed, too, at the fluency and truth of her own lies; at the blurring between fact and fiction, and how she no longer cared or remembered what she did or didn't do. But she couldn't forget a single one of her parents' offences.

~

'She looks like a bloomin' after-dinner mint' – that's what Wallace had said of her newborn Kamelia, all sleepy and slumped in his arms, drunk on breast milk. He was meant to be holding her upright, burping her. One hand here, the other – never mind. Why didn't he know that? Of course, she was still learning herself, engorged and bleeding, but grateful, oh so grateful. *This is what you've always wanted. Isn't it?* she asked herself and Amir, who had walked about in a stupor since the baby's arrival, doing sit-ups and averting his gaze. She was tucking her soggy-self back in, not wanting to reposition her father's hands to stop her baby's head from flopping . . . 'Please don't, Dad. No, no, it's okay.' At least he was holding her daughter, the way he'd never held his – her. In that moment, couldn't he marvel just a little bit at her creation? Not compare her to a friggin' chocolate?

When she reached out to grab Kamelia from his arms and he refused to let her go, it was as if she were the crazy one and he was – what? Their saviour? As she was prising her daughter from his arms, when Kamelia was neither in his nor hers but somehow suspended, startled, squealing between them, Bernadette screamed, 'Give her to me, you racist fucking pig,' to which Wallace Bird calmly responded, 'Steady on there, BB, and mind your language. I love after-dinner mints. And your mother and I aren't racist, we rolled out the red carpet when that fella of yours swanned in here from the jungle.'

Leslie couldn't believe Bernadette hadn't said anything – 'not a single word' – before she returned from a backpacking trip to Borneo with Amir on her arm.

'Quite the souvenir – all teak, petite an' effeminate; more sheila than me wife,' according to Wallace. Amir Khan 'pranced about like a poofta and, strike me pink, it turns out the little black fella's a Muslim. Mark my words . . .' he said to Bob Savage, on the tarmac of his service station.

Bob and Wallace stood in silence, Bob with his hands in his pockets rocking back and forth, while Wallace leaned against the unleaded bowser, its faint vibrations against his nether regions stirring memories of Bernadette as a youngster hauling home other useless things. When Bob offered to intercept the nozzle, Wallace shook his head and said, 'She'll be right, mate. If only her mother had allowed her a pup as a kid, she mighta got it out of her system. Fill her up.'

Pickled pork was what Bernadette remembered. And shag pile carpet, patterned linoleum and being pregnant with no one knowing. Which was the same as not being pregnant, except her nipples were tingling and bile burned the back of her throat from vomiting four times already the morning of her mother's 'meet the family' lunch; one purge from the baby, one for the floor and twice in dread of going into battle, introducing Amir – whom she'd acquired, initially at least, to incite Leslie. But the moment she stepped over her parents' threshold, through the autumnal shag pile – sprouting no less than two varieties of mushrooms, thanks to Wallace's recent incontinence – onto Leslie's cracked lino, where the worst gashes, thirty to fifty centimetres, were covered up by mismatched carpet offcuts that slipped the second you stepped on them, Bernadette relinquished her autonomy and adulthood, growing down in years. Up in her fears. And fondness for Amir.

~

Of all her childhood memories, it was her siblings swivelling on offcuts that Bernadette remembered most fondly. One Christmas choreographing a dance to 'Let's Twist Again', each of them singing, skating and giggling across the linoleum on their own little Berber stages, in formations she alone configured, first on paper then in rehearsals, which provoked peals of laughter from their father and infuriated Leslie, smiling through a clenched jaw, jumping up the second the debacle was over to reposition her mats.

As an adult, Bernadette despised the worn cover-ups, which said what she couldn't about the family, their lot laid bare, their foundations exposed, the moment her blathering mother opened the door, panting and hugging one minute, then down on all fours the next, crawling behind you, scolding and straightening her precious 'prayer rugs', as Wallace called them. There was one in the entry, three in the family room and a late addition, a small fluffy burgundy one, oval, not unlike a toilet seat cover, that sat in front of Wallace's Jason recliner, a gift from Lana, his special girl, number one on the speed dial, which absolutely no one was allowed to touch and that Wallace kicked aside to scratch his tinea on a particularly toothy lino fissure, a concession Leslie granted him if he would just stop, once and for all, blaming her for slipping over and smashing his hip. And if he would just put it back after his scratch. Which he never did.

Leslie would never forget the long walk home from church when Wallace had failed to pick her up. Nor having to disturb poor Shirley next door, flustered in brunch coat and rollers, unable to locate the spare key immediately. Leslie apologised profusely for calling on her kindly neighbour at the ungodly hour of 7.30 pm. Nor would she ever forget the sight of the little mat all skew-whiff and Wallace spread-eagled on the living-room floor, moaning, blaspheming and florid, the colour of a Dixie

Knight, her favourite *Camellia japonica* – which, incidentally, he was meant to be pruning, not sitting in front of the TV watching football, gorging on Blue Ribbon Neapolitan ice cream. Chocolate and vanilla, mostly. He was getting up for seconds when he slid. Caroline called it karma, Leslie called it justice; eleven weeks in hospital, two operations, a hip replacement, a blood transfusion and a staph infection so serious Wallace almost didn't make it.

Sitting with their heads in their hands and their backs to Wallace – high on morphine, hanging by his elbows from the traction frame above his hospital bed, naked flanks quivering, over a pan – Caroline had asked her mother, 'Wouldn't it be easier to just replace the lino, Mum?' To which Leslie responded, 'Why would I do that, when the rest of the floor is just fine?'

Removing a can of Glen 20 from her handbag, Leslie spritzed the ward.

~

Bernadette had pre-warned Amir about her mother's carpet offcuts, which he navigated more deftly than the duelling air of indifference and bigotry that circulated about the Birds' dining table.

'The little bastards used to prayer rugs – leave 'em right where they are,' Wallace instructed Leslie, when Bernadette insisted on their removal before his first visit.

After days of profuse fretting and phone calls from her father – 'Does this bloke of yours speak English?' (As if the Birds would even notice Amir's minimal grasp of the language, the way they squawked over the top of one another.) 'What time are you gettin' here? What time are you leaving? Is he legal? Just how dark is he, BB?'

'On a scale of cappuccino to expresso?' Leslie called out, from the kitchen, blushing, bandying baristas' lingo in front of Wallace, reeling at his wife's genius.

Wallace lost interest in Amir a minute after he arrived, refocusing his attention on the football as Leslie, fresh from the sink, held up her damp hands as an alibi for physical contact. She dried herself on her apron and fussed with the down lights. Claiming to forget she'd been told Amir, a veterinary assistant from Borneo, was Muslim – speechless over his hue (short black) – Leslie boiled pickled pork and served it with cauliflower, carrots and white sauce beneath bare glaring globes to satiate her concern that things suddenly seemed so dark. Wallace slurped the meat, removing his dentures to retrieve a piece of butcher's twine, while watching his beloved Tigers on TV, blaring throughout the meal, as he thumped the table with his knife and fork, barracking toothless. 'Go on, get him, ya mongrel bastard – he's been doin' it all day. Eat up, Amo; you haven't touched your plate?'

'It's Amir, Dad!' Bernadette remembers yelling above the football, and her mother asking Amir if he'd like to borrow her nail clippers and if he might know her gynaecologist or the fellow who worked up the road at the 7-Eleven, just as Wallace muted the game, reinserted his dentures and said, 'Jeez, there's no need to shout, love,' before grabbing his car keys and leaving for Westfield Top Ryde to search for something halal.

After having no luck at McDonald's or KFC – whom, he learned, only served halal in their George Street and Punchbowl stores – Wallace took the food court cleaner's advice and grabbed a kosher chicken from the kebab shop and raced home to stand at the head of the table and invoke the Torah as he squeezed it from its foil bag; it plopped and skidded across the dining room table, landing in his new little mate's lap.

'Great catch,' Wallace said, winking at Bernadette.

~

Leslie decided to inquire no further into the layette's whereabouts, suspecting neither story nor hand-me-downs had been cherished by this selfie-obsessed machine-made generation, who didn't seem to mind one bit their husbands seeing every last stitch of themselves. Nor it seems, did they (Bernadette?) mind leaving their mother's precious pastel knits in the boot of the car before on-selling it to a woman named Marilyn in Taree, a breeder of champion Cavalier King Charles spaniels who uncovered the soft woollen loot in a plastic bag and put them to use in her whelping box.

Instead, Leslie took her search and rescue mission undercover, by discreetly attending the first Saturday of Bernadette's open for inspection, posing as a potential buyer for the very house she and Wallace had funded without any of the other kids' knowledge, much to her horror. Leslie was mortified by Wallace's big idea to hand out dollars they didn't have by up and selling their precious weekender in Batemans Bay. Her lifelong desire for water views disregarded, her blue reward squandered; before their renters moved out and the Birds could retire and move in, all so Wallace could be the dopey knight in shining Commodore secretly doling out their savings; half of which would end up in Borneo and, later, a seedy bath house, care of Amir.

Leslie questioned the agent about who the owners were and why they were selling; telling him, when he said they were highly motivated due to an impending divorce, that this was the sort of thing that put people off and he ought to keep his mouth shut and opinions to himself. Then she asked him his thoughts on grubby facial hair and lectured him on the invasion of Indian myna birds.

'You know, our council's using traps. They're one of the world's most invasive pests, a threat to our native species with their disease-spreading and corrosive droppings. They're highly territorial, taking over tree hollows, even plugging up nests they're not using, forcing Australian birds out of their homes and – oh Lord, what's that smell?' Leslie interrupted herself, holding her nose, sniffing around the dining room, straightening chairs and the fringe on the floor rug, checking the soles of her shoes. 'Is it pronounced cue-min or come-in? And why do we need it? We got by just fine without stinky spices and Indian mynas flocking in ruining the place. My husband tells me that with the right sort of permit, you can shoot them dead on your own property.'

The agent ran a hand over his slicked-back hair and excused himself to feign a phone call outside.

With the house to herself, Leslie wandered through the musty rooms, past the dreamcatchers, green tea candles, and motivational fridge magnets (*Be the change you want to see in the world . . .* 'What a load of old trollop,' she said aloud) and rifled through her daughter's dishevelled closets and chest of drawers, searching for her knits. With the toe of her Homyped she levered up off the floor what she thought was an overstretched red hair elastic but was in fact a G-string. Heaven forbid! She hurled it towards a pile of other unmentionables behind the bedroom door, marvelling at a full-length mirror, wondering if it had ever been used, how Bernadette could possibly leave the house looking as she did, dressed in what was once considered exercise gear – singlets, t-shirts and tights – which did nothing but amplify her considerable form.

Leslie thought her daughter's impending divorce was a disaster, what with the shame of a failed marriage and Amir walking away from their Glebe bakery – an oven full of hot cross buns and the plum job Wallace had handed to him on a plate – to waste his time at university, furthering his veterinary studies. This despite Bernadette's attempted sabotage on the day of his enrolment interview. According to Caroline, Bernadette had taken all of his clothes and hurled them out of the window onto the footpath, leaving Amir with two options of what to wear to his meeting: his Star Wars pyjamas or a bright red t-shirt emblazoned with an *Anchorman* quote (*'I'm kind of a big deal'*) and a pair of tight white capri pants sprinkled with olive oil either side of the fly, to cast doubt on his hygiene and plumbing. Horrid enough – but nothing compared to what Bernadette packed him for lunch.

Wrapped in aluminium foil, inside a Ziplock bag, a crusty baguette from Bird's Bakery encased the solid steaming contents of their youngest's nappy; smeared lengthwise. Bernadette placed the poo sandwich inside his satchel, along with a note – a note Amir saved and later submitted with photos of the sandwich as evidence in the Family Court's couples counselling session, which both parties had requested the same support person attend – Caroline. Who else? She was hardly Bernadette's first choice, probably her last, but she wasn't going to let bloody Amir rat her out without seizing a chance to set the record straight and maybe even teach her stupid, stuck-up, childless sister a thing or two about judging someone else.

'Have you ever heard of EI? And why are you so short again, Gomey?' she heckled Caroline, towering over her and Amir as they walked towards the Family Court in Parramatta.

Caroline wanted to run, stop, hide, stand on tiptoes and tell her sister to fuck off and stop calling her that stupid fucking nickname.

'I don't know – you tell me,' she said, shrugging and shrinking herself even further.

'It's passive aggressive,' Shelley said of Dette's taunts. 'She's the least emotionally intelligent person on the planet.'

'It's aggressive aggressive,' Michael corrected. 'She's a psycho, and its criminal what they've done to those kids. And you're an idiot for agreeing to go to their counselling sessions.'

'But a lucky idiot. I'd kill for a front-row seat,' Shelley said, salivating. 'Call me the minute it's over!'

Once inside the court building, the three of them sat on green leather chairs in a room that felt more dental than judicial to Caroline, caught between Bernadette and Amir; who refused to look or speak to each other, speaking through her instead. Akin to undergoing a root canal without an anaesthetic, Caroline sat frozen in agony with her mouth gaping open. Utterly bewildered to be bookended by such intense hatred. And something more. Indifference, was it? She'd read somewhere that it was worse than hate. No, not worse than hate. Maybe 'indifference is the opposite to love?' Whatever it was, it seeped in from both sides, and gave her migraines.

The irony wasn't lost on Caroline that when Bernadette met Amir in Borneo – he was working at a primate enclosure, she was visiting the orangutans – that she couldn't speak a word of Malay, Bahasa or Tamil and Amir could barely speak English. That her sister had dated, for a year, without speaking, a trilingual man habituated to wild creatures.

'Communication, it seems, wasn't high on their agenda, until their baby girls arrived and were used as artillery and propaganda, until they protested and were subdued with methylphenidates, so their psychotic parents can get some peace and quiet,' Caroline lamented to Wallace and Leslie, after another gruelling day of grisly testimony.

'Don't go getting yourself so upset, love. They're just idiots and ratbags who need a good hiding.' Wallace meant the kids. Leslie nodded.

Caroline lost it and roared that 'idiots and ratbags' were descriptors best applied to them – her parents. 'And to anyone else who fucks up your DNA, then gifts you with acronyms.'

Foolishly, she had driven in a daze straight from the courthouse to her parents' place in Ryde, seeking some sort of consolation, and found Michael there, moping in front of the TV, hugging Trevor – or, rather, what was left of Trevor: long tufts of chihuahua ear hair and his ashes stuffed potpourri-like inside a pillow that Shelley had screen-printed with his little face. Wallace was reclining, trying to access the photo gallery on his phone, stabbing at the screen, accidentally taking thirty-seven selfies, while Leslie served up dinner, complete with the metal clamp from the end of the extruded sausage mince she'd partially defrosted and mixed with breadcrumbs, diced onion, carrot and a dash of Worcestershire sauce, topped with plastic cheese sliced into strips, cut on the diagonal, baked then popped beneath the grill for a minute to brown, before adding a curly crown of bloodied butcher's parsley.

'Meatloaf,' Leslie called what tasted to Caroline exactly like her parents and cracked her back molar in half. Caroline shrieked and spat out a chip of tooth and metal as Wallace wailed, 'Jeeeeeesus Christ,' and put his hand inside of his own mouth, extracting top and bottom dentures, his face caving in like a baked apple as he tapped his teeth hard against the table, dislodging a steel staple. 'What are you trying to do, Les, kill us?'

Leslie shrugged.

Michael picked up the staple, wiped it on his trousers and offered it to Caroline. 'Looks like the other half of yours – wanna make a wish?'

'No, but you can,' Caroline was weeping, holding the side of her face.

'I wish people would wake up to themselves. Wake up to what's going on in this country.' Michael let rip. 'It's an absolute disgrace that we could fill the MCG with kids under twelve on Ritalin. We have one of the highest prescription rates in the world. There wasn't a thing wrong with Dette's girls until her marriage turned toxic – not like the hordes of kids I see at work with genuine disorders. The middle D in their ADD stands for divorce. Divorce is what fucked them.'

'Hear hear,' Caroline cheered, clinking staples with Michael.

Proud as punch of her little brother and shocked by his valiant effort to enlighten their parents and fight for Dette's girls, when he never ever said boo or fought for himself.

Michael looked at his mother – a furious old woman with her hands cupped over her ears and her head bent low, mouthing to his dopey father to keep his ears blocked too.

Michael grabbed at her shiny red fingers. Leslie resisted. He peeled them back and screamed into her ear, 'What are you doing, you stupid woman?'

'Wishes won't come true if you say them aloud,' Leslie said calmly, clamping her fingers back over her ears and glaring at Wallace, who had risen from the table to grab the remote.

Caroline tried to convey the meatloaf molar affair to Toby, who stopped just short of saying she deserved a whopping great dental bill for making light of her family's madness and ignoring the toll on her own mental health – and their marriage – of decades of futile peacekeeping. 'I just don't know what you were thinking, going straight from the courthouse to your parents' place when they're such friggin' idiots.'

'I know – but they're my friggin' idiots. And please don't call them that.'

'Hadn't you had enough shit sandwiches for one day? What did you expect them to say?'

Caroline shrugged.

No one knew better than her the impossibility of edifying her family or articulating the complex feelings she had for them. 'I guess

I just wasn't thinking,' she said. She was as surprised as him that she'd ended up at her parents' table, chewing metal. She was sure she'd already given up on explaining things to them. 'Especially after the last time I tried, and ending up sobbing down the phone line: *I'm done with you lot. Do you even love me?* Remember that? How neither Mum nor Dad answered me, and I hung up?'

Toby nodded.

'Then a while later, maybe half an hour, Dad called me from the car, on speaker, saying, *What do you know, CB?*

'And I said, *Nothing apparently.*

'And he said, *Make no mistake about it, CB, you've held this family together.*

'And I said, *Yes, Dad, and it's torn me apart.*

'And then he said –'

Toby interjected, '*Before you duck off, love, can you do us all a favour? See if you can whip ten kilos off your sister. I reckon she'd look real beaut a bit lighter; might even nab herself a younger bloke, like one of them cougars.* Of course, I remember that – and that you weren't sure if he meant Shelley, Bernadette, or Lana.'

~

Lana might be only half Bird, but she was all the proof Leslie needed that what was inherently wrong with their flock was entirely genetically Wallace's fault. To be born a Bird was to inherit not only their mangy plume, posture and habits, but a molecular deficit that generations of hard living and soft thinking deposited in their blood, an itch and an appetite bar none – that sealed one's fate as a Birdbrain.

Leslie was less aware of her own lot's legacy. The Maloney broad hips, deviated septums, thin lips and skin. Clingy, pious Catholics, prone to abandoning their children, poor circulation, spectacular stupidity and hatred. Awful, really.

Leslie let slip, whenever possible, that Lana was 'an older working mother of two kooky kids, idiotically named Paris and Sage. As if a herb and a city could save them from their fate?' She sneered that Sage was a veteran of a sixty-hour childcare week since he was fourteen months old, and was turning six when he imploded on a train from Mascot to Carlingford, when Lana gave in to 'his impossible need for her' and instructed the illegal Spanish nanny to leave five-year-old Paris in the care of the neighbours and bring Sage to the city, to meet her each day after school, homework, piano practice, and bath time, in his pyjamas, dressing-gown and slippers, by foot and train; on a three-hour round trip to Qantas where Lana worked full time as a project manager at their new childcare facility.

'According to LinkedIn,' Caroline told Leslie, 'Lana got the job because of her "exemplary skills at bringing stakeholders together to improve services, while simultaneously nurturing the broader environment, particularly diverse communities of educators, carers, children and their families", and her stated goal was "to produce outcomes that were exemplary exhibits and a collective optimal solution for all."'

'What a load of old poppycock,' Leslie said. 'If you ask me, she got that job, rather selfishly, because Viktor quit his to stay home in bed and she's too old and lazy to look after her own kids.'

Born of despair, Lana's 'collective optimal solution for all' – having found love in her forties, with a beautiful melancholy man and vowing to care for him in sickness and in health, till death do they part – was to bring her anxious son to the city on a crowded peak hour train, so mother, child and fractious commuters could spend the 'quality time' together that he craved. Lana said, of the night that Sage erupted after finishing eighty-sixth out of eighty-eight in his school cross-country carnival, then walking two kilometres to Carlingford Station with the nanny and standing on the train to and from Mascot, that he was desperate to just sit down and cuddle his mother. But when the passenger beside her finally got off at Clyde, Lana was still on the phone to her accountant and shooed Sage away. The nanny failed to restrain him and then finally lost it herself, telling Lana and anyone else in the carriage who cared to listen what she really thought of Australian parenting. 'You people care more about chickens than you do your own children, with your grain-fed, free-range, hormone-free shit, but not a single care for your kid's constitutions.'

Who me? was written all over Lana's stunned face as the nanny continued her denunciation. 'Children's behaviour tells their parents everything they need, but don't want to know.' Sage kicked and howled and launched himself at Lana, who pushed him away and excused herself from the hysteria, to get up and stand by the train doors and say to other stunned commuters, 'I wonder where the poor mother is?' Then she got off, alone, at the next stop. And sobbed.

Within a week, the nanny was sacked. 'Because she smoked.' Lana told anyone who asked to mind their own business when they queried how she was coping since Viktor's departure.

'I'm afraid he's not here,' she would say to people who didn't know what had happened, when they called to speak to her husband. 'Well, he's not here, so what's wrong with that?' she roared at Caroline, fending off her incessant questions, 'Have you ever considered you go looking for trouble, Caroline?'

Have you ever considered I'm looking at trouble? Caroline thought but didn't say.

~

Before custody was granted, Bernadette insisted all three of her girls were co-morbidly defected and as such required a formal diagnosis of what was effectively her own disorder – oppositional defiance – because when ODD coupled with ADD it ensured funding that she later used for her research studies and school assistants. The poor suckers whose job it was to stand around in classrooms spouting best practice drivel, trying to keep little zombies safe from themselves and others as they railed against the system while drugs coursed through their tiny bodies – causing Kamelia, for one, to only ever enter rooms by their perimeters, with both hands on her head scrubbing her stubble, pacing only in straight lines, as diagonals were off limits to her precious mind. Skewed by tics, loss of appetite, self-loathing, itches and insecurity – on a good day. On a bad day she pulled fists full of hair out and swallowed it until she gagged and threw up hairballs in the room she shared with her baby sisters.

'All but once I ignored her,' Dette said. 'The first time she did it, *I* took her in my arms and held her and *I* told her it would be okay . . . but then she did it again – and vomited all over the bed in the middle of the night. I didn't hear her until all three of them woke me up howling like fucking cats. Can you imagine waking up like that, Caro? Walking in and finding your daughter choking, covered in spew? The stench was unbearable. I can't tell you how disgusting it was. So *I* carried her to the bathroom and sat her down next to the sink, turned the tap on, opened the cupboard, got out the scissors and told her I just wanted to . . .' Dette exhaled.

Caroline inhaled. Deeply. To this day she's never heard anything more disturbing than what her sister said she wanted to do to her daughter, before hacking off great clumps and chunks of her hair.

'There were just a few knicks,' she said. She'd used Amir's razor to shave off the rest of her five-year-old's hair, but it was blunt.

'Tell the busybodies you've got nits,' she commanded Kamelia – who didn't know what nits were, but wouldn't soon forget when a note was sent home to the entire school warning of the outbreak. 'Every pharmacy from Epping to Eastwood, sold out of treatments,' Dette said smugly, as if she had done local businesses a service by disfiguring her daughter. 'One stupid mother mixed her own aromatherapy treatment. Doused her kid's head in neat coconut and vanilla oil and wrapped it in Glad Wrap. Apparently he passed out and landed in hospital. I suppose I'll get the blame for that too?' Dette said laughing – as if she were Mustafa, not Scar, and everyone else was mad.

Caroline laughed a little too, because she didn't know what else to do in the face not just of what Dette had done and said she wanted to do to Kamelia, but the way she said it. The flash of something Caroline had seen before (on TV? in the eye of despots?). Not being a mother herself, she couldn't understand how a mother could say she loved her children while secretly hating and wanting to destroy them. That love and hate could exist simultaneously was a truth she couldn't comprehend. Maybe it was why she hadn't conceived herself? Perhaps Dette's heroic *I*'s were a warning? Leslie was always going on about mothers who loathed their own daughters, and how it was something she, who loved her own so dearly, could never for the life of her understand.

'The genius of a mother who raised girls with such low self-esteem they don't recognise their own mother's envy,' Toby said, urging Caroline not to call Leslie.

She ignored him, but hung up when her mother answered and she realised where she'd seen the flash before. Not only terrified, Caroline felt a seismic shift in her feelings. And felt something sever. As if whatever had bound them all together was now slithering between them on the ground, waiting to strike.

The officials agreed to Bernadette's request for a diagnosis, since as well as being a giant, dangerous bully, she was as smart as a whip and had all of her PC and BS down pat, even authoring a government-funded thesis titled 'Under Rage Girls', which Toby referred to as her memoir.

Winning custody seemed neither here nor there to Dette. What appeared to matter most, what would signal victory, was that her girls were who *she* said they were. Disordered – by the letter of the law.

Reeling in her sister's wake as they left the courthouse after receiving the rulings, Caroline was thinking, *What the fuck?*

'It's easy. You just have to tell people what they want to hear,' Bernadette said. 'Try to keep up.' And then, as if accepting a Nobel Peace Prize, she said she felt most inspired to come up with answers to everyone's stupid questions when she was standing at the courthouse windows, gazing west across Parramatta Park. 'It's quite beautiful, you know. You should try it sometime.'

Along with thinking her sister was off her rocker, Caroline thought that 'coming up with answers to endless questions' almost perfectly described her own painting practice; with the exception that what inspired her was not easy but painstaking – to show people what they didn't want to see.

No one but those present at the court ever knew what the note in Amir's briefcase said, but they could guess, after police and psychologists were called in, statements taken and the children removed from Bernadette's custody.

Leslie was speechless.

The poo sandwich was not only the final nail in the coffin of Bernadette's marriage but any hope that Leslie harboured for her. It was, as Caroline liked to say, when shit got real for her sister, who quit her job and university studies and fled up the M4 to Katoomba, leaving Amir and the girls to fend for themselves, while she found yoga and some more gripes. The trips back and forth to Sydney, peak hour traffic on the Great Western Highway, the cost of child care, meds, unemployment and keeping company with the loonies of Katoomba in a derelict guesthouse on Lurline Street. 'The place has gone to shit,' she said. 'Full of dreads and dregs wandering about mumbling to themselves, mental as anything, breeding like rabbits.'

'If I wasn't before, I am now convinced it's nature not nurture,' Leslie said. 'I was always there for you kids. And Katoomba was glorious in its day. We used to catch the train up there for high tea at the Paragon. Scones, jam and cream. Shows at the Savoy. Before Peter Allen's baby smiled at him and he left Liza for Rio, it was the bee's knees. How they could ever do that to a place? Dumb it down and breed idiots. And your sister – how she could ever walk out on her girls is beyond me. Do you think it's the blood rushing to her head when she's standing on it? And how does she do that, stay upright when she's so huge? You'd think she'd fall.'

'Oh, but she has,' Caroline said, swallowing everything she wanted to say to her mother except: 'Some of my dearest friends live in Katoomba.' And then later, while making Leslie a cup of tea, she couldn't help adding, 'There's got to be few things worse than the prison you put yourself in and don't understand, Mum. None of us have a clue what goes on behind each other's closed doors.' Which was true for most but not entirely for Caroline, who'd be forever grappling with what she knew her sister and brother-in-law did and didn't do to each other and the hideous mess they'd made of their girls. Oh, and what Amir had revealed of himself the day Caroline stepped inside her sister's hospital room, just hours after her very first birth.

Perched sideways, shivering in shock, on a chair in the corner of the room, Dette sat jaundiced and decimated after twenty-six hours of labour, which included a third-degree tear, ventouse and forceps extraction, and a full blood transfusion, while Amir lay on the bed shaking his head. He wasn't saying, *Can you believe it, your sister's a warrior, I'm a father, you're an aunty – look at our beautiful baby girl!* No. Rather, he eased himself to the edge of the bed, stood up gingerly, made a production of gathering in the waist of his pants, walked over to Caroline, grabbed her by both shoulders and whispered into her ear, 'Dette disgraced herself.'

'Oh,' was all Caroline could think to say, before pulling away from his grip and leaving the room without even speaking to her sister or looking at the baby.

Amir followed hot on her heels, tightening his belt, calling after her, 'Hey, hey, wait up – I want to ask you something.' She quickened her pace, but still heard him say, 'I've lost three kilos.'

Dette still hadn't forgiven Caroline for racing off and then returning all weird sometime later, appearing not the least bit interested in her or the baby, looking no one in the eye. 'Topping up the parking meter,' was the excuse she gave to explain her quick exit, the time spent wandering dazed about the hospital car park and to protect her sister, who was convinced Caroline had stormed off out of jealousy.

'She can't bear to see me this happy,' Bernadette said to her mother, who had arrived with Wallace for a visit.

Leslie nodded, despite adjusting to the sight of her first granddaughter.

'Does she even feel like yours?' she asked, peering down at the baby as Bernadette unwrapped her on the bed.

Caroline jabbed Leslie and Leslie yelped, clutching her side, claiming child abuse, just as the paediatrician walked in to check Kamelia's reflexes.

When he placed his middle fingers inside her tiny palms and raised them, she gripped so strongly she was lifted up off the bed. Wallace said, 'What a bloody beauty,' and wiped tears from his eyes, as Leslie gasped and pointed to the base of her tiny three-hour old spine. 'Oh dear, a birthmark. I guess we should be grateful it's not somewhere more visible.'

'On the contrary . . .' The paediatrician turned Kamelia firmly and gently in his hands, explaining that what looked for all the world to Leslie like an ink splotch was in fact a Mongolian spot. 'She's absolutely perfect,' he said. 'It's just melanin that will disperse over time.'

Which set Leslie thinking, *If I only I had a tissue, we could blot it up and everything would be just fine.* 'Does anyone have a Kleenex?' she asked.

'I do,' Caroline said, taking one from a packet in her pocket and handing it to her father, who wiped his tears and blew his nose.

Caroline suspected from that day forwards that Amir was done for, and in the years afterwards, when her sister was taking leave of her senses and children, nothing would dim her memory of his pettiness and narcissism. Almost nothing. In her mind, Dette's poo sandwich was an unnerving masterpiece. One that could have been halved with Leslie – like they do with foot longs at Subway.

Leslie continued attending the open houses at Bernadette's place and searching for the layette, to no avail – but didn't leave empty-handed though, after her fourth visit. A week before the scheduled auction, when there'd been barely any interest and no contracts handed out, she met a lovely expectant couple who startled her while she was rummaging through Bernadette's linen cupboard.

'Well, would you look at that – great storage!' Leslie said, restacking towels and sheets she'd taken from the shelves. 'Bedspreads take up so much room, don't they? I was just checking to see if mine would fit – and I think it would, folded sideways. It's a fantastic house. Have you had a look around? It's a tad messy and whiffy but would come up a treat with some elbow grease. What can you expect but mess, what with mothers working outside of the house these days? In my day it would have been unthinkable. We worked inside the house, did everything your machines do by hand. And we didn't need spices to curry favours from our husbands. The agent's been telling me about the lovely couple who live here, how they've been blissfully happy in the area and have three dear little girls named after flowers. You'll probably see on the bedroom door they misspelled Kamelia. People don't seem to care about spelling, flowers or making fools of themselves these days.' Leslie glared at the woman's protruding belly.

'I wonder why they're selling?' the husband asked, looking towards his wife, who was rubbing the small of her back and giving him her best *she's nuts – quick, let's get out of here* look.

'To open a yoga studio up in Leura, I believe. The wife's an instructor, isn't she?' Leslie said to the agent, who had appeared behind the couple. But before he could answer, Leslie leaned in towards the wife. 'Do you know what you're having, dear?'

'No, we'd rather a surprise.'

'Oh, so would I – I'm constantly surprising myself. Places like this with such wonderful karma' – she could shoot herself later for using hippie talk – 'rarely come on the market, do they? Now, do you mind if we have a word outside?' Leslie took the agent by the arm, and spoke extremely loudly about making an offer.

~

Leslie couldn't be sure which bit was the clincher but the pregnant busybodies bought the house before auction. Bernadette wasn't grateful – not then, not ever, and especially not back when Leslie and Wallace sold Batemans Bay to finance the mortgage of this house Leslie was now helping to sell. Bernadette took the money without a thank you and then complained bitterly about Harry, Wallace's lawyer. The way he incessantly slurped chocolate thickshakes through a split straw, wearing tight white jeans, high-top sneakers and a gold medallion, really annoyed her. She referred to the buyers of her house as Bonnie and Clyde, though according to the contract they were Anna and John Thompson.

Six weeks later, when they exchanged and the For Sale sign came down, Leslie found herself driving about the neighbourhood again, thinking about her layette, and most particularly its delicate lacy collar. How deft Mrs Portelli's hands had been. How beautiful her baby, Alicia.

Leslie wondered what had become of the mother and daughter as she pulled up to the kerb and parked. She got out of the car and glanced about Bernadette's garden, at the grevillea and hibiscus; at the flowerbeds – now empty – she and Wallace had planted with the girls' namesakes for their first family Christmas. As a parting gesture, Amir had pulled them all out and left them rotting on the footpath.

Kamelia had loved the red sasanquas they'd chosen together, the scattering of poppy seeds that later bloomed orange and yellow. She'd loved digging beside her grandparents and the little spade and watering can they'd bought her – oh, and the tiny gardening gloves. Bernadette reported she'd even worn them to bed. Bless.

Either side of the front verandah, Leslie spotted the faded newspaper they'd torn up together as mulch. A few yellowed strips from the TV guide, ribbons from the sports pages, and half a headline about Julia Gillard and misogyny. Leslie winced remembering the speech; as if it wasn't bad enough having a female prime minister, they had to have one who was name-calling. She stomped on the strip until it merged with the others at the base of the peace lilies Wallace had planted after the baby was born; all of which had come to nothing, like Kevin Rudd and Bernadette's marriage.

What have I got to lose? Leslie asked herself, as she knocked on the front door.

Heavily pregnant, Anna Thompson was a little taken back when she saw the madwoman from the open house standing on her doorstep, all teary-eyed (hay fever, she explained), saying she had been driving past on her way to the shops and decided to stop and say hello and see what had been done to the place.

Flushed with baby brain and the effort you make when you're trying to convince yourself your new neighbourhood's worth all of the upheaval and stamp duty, Anna welcomed Leslie inside and offered her a cup of tea, apologising for the mess as they passed Bernadette's lounge room, littered with moving detritus, and entered the kitchen, where stacks of dinner plates swathed in butcher's paper sat half unpacked on the countertops.

'Everything's going in at eye level, I'm afraid,' Anna said, rubbing her enormous bump. 'I've been struggling to access the lower cupboards.'

'Yes, well, I can certainly see that,' Leslie said, flinching at the display. During her own pregnancies, she had worn a modest smock and no one would have known how pregnant she was. The one time her condition was mentioned in a maternity shop, she was praised for her posture and told she could have been a model. But seeing as she'd never seen the house look this tidy before, Leslie ignored Anna's immodesty, pushed up her sleeves and offered to help. 'Here pass it to me, Bonnie.'

'Bonnie?'

'Sorry, what was your name again, dear?'

'Anna.'

'Anna, of course. Anna, let me help. You sit down. Let me get the tea.' But Anna insisted she'd make it herself. 'Alright then. Earl Grey with a splash of milk, please,' Leslie said. 'You know, you never really get over losing a house, Anna. People think it's the cost of the building and pest inspections that sets you back when you miss out on a property, but that's nothing compared to the loss of all the time you spent imagining yourself living there; where you'd go to church, shop, walk, the friends you'd make, how you'd lose weight, read more, start a book group – one where people actually read and listen to one another. Imagine that! You know how a house gets into your mind? Well, it does mine, at least. There was a place my husband and I fell in love with down in Batemans Bay, on Beach Road, near the golf course, with a circular lounge room, a verandah and one-hundred-and-eighty-degree views. The main bedroom had an ensuite.' Leslie paused, swallowing a lump in her throat. 'So, you can just imagine what that would have meant to an old bladder like mine, having to sleepwalk only a few steps at night. Not to mention the view from the toilet of whales breaching just fifteen metres from shore. On blustery days, you'd go in there just to sit and watch their acrobatics. How can I ever explain to my husband that my sighing in bed at night is not so much from my incessant toileting, as toileting *here*, not *there*, in Batemans Bay, where we should be living out our final years? Never mind. He claims the glut of fresh prawns from the co-op would have been fatal for his cholesterol and some piffle about how it would've been "too damn far from his beloved grandkids".'

'How sweet,' Anna said, wondering how this poor grandfather fared with the ogre in front of her.

'Positively saccharine.' Leslie grabbed a piece of butcher's paper, scrunched it up and rolled it about her palms.

'It sounds like he really loves his grandchildren.'

'Oh, for a minute or two he does,' Leslie agreed, tossing the paper ball towards a pile on the floor, making it clear that Wallace Bird never loved his grandchildren more than when he saw them walking towards the door to leave. She told Anna how Wallace made a habit of dashing off in their company to satisfy some sudden urge to lie down on his bed and think about how much he loved them, or to stock up on blood and bone at the nursery, curry at the food court, or to check on his tyre pressure at the service station, where he regaled strangers with stories she'd told him about something the grandkids did, making it sound like he had been there and that he cared.

'He loves them in retrospect, rather than in person,' Leslie explained. 'He's fed up with them after a few minutes. Just like he was with our kids. We hear the beach house sold to a bald bank manager, but I swear I've had more parties in that place than he ever will or than I've ever had in my own home. Wonderful parties where everyone just got along, sitting out on the verandah at sunset. Pelicans swooping by. Grandchildren swimming at the beach, then falling asleep. The best sort of place in the world to retire to, it would have been. Funny how we never lived there, but it lives on in me.'

Leslie felt her knees buckling as she took a stack of soup bowls from Anna and opened a cupboard that she'd personally lined with pretty paper she'd found at Spotlight, thinking stupidly – oh so stupidly – that little pink carnations and baby's breath on a mauve-striped background might soften or ease things for Bernadette and Amir in perhaps the same way Wallace had thought doling out their life savings might. Fool. Leslie had poked her tongue out at Wallace so long and hard it had cramped. Who knew the tongue was a muscle, second only in strength to the glutes, according to Martha?

When Wallace said there wasn't a damn thing Leslie could say to stop him putting a roof over his grandkids' heads and that it was none of her business anyway what he did with his money, she fumed, 'None of which you'd have if I hadn't saved it and stopped you wasting it.' *His* money. The buffoon. That was the bit that cramped her tongue. And triggered her temporomandibular disorder – six weeks of meds, heat packs and nil by mouth resulting in nil by weight loss; as if her body was just fat and that was that.

When she complained, Martha asked her if she knew what caused her latest bout of TMD, and Leslie said, 'I don't believe in reincarnation, Martha, but when I die, I want to come back as a stranger waiting for a bus in the rain at the end of our driveway. It has to be raining for Wallace to get up off the arm of his chair in the study, where he sits peering out from beneath the roller blind waiting for the clouds to break before hobbling downstairs to the garage, to raise the roller door and his Tigers umbrella, to offer shelter to strangers waiting for the bus. He accompanies them inside and lets them dry off between the mower and recycling bins until their bus arrives. The drivers all know that if it's raining and the garage door's up, Wallace's valet service is underway. It's just bizarre how he's aged and developed a kindness to strangers he's never shown to any of us. Except Bernadette.'

'It's not kindness, Les, it's fear,' Martha said. 'Remember how nostalgic and sweet he was at sixty-five, all watery-eyed, out of work and on the wagon, after his open-heart surgery? You could just imagine they hadn't closed it; heart more, not less, ventricles and valves pulsing just beneath the skin, like a baby's fontanelle. Maybe Wallace Bird is starting all over again, reborn, through generosity to strangers?'

'And strangely Bernadette?' Leslie cocked her head.

Martha brayed. 'Can't you see, Les? There's no bigger stranger to him than Bernadette – and it's bucketing down in her life.'

'But she makes it rain. Every single stupid thing she's ever done has accumulated and caused this deluge.'

'Regardless, I reckon he's terrified of her. You all are. If she blows up, it all will.'

'All of what?'

'All of this . . .'

Martha stood in Leslie's lounge room waving her arms about, simulating an explosion, clapping then parting her hands, softly like a priest; pointing past the kitchen to the front door and beyond, to the aforementioned bus stop out the front of 6 Quarry Road, then towards the pale eucalyptus corrugated Colorbond surrounding the backyard; to the Hills hoist, besser-brick barbecue and incinerator; to the caravan and boat that never went anywhere – the boat Wallace bought through the *Trading Post* and left out in the yard until the grass grew up and over starboard, which did nothing to deter him from inviting friends over 'for a day out on the boat'. When they arrived the first time and realised that meant on land not water, they chuckled and traipsed on in anyway, from the front door around to the side, as per Leslie's detour signs, hauling eskies and towels across the pebblecrete patio up onto *Old Mate*, as Wallace had baptised the boat. Much to Leslie's horror, people arrived in beach attire and left the side gate unlatched, meaning any Tom, Dick or Harry could (but never did) waltz in unannounced. The thought of that much flesh cavorting in her own backyard kept Leslie Bird indoors with her head bent low making hors d'oeuvres – cream cheese and gherkin Jatz, cabanossi grilled on Coon-topped toast, and prunes wrapped in sweaty bacon, all arranged on recycled Pavlova Pantry platters and passed out of the sliding window while Leslie looked the other way. 'Years before McDonald's copied with their drive-thrus,' she boasted to friends.

The kids thought the boat was a hoot and encouraged their father to keep up the dream of one day repairing the rusted old hull and making her seaworthy.

The very first thing Wallace did whenever he arrived home was take a quick squiz to check his *Old Mate* was still there. 'Oh, hello, my lovely,' he'd say, and Leslie would roll her eyes and reply, 'Settle down, Romeo,' thinking he was talking to her and not his prized possession, which Wallace was terrified she'd have towed away one day, after catching her cutting an ad from the paper for a haulage company. It still amazed him she hadn't called them. He couldn't fathom why, but he figured the best way to stay on her good side was by never mentioning her hoarding of every goddamn thing that ever belonged to the kids. If he even got close to looking like he was thinking about raising the subject, all Leslie had to do was glance meaningfully towards the backyard.

The view from *Old Mate*'s deck was the back of the Birds' red-brick house, with fairy lights strung across the pergola and aluminium sliding doors that Wallace had installed for an indoor-outdoor feel, until Leslie insisted they remain closed and the vertical blinds drawn, to save her peripheral vision not only from the boat people but from Wallace's collection of lawnmowers – seven at last count, also acquired through the *Trading Post* and word of mouth, with the intention of one day, when he retired from baking (many years ago now), of taking a welding course at TAFE so he could solder them together and cut down on mowing time. But with the boat taking up most of the yard they stayed separated, exactly where they were. *Just like us*, Leslie thought standing out in the yard one day, hanging her washing out in the only way possible that ensured her smalls had privacy and that the bedsheets didn't flap up and tangle on Wallace's cleats and get rust stains.

'All of it – all of this, Les,' Martha said again, swirling her arms about in widening circles.

Martha, who didn't have a family of her own, thought 'all of this' meant family. Six chairs at a dining table, mismatched crockery and partners, full loads and washing lines, big cars, boats, prams, bunk beds, sectional sofas and lawnmowers, fated to be welded together.

~

'What about over here then?' Leslie said, pointing towards the Westinghouse oven when Anna Thompson, arching and rubbing the small of her back, unpacked a nest of casserole dishes. 'That's where I keep mine at home.' Easing the oven door open, Leslie immediately spotted two filthy baking trays inside. Almost unrecognisable, but most definitely hers. *Goodness gracious.* Her heart skipped a beat and then pounded in her ears.

Tuna bake was the last thing Leslie remembered leaving, when Amir was living here alone with the girls and Bernadette had banned her parents from visiting.

'No need to make a song and dance of it, Les,' Wallace had said. 'Let's just get over there. Those kids need us; need their Whoppy and Lanny. And what Dette doesn't know won't hurt her.'

Such sad, naughty little girls, missing their mother, Leslie thought, crying on their way to and from school. Poppy insisting on propping her teddies up against the back windscreen, so she could wave goodbye to them as Leslie drove away, though they inevitably fell onto the floor. Leslie would watch in the rear-view mirror as Kamelia tried to console her sooky sister. There were more tears in the afternoon if Wallace wasn't standing outside the classroom in the exact spot Poppy had chosen, so that when her teacher opened the door, she would see her Whoppy immediately. Heaven help Wallace if he was late or even had turned his head the other way to chat to some other grandfather on pick-up duty.

Kamelia's hair-pulling had escalated to scalp-picking, so Leslie smeared her head with calamine lotion and knitted her a yellow beanie to cover the scabs that bled along her centre part. The youngest, Lily, walked around with her eyes shut tight, bumping into things. She was Leslie's favourite customer. Loved her Lanny and frittata. In fact, that may have been the last thing Leslie cooked and was still baked on in Anna's oven. Perhaps the blackened frill of mould spores was burnt egg?

When Anna excused herself to go to the toilet, Leslie opened the oven, removed the trays and stuffed them into her bag, calling out, 'Oh gosh, I've just seen the time, Anna. So sorry – I'll have to run. Hooroo. All the best with the baby.'

Safely outside in the car, Leslie exhaled slowly and emptied her bag.

Two filthy baking trays. Not the layette – but something.

Not nothing.

Neither One Prepared

'Where should we start?' Leslie asks, wishing the moment she had that she hadn't, given that *where*, could only mean *here*, right here, as there was nowhere else to unpack the mountain of boxes in this, Bernadette's new one-bedroom apartment. *Apartment's rich*, Leslie thinks. *At best it's a bedsit. At worst, solitary confinement.* 'What I mean is: which stack should we tackle first?'

Bernadette shrugs and hands her mother a knife to slit the masking tape securing the tops and sides of the nearest box. Leslie uses it and offers it back, 'No thanks,' Bernadette says preferring to use her fingernails instead. Belle, on her thumb nail, in a yellow ball gown from *Beauty and the Beast*, easily slices open a box labelled *Bathroom Miss. Miss*, Leslie guesses, is short for *miscellaneous*. No doubt Bernadette wouldn't have a clue how to spell it. Leslie sighs and shakes her head. To her great shame, all of her children are appalling spellers. When she'd challenged their teachers, only to be told getting ideas on the page was more important than grammar, she knew for sure the place was going to hell in a handbasket. Just like Olive Kitteridge had said it would.

Bernadette ignores her mother's sighing as she unpacks towels, toilet brush, ear cleaners, face wipes and dental floss. Leslie unpacks books. Cooking. Self-help – *Start Where You Are*, *When Things Fall Apart*, clearly unread, Leslie thinks. As they work their way through the boxes labelled *Clothes*, *Lounge* and *Kitchen*, she cheers herself by humming along to Angela Lansbury warbling one of Kamelia's favourite songs from the movie stuck fluttering across Bernadette's fingernails and now in Leslie's head.

'Tale as old as . . . la la la la . . . barely friends . . . somebody, la la la bends, unexpectedly.'

'Can you not?'

'What?'

'Hum.'

'Oh, sorry – I didn't know I was.'

'Well, you were. You are still. For god's sake.'

Leslie rolls her bottom lip inwards then bites it to make a point of not humming. Then puts a finger to it to dab for blood that isn't there, but might well have been if she'd bitten with any force.

'Don't over,' Bernadette barks. Less the ferocious guard dog of before and during her divorce, more mongrel with a bindi stuck in its paw, she rips open a box marked *Dinnerware.*

To *over* is to exaggerate. According to George, all the Birds *over* and now say it. *Don't over. You're overring.* Now was a time for under-ing. Of not speaking. Of lying low, unpacking quietly while the traffic roars by outside on Parramatta Road, not letting you forget for a second where you are and would rather not be.

Leslie spots Lumière on Bernadette's middle fingernail and thinks how well positioned he is, being a French candelabra and all. She wants to ask how she applied the sticker, how long it will last. Can she wash up and wear them in the shower? Leslie wants to know everything about Bernadette's new . . . fingernails.

'Create the Life You Want for $99' was the hook that sucked her in to sign up as a consultant for Jamberry Nail Art, after she met a pretty Becky at the Blue Mountains Co-op sporting a full set from *Aladdin* was the gospel according to Shelley. 'And, with a bit of luck, she'll make a fist of it, so just let it go, Mum. Be grateful she's staying on in Sydney, near enough to see the girls.'

'Every second weekend under supervision?' Leslie plucked the inside of her mouth making a popping sound.

As she watches Bernadette flipping and slitting boxes with such dexterity, it occurs to Leslie that a career as a removalist might be a fallback, if people wanting a cast of Disney characters stuck on their fingernails by a grumpy know-all divorcee who'd abandoned her husband and children for a dump in Camperdown were thin on the ground.

Just a little . . . la la . . . scared . . . la la la . . . Nobody prepared, la la la . . . the Beast . . .

'Oh, for Christ's sake, stop the humming!' Bernadette bellows, storming towards the sink.

Leslie apologises again and lifts the yoke of her jumper into her mouth as she continues unpacking, thinking about her first-ever trip to this building to visit Alex; just after his reassignment surgery, when they hit it off and started their monthly book group.

How it was Alex's Jo-Dee, who'd mentioned this apartment was vacant when Leslie had wept at her basin over Bernadette's circumstances, reasoning that, after years of haemangioma discretion, Jo-Dee could not only be trusted, but had enough troubles of her own not to judge others. Jo-Dee Lane had put a finger to her lips and turned a little key that wasn't there, indicating Leslie's secrets were safe with her.

'It's like going to confession,' Leslie once told Martha, who wasn't listening, embittered by the thought of her sister confiding in someone else. 'Except you get conditioning treatments, not penance.'

'Goodo.' Martha had said.

Leslie mentioned neither her friends nor the building when Bernadette announced she was downsizing and looking for a place close to uni and Jamberry's warehouse, where she could stock up on stickers, pliers and solvents. *And children and transsexuals,* Leslie wanted to say but dared not, for fear of exposing Bernadette's wrath and Alex's private business.

It was too late now to tell Bernadette she'd be sharing joists and plumbing with dear Alex and Jo-Dee. Maybe they'd meet one day in the basement and divvy up dirty laundry? Then Bernadette could tell Leslie all about her beautiful unusual neighbours, believing she'd found them all by herself, not via the real estate clipping Leslie had quietly slipped into her handbag a fortnight before Bernadette called to say she was moving to Camperdown. She gave Leslie the address and asked if she was free to meet her there to help unpack: 'So long as you don't say anything. Can you do that, Mum? Can you just show up and shut up, for once in your life? . . . Mum? Are you there?'

'Yes. Just a sec.' Leslie had been struck speechless by the address; this was the first time in her long life that one of her children had ever taken her advice. She wanted to burst with joy. 'Of course, I can be quiet.'

What was there to say, anyway, that wasn't already being said by a mother and daughter standing side by side; the why of where they were, as unknown to themselves as they are to each other.

And how alike they are in their creed – that silence is loyalty. And if they believed for a moment their children were as damaged as they and others say they are, they could never have lived with themselves, let alone stood together in a bedsit one floor above Curvaceous Brides and a kebab shop, six sets of traffic lights and one speed camera from the university where Bernadette will continue to research rage; two intersections west of Jamberry, where she'll load up on the Disney stickers inspiring the film score playing louder in Leslie's head than the reality in front of them – two lives so disparate and yet the same, packed into boxes. Bernadette's piled up all around them; Leslie's at home in the boot of her car in the garage.

Painstakingly collected from supermarkets and arranged over many years into a cardboard maze, Leslie panicked if one of the precious boxes she used to transport her groceries home wore thin and had to be replaced. From Coles to Woolworths to Franklins to the independents, she drove with the exact dimensions in her mind's eye and only really recomposed once the gaping hole in her boot was neatly filled.

Leslie Bird's boxes were not to be disturbed under any circumstances, as Bernadette had learned a few years earlier when she'd arrived from Borneo wearing six-week-old Lily strapped to her body and with Poppy and Kamelia dangling off either forearm.

~

Twenty-nine hours in total (counting delays) it took Bernadette to fly to Sydney via Singapore from Borneo, when she'd left Amir and his parents on the outskirts of Kudat, where they farmed goats and chewed the tobacco that rotted old Mr Khan's teeth and gave him heart disease. Amir had stayed behind to care for his father, while she travelled home.

Quite the convoy, three girls under five and four suitcases. The largest had no wheels, and Bernadette straddled it to sit and breastfeed, bunny-hopping along in the queue snaking through Kota Kinabalu Airport, as Lily fussed and pressed her tiny feet against Bernadette's inflamed caesarean wound encrusted with a paste that she *hoped*, the baby nurse had said, would extract bacteria the same way antibiotics would have, if anyone had dispensed them on the night her stitches ruptured during an asphyxiation incident that may have left her girls motherless (if Kamelia hadn't been woken by Bernadette hurling a mug of tea against the wall and summoned help) when, two hours after Lily was born, still anaesthetised below the chest, Bernadette found herself gasping for air, suffocating, without any body or voice.

Not unlike how she felt as a big white woman with child, living in Borneo without any of their languages or gods.

Fluid on the lungs, they said, caused the choking.

Fluid that migrated when the doctor and nurses, in the midst of Bernadette's C-section, lifted her up off the bed and tipped her onto her left side to raise her blood pressure, which plummeted as soon as the scalpel sliced her open. Her voice and field of vision narrowed like a bung picture tube. She'd tried to tell Amir about the pressure, the rush of air, what she was feeling – that she was fading – but he was too busy fussing with the ties on his scrubs and joking with the staff in Tamil to read her pale lips as she was tilting. Her innards lurching outwards, utterly in their hands, she was sensing not just Lily departing her body but her very self.

She felt it again, later, on the ward, when a crabby woman, who couldn't possibly have been a nurse, thumped her on the back and demanded in Bahasa that she breathe, breathe, before heaving her onto a grey vinyl chair, (where she left her overnight) in order to strip the damp sheets from the bed. As the hours wore on and the epidural wore off, Bernadette felt more of herself waning.

The crabby woman returned only once at dawn to lift the blinds and leave what looked like a photo album by the end of the bed where Kamelia slept with little Lily slumped across her tummy, like a tiny sack of grain.

Bernadette hadn't planned to give birth in Borneo, on what was meant to be a family sabbatical to visit Amir's poorly parents before Kamelia started school. Nor had she intended to depend on her five-year-old to stay by her side after the birth and help with the baby so Amir could return home to shepherding his father, goats and Poppy, who was inconsolable after seeing her mother carted off earlier in the morning. Bernadette's intentions had departed with news of the unplanned pregnancy and arrival of renal colic and vaginal varices, so serious, she thought the doctor said, via the translator standing beside her during an internal examination, that this would be her last baby and could he perform a caesarean and tie her tubes?

'Tell him no, thank you,' Bernadette said, squeezing her eyes and knees closed, sobbing that she wanted to go home. That she wanted Leslie. Which surprised Bernadette almost more than Amir.

But she was too pregnant to fly home.

Flying would endanger the baby, they said – those who didn't know how dangerous it was to find yourself pregnant and ailing in a third world village, living in a constant state of confusion and exhaustion with Amir's parents, their bleating goats and two small children who were picking up the local dialect faster than she could rattle through her own little list of Bahasa words – *yes, no, hello, good, thank you, goodbye, goodnight.* Or one of the few sentences she memorised. *How are you? Where's the toilet? Only looking. One chicken, please. How much is it? I've got the shits.* Forsaking conjugation, she tacked yesterday or tomorrow onto a sentence, occasionally adding both, 'Yesterday I've got the shits tomorrow.'

An unbearable month later, with the breech baby's head jammed beneath her breasts and reduced fetal movement, she conceded, yes to the C-section, via another translator*, a 'sexpat' – locals called mid-lifers who got laid by young villagers* – an ex NHS midwife, who visited her from a neighbouring farm with bovine ultrasound equipment caked in pig muck, that she placed onto

Bernadette's belly before calling the doctor, who instructed her to transport Bernadette to a small clinic two hours down the coast, where he'd secured an operating theatre. There, Bernadette would be stripped and scrubbed of pig shit and painted with antiseptic the same colour as the meconium staining Lily when she's finally delivered; one of the doctor's shoes will be resting on the bed, whilst both of his hands are wrenching the baby, finally yanking her from the womb, into the world, whilst the bed is rocking. Bernadette watched the whole thing in the reflection of the six stainless-steel surgical lights mounted on the ceiling.

The green sheets draped over a screen in front of her face were meant to keep her from seeing what would feature in her dreams for years to come.

No one in the operating theatre had realised that all you had to do was look up to see what you weren't supposed to.

Her most frequent nightmare was of an autopsy executed in the centre of a vast library where Bernadette was laid out on a concrete table, deceased but watching intently from high up on the ceiling, as a parade of family and friends filed past the towering bookcases to forage about her insides, extracting organs that were recorded by a clipboard-wielding Amir. The nightmare seemed self-explanatory except for the bookcases, which were crowded with trophies of cats. This baffled Bernadette until she wrote it down and sounded it out, *cat-as-trophies* – catastrophes! 'Isn't that incredible?' she said later to Leslie, who agreed it was indeed uncanny that even Bernadette's dreams were misspelled.

Inside the photo album, left on the end of the bed, were pictures of twinkling constellations set against a black velvet sky. Bernadette thought she was agreeing they were beautiful when a woman in a white uniform repeatedly pointed at the same page, over and over, saying something in Hindi, then putting out her hand and asking for money. Bernadette hadn't slept for three days and was sick of nodding and wanted her to go away so she opened her purse. It wasn't until the woman returned and lifted Lily from her arms and positioned a piercing gun by the side of her tiny head and went bang – bang, that Bernadette realised; they were studs not stars glittering in the album.

When her shock subsided, she learned from Amir that it was customary to garnish baby girls, even before the placenta was delivered, the third stage of labour in Kudat was ear piercing; as much for adornment as branding.

~

When Leslie saw Lily for the very first time strapped in a sling, splayed like a Portuguese chicken against Bernadette's ample bosoms in the arrivals hall at Sydney Airport and blurted, before saying hello, 'What have you done to her ears?' she tried explaining to her critics, it was simply because she was teary and flustered. Overwhelmed by a whole raft of things from Bernadette's cleavage to the flight delay and all of the endless waiting, checking and rechecking that her parking ticket was still tucked securely inside of her pocket, *not to mention the lid on her graphite powder*, while her old eyes scanned the arrivals board and hall and witnessed the most moving of reunions. Leslie Bird cannot begin to tell you about the unlikeliest-looking people in the world that she saw throwing their arms around one another. One family in particular that took her fancy still had her attention when Bernadette arrived. 'So, what else could I do but ask Bernadette and the girls to join me, so I could show them this funny little man? Honestly, you just had to see him from the front, he was *so* unusual! And all I said was, *If you hurry up, we might catch him.* Come to think of it, it was that – and not the ear thing, that I said first,' Leslie stated defiantly, 'And it's not like Bernadette threw her arms around me, either.'

Bernadette had stood still, speechless, shaking her head, when Leslie gave up chasing the little man and begrudgingly changed the subject to the ungodly hour she'd driven to the airport and the price she'd paid for a cappuccino that still wasn't hot enough despite specifically asking for the water to be boiled, while knowing full well that if she'd just got up ten minutes earlier she could have made a nice hot thermos for herself – but she was just too tired. So tired she'd probably have to nap when she got home, after tossing and turning all night rehearsing the drive to the airport after Caroline instructed her to stay in the far right-hand lane for the short stay car park and not to go into the big one, which you can never get out of apparently – which reminded Leslie that her parking ticket was due to tick over into the next ridiculous hour, so if Bernadette and the girls could please just try to keep up and stop dawdling, she might just reach the machine in time. Meanwhile, they could join the taxi queue, and they'd probably all arrive in Ryde around the same time. 'Welcome home, girls!' Leslie said excitedly.

'Sorry?' Bernadette managed to say.

'No need to apologise, darling. It's not your fault that the flight was late and you didn't have time to tidy yourselves up before landing. You can have a good scrub when you get home.'

'Wait. What? I'm not sorry for that, I'm . . .'

'Overcome?'

'No! I meant, aren't we coming home with you in your car? If not, why the hell are you here?'

Leslie frowned and did a little charade thing with her hands – half praying, tapping her fingers against her mouth, half outlining a box, boxes; lots of them, before biting her left knuckles, and whispering, 'I don't think your luggage will fit in the boot.'

'Why not?' Bernadette screamed. The baby startled.

'Oh, poor thing.' Leslie peered into the sling. 'Maybe she's got a little pain. Have you got a little pain?' she asked Lily, before turning and starting a slow gallop away from them towards the machines, waving one hand above her head in farewell. 'See you at home, girls.'

Bernadette knew what Leslie couldn't say – that she couldn't possibly part with her boot full of empty boxes. 'One of the neatest configurations ever assembled,' according to Aunt Martha. The Batlow apples box was the last piece of Leslie's cardboard puzzle, and had taken her nearly a month to source.

If Bernadette could have, she would have turned around right then and there and taken the next flight back to Borneo.

~

As the smell of kebabs wafts in through the windows, Bernadette notices that not only is she not hungry, but she'd already had more than a gutful of Leslie.

Caroline had been right to say it was mad to invite their mother to help. *And Caroline would say that,* could *say that because she had Toby, and friends, a cosy life, and believed wholeheartedly that her 'art' – rendering others in her stupid paintings – was a sign of empathy, when in reality she didn't have a clue what it was like to live inside another person's skin. Thinking she did was fiction. Idiot.*

'What about these?' Leslie asks, pointing to the last pile of boxes, stacked beside what will be Bernadette's bedroom. *If you can call a wall with a sofa bed and a folding screen a bedroom,* Leslie thinks. *Heaven help anyone who thinks they'll fit three little girls in there as well. Maybe that's the plan? Unmother them – officially, then blame the apartment.*

'I guess so. Yeah. No. Actually, no. No, thanks. Just leave them. Can you just leave them? Please, Mum,' Bernadette begs, after spotting the side of the second box, marked *Baby Clothes 0–1.*

But it was too late. Leslie had seen it too.

Bernadette tried to intercept it. 'That's okay, I'll take that.'

'Don't worry, I've got it,' Leslie says, wrestling it towards herself, the two of them struggling, tugging, Bernadette looming, Leslie losing her balance, letting go of it abruptly. Bernadette stumbles a few steps backwards then rights herself and places the box on the sofa bed.

Leslie points to it and says, 'I've been meaning to ask you –'

'Don't,' Bernadette interrupts, making fists of her hands and ropes of her jugular veins.

'Don't what?'

'Don't ask me. I've already told you a million times I haven't seen it.'

'Seen what?'

'Your bloody shit green knit thing. Isn't it the only reason you're here? To snoop. Oh, and to gloat of course.'

'What a dreadful thing to say about your poor old mother, who's only ever tried to help you. Honestly . . .'

'Honestly? Help me? Jesus. And while we're at it, I've been meaning to ask you something: how the hell did you ever think I'd remember her?'

'Who?'

'Oh, for Christ's sake, Mum, your stupid Portelli woman, in room two hundred and whatever.'

'It was two thirty-four, but never mind.' Leslie shudders, 'Please don't blaspheme. I think it would be best if I just collect my things and get on my way. Your father will be waiting for his dinner.'

'Suit yourself.' Bernadette opens the door and holds it, staring at the floor, waiting for her mother to finish faffing and almost exit before slamming it with such force it lifts Leslie's curls and almost knocks her over.

Shaking. Shocked. Unable to move. Leslie tries to catch her breath. Camouflage her neck. She feels hideously exposed and suddenly sorry and wants to knock on the door across the hall and apologise to poor Alex, who couldn't have helped but heard the racket. But what would she say? *Hello, darling. Sorry about the noise. I hope your glassware survived the slamming. I hate my daughter. My daughter hates me. When's our next book group? Goodbye.*

No, of course Leslie can't knock. Doesn't want to knock. Considering it is proof of just how discombobulated she is, leaning hard against the wall, both hands clutching her chest, which feels as if it contains a flock of ruby-throated hummingbirds. Her fingers are tingling. Her mouth is dry. She tries to slow her breathing and count all the women in her family who had met their ends with massive heart attacks. Late at night. Alone. In an armchair. All neat, tidy and privatey. As the pain moves from her chest to her throat, she wonders if this is her time. Or if this is angina? (And why someone can't think of another word for it.) And who would find her? God forbid, sprawled in a dingy hallway. She can just imagine Bernadette stepping over her. Calling the council. Asking for waste management. Booking a hard rubbish collection. Saying, 'Whitegoods,' when asked what needs removal – describing a large old freezer in the hallway. 'Rusted inside. Double doors. Oh, I'm not sure. About one or two cubic metres?' Then frowning and saying, 'Oh, I see. Well, if you can't pick up on Parramatta Road because it's a clearway, what about the laneway at the back of our building? Yes, I'm sure there's access. The kebab shop's got a big dumpster, so you must be able to get a truck in.' More listening, frowning, then giggling. 'No, I'm single. Yes! I've just moved in, I don't know anyone yet. But yes, I guess you're right, it's as good a time as any to meet the neighbours. I'll pop across the hall and knock and see if they'll help me haul it outside.'

And when Leslie imagines the waste man telling Bernadette that many of their pick-ups are taken before council can retrieve them, she can almost hear her youngest agreeing to take his advice and, rather than attaching a sign to the freezer saying *Free to a good home*, writing *Out of order*. In permanent marker, so the ink won't run if it rains.

Leslie wonders if she should start wearing one of those Medic Alert thingies? Heavens.

When her fluttering finally eases, and it appears she'll live to tell Wallace all about this dreadful business, Leslie sighs, lifts herself off the wall and slowly makes her way downstairs to the bus stop, lamenting Bernadette's belligerence and stewing over all the things she wished she would have said to her . . .

You were there in room two thirty-four, you ungrateful foul-mouthed hippie. Before you went and ruined yourself, lost your girls and your marriage and ended up in this dump with your stupid stickered fingernails. You were there in my arms – in hospital – cradled, fed and burped every four hours, as soft-soled nurses moved around us, plumping pillows, stroking tiny feet, keeping dozing babies suckling, coaxing jaundiced cheeks and cracked nipples until just the right connection created the let-down that contracted uteruses, expanding newborn tummies – yours and Alicia Portelli's.

Leslie thinks it's beyond cruel of Bernadette to have forgotten all of this.

~

After the trespass and indignities of marriage, pregnancy and labour, nothing in Leslie Bird's life would ever surpass the sanctity of the maternity ward – the pastel fruit of wombs and fontanelles quietly closing and no men (bar the doctors, who were gods, so didn't count). The bliss of bonding with multiplying women who had endured the same long self-divisions, before returning home to mouths to feed, a household to run and a husband's needs (which would see Leslie back on the ward in eighteen months). The communing was heaven, as opposed to having a nappy stuffed in her mouth by a pink lady in a mixed surgical ward where, confined alongside hernia and bunion patients, Leslie had spent a month sobbing after her very first birth, fifty years ago in a few months. Not that she was counting or commemorating month birthdays for half a century; the birth never mentioned, save for Wallace, staring at the road behind him, thinking of Sammy, freckles, Florence and leaving Grenfell; not Leslie, beside herself and him with her empty arms and belly still huge, as if what happened hadn't. Saying, as he lit up a Benson and Hedges on their drive home from hospital, 'Never mind, love.'

Never mind that Leslie had conceived, carried, delivered but never seen or held her baby boy born blue; rugby-passed by a midwife to a nurse to an enamel bucket, making a noise that had never left her and kept her from piers, fish markets, florists, anywhere enamel might receive weight. From the bucket, her son slid to an anonymous grave at the very edge of a cemetery, as mother's arms and consecrated ground were not for stillborn unbaptised Catholics in the 1960s. Buried alone or in the coffin of a stranger in tandem disposal, in order that the little ghost not torment its parents with reproachful lamentation, he decomposed, she supposed, having never asked after being told: 'It's for the best. Move on. Have another one.'

And this from Wallace's mother: 'You can't die if you weren't born alive, can you, dear?'

Fed a tray of tablets, Leslie had her bosoms bound to prevent mastitis when the milk came in and had nowhere to go.

'A few tears are normal on the third day, what with the hormones and all,' the dour duty nurse said. 'But would you mind keeping it down so as not to disturb the other patients? Mr Carlin here has had an awful night with his big toe.'

'Milk and sugar?' a pink lady serving tea and arrowroot biscuits inquired, drawing the curtains around Leslie's bed then leaning in and whispering, 'This will help.'

For a split-second Leslie anticipated a hug, not terry towelling stuffed in her mouth to silence her sobs.

You can die and still be alive, Leslie decided at twenty-eight years of age; biting the sheets a fortnight later when Wallace reached out in bed and heaved atop her before she'd finished bleeding.

Never mind.

In time it became a place, like Peter Pan's Neverland, conjured by Leslie not to preserve childhood but the state of holy matrimony; Nevermind appeared just off the coast of her marriage from the wedding night and was sensed whilst they were dating. Once at Luna Park on the Turkey Trot, and later when Leslie was in Wallace's Volkswagen admiring her engagement ring, and his dog humped her haemangioma and Wallace mounted the gutter, crashing.

Never mind.

Whenever Leslie said it, thought or heard it, whatever it was that took her breath and words away, she dispatched to this place, where it merged with other dissonant thoughts into menacing contours that floated in her mind's eye like a giant iceberg. Ninety-one per cent of itself concealed beneath the surface.

Life, Leslie, Marriage.

Tenanted

'How do you stay married so long?' they asked.

There were two types who probed her and Wallace's longevity – desperate or sarcastic, Leslie thought. They revealed themselves as one or the other, by stressing the *do*, the *you*, or both, usually at anniversaries or weddings.

At Bernadette's ghastly reception, back in 2005, just before the Cronulla riots, in the low-ceilinged, maroon-and-gold-carpeted Indian restaurant, Wallace stood sweating, awaiting his applause, thinking, *What the hell's wrong with these people? Maybe they can't hear me?* He was nearing the end of his speech as father of the bride, having just shouted: 'I don't care what colour a man is – no son-in-law of mine's going to waste his bloody time on books at Sydney Uni. A man needs a career; needs to make a crust . . .' He tapped the microphone – 'Testing one, two, one, two' – as the audience, who had been stunned silent, broke into gasps when Caroline jumped up and tried to pull him off stage. Wallace refused to move, telling Caroline it was no one else's business if he wanted to install Amir as an apprentice at their Glebe bakery. 'And I'm paying for this shindig,' he added, 'so I can bloody well say whatever I want.' And what Wallace most wanted to say, as he moved back towards the microphone, shoving Caroline away, was what he had planned to say: 'Now, would you all please be upstanding and join me in toasting me daughter Bernadette. I don't know what it is about brides on their wedding day, but they all look nice. Cheers, love. To Bernadette.'

The guests looked at one another and clinked tentatively. 'To Bernadette.'

The band had resumed playing when Wallace interrupted. 'Sorry, fellas – there's just one more thing, before I duck off. I wanna share a little secret with youse. Everyone's always asking me – aren't they, Les? – asking us what's the secret to staying married for so long .'

The guests looked over to Leslie, who was staring at her lap, one hand in her pocket pressing on the lid of her graphite cannister, as Wallace continued, 'I've thought about it long and hard, and the answer is . . . can I have a drum roll, please?'

The band obliged.

Leslie looked up and, after an endless pause, Wallace exclaimed: 'The secret to staying married . . . is marrying the most wonderful woman in the world!' (This, about a woman he'd elbowed and called a cow only ten minutes before.) 'So, I'd like you to join me in toasting me own bride – the greatest housekeeper that ever lived. You wouldn't believe how tidy our joint is. A man doesn't have to lift a finger. Cheers . . . cheers to me bride, Leslie.'

The room erupted.

Leslie nodded, smiled, then felt herself stirring, having finally heard the answer to her own interminable question. As Wallace said 'world' and the Bollywood drummer hit the snare drum – *ta da!* – it blazed into her consciousness that the secret to staying married was implicit in the question. It was staying. Simply staying! Staying – not leaving. Staying put. Plain and impossible. Pick and stick, George would call it. Sticking it out and staying, even when your youngest daughter was prancing about in the Taj of the Valley Indian Restaurant, Penrith, after marrying an effeminate little creep in the local courthouse, much to Leslie's horror. And horror doesn't come close to describing the wedding, the uncivil ceremony: the surge, the heat, the yank forwards and jerk backwards, as if everything connecting them was straining, the umbilical bungee cord threatening to snap and release her as a mother once and for all. Leslie held on to the back of the seat in front to stop herself from toppling, collapsing, watching her own flesh and blood in flimsy lemon chiffon, beaded ankle bracelet, open mouth kissing a scruffy Indian, before bride and groom tore band aids off each other's ring fingers and raised them towards the room, in the biggest up yours; revealing not only freshly tattooed wedding bands, but that they were now not only legally wed, but expecting a baby, too. Bernadette cupped her belly. Amir bent and kissed it. Leslie fell backwards, her bowels lurching. Shotgun: she should have guessed. She wished she had one loaded in the back of the Camry.

Horrified she was, from the moment she'd arrived and had to leave the car parked out on broad, treeless Henry Street, its breadth suggesting someone had higher hopes for Penrith than the drongos littering the footpath, asking Wallace for a light, while she slipped and tripped up the gutter in the stupid new shoes Bernadette insisted she wear. 'Anything but those ghastly sandshoes of yours. My mother only owns one pair of shoes,' she told the women in the Comfort & Fit store, and they all cackled as if Leslie wasn't sitting there with her big, red, bunioned toes protruding through the used, nude disposable try socks that laddered the second she put them on. Why they made them so tiny was beyond her. 'They look fabulous – just wiggle yourself a little more forward,' the stupid woman instructed, tightening the straps, ignoring Leslie who, eyes skywards, was wincing in pain. 'The leather will stretch,' she said, which it didn't, after Leslie gave in for no other reason than to stop the humiliation and bought them and wore them, as she was told, on the carpet at home, all the while plotting to return them the minute the wedding was over. With that in mind, she protected their soles with thick layers of sticky tape, so when she slipped and tripped up the gutter and scuffed the buckle on the right shoe, her plan and the day were ruined, long before she learned of the pregnancy, even before she joined the smoking, tattooed, toothless rabble dawdling into the courthouse foyer where, displayed in magnetic letters on a noticeboard, among the hearings, mentions and motions of the day – a loose motion, an explosion, is what Leslie feared when her stomach dropped upon seeing it there in black and white, plain as day – spelled out: *Bernadette Grace Bird & Amir Bin Khan. Wedding. Courtroom 3.*

Leslie was still acknowledging the raucous applause that had greeted the finale of Wallace's speech; luminous now with her 'stay' revelation. 'Thank you, yes, cheers.' She raised her glass and then her voice, leaning in towards Wallace's good ear as he settled himself back down at the table. 'Marriage vows should be changed immediately, Wal. Do away with take him and take her, for better or worse – it always gets worse. There's only one thing to honour, promise and obey, and that is to stay! Stay when you would much rather leave. Stay when you can no longer bear each other one more day. People are greedy – they want to be married and happy, but someone needs to tell them, *You can't be both!* They should sit couples down with God as their witness, strap them in and make them listen to the worst possible versions of their future selves, as described by the cranky elders of both families, and then ask, *Who's staying? Will you, so-and-so, stay, when the worst of life comes your way?* And the answer won't be, *I do*, but, *I will. I will stay.* What do you think, Wal?'

As Wallace deflated, Leslie leaned down until her chin was resting on the table, unbuckled her shoes and then wriggled her toes free. Bugger Bernadette. Bugger everyone.

> *Love is never patient or kind. It envies. It boasts and is proud. It dishonours, is self-seeking and easily angered. It keeps records of wrongs and delights in evil and rejects the truth. It does not protect, trust, hope or preserve. Leslie Bird. 1:01.*

Wallace had returned from the stage, floating on air; feeling somewhat the celebrity after the riotous reception his speech received, his hands and cheeks were red and tingling from guests high-fiving and gushing. He particularly enjoyed the accolades from Uncle Bhadra, the Khan family's sole representative at the wedding, if you didn't count the life-size cardboard cut-out of Amir's parents, which Shelley had kindly organised and printed. It turned out a little too shiny, making it hard to see Mrs Khan's face, but otherwise it was splendid and hauntingly life-like. Shelley propped it up at the registry office in the front row for the ceremony and then placed it on its side in the back of Leslie and Wallace's Camry, making Leslie feel they were getting on just fine with the new in-laws. Afterwards, she would mention to strangers that they'd shared a car ride from the wedding to the reception at the Taj, into which, incidentally, Wallace had carried Mr and Mrs Khan from the car under his arm. The father was short, like Amir, but almost as tall as Wallace on account of his turban. 'You sure know how to use a pause, sir, and an apostrophe,' Uncle Bhadra had said. 'I can't read in English, but if I could I would want it to sound like your voice in my head. It was the best speech I've ever heard, sir. Would you mind providing me with a copy of it for my family?'

'Did you get an earful of that? He wants a copy. And called me sir – not once but twice,' Wallace broadcast with two fingers in the air, to no one and everyone at his table, ignoring Leslie's sour revelation about staying. No one was more accomplished than Leslie at extinguishing his joy.

'So, what do you think of my idea, Wal?' Leslie pressed him.

Wallace slumped in his chair, inhaled deeply then exhaled loudly, placing both hands on the edge of the tablecloth, looking like he was going to stand up or tip the table over. The rest of the Birds made their escape. Even Caroline, with her voracious appetite for drama, left her parents to their argument.

'What do I think about your idea, Les? I think you're mad and cruel. And that everyone loves me. Look at 'em all, still laughing about my speech. I think you're jealous. I think a man tries to pay his wife a compliment in front of all of her family and friends, and she doesn't even have the decency to thank him.'

'Keep your voice down,' Leslie said, smiling through clenched teeth.

'Yeah, sure, whatever you say, love. How about these for vows? *Do you, Amir, promise to stay with Bernadette when she's old and crabby? When both hips are gone and she hasn't let you near her for decades? When you try to talk to her about your needs and she tells you you're disgusting; disgusting could be your middle name she calls you it so often. Will you stay with a woman who'd rather whinge incessantly about her ailments than get them fixed? Barely a day will go by when you won't hear her bitch about her bunions and children. Even her closest friends will cop a caning. Will you stay with her when she forces you to give up all of your friends? Your favourite TV programs and clothes? When she insists you wear what she wants to look at and not what makes you comfortable? And that goes for sitting and standing, too. She'll choreograph you. Comfort's not her goal. Get used to correction, mate. And when she finishes coddling your children, which is about the same time you'll retire and have time on your hands, she'll set to nagging you twenty-four seven. Reckon you'll stay around then?* There, that ought to sort the wheat from the chaff, don't you reckon, Les? I'm out of here.' Wallace stood and slammed his chair into the table to go and sit with Bernadette's dizzy bridesmaids.

'Good riddance,' Leslie muttered, only half-listening, too busy fleshing out her stay theory to worry about Wallace's nonsense; she imagines pictures of the bride and groom aged up by the likes of one of those awful apps Michael uses – the one that renders you ancient, spotty and goiterish. The pictures could be used on the cover of the orders of service, she thought, and blown up to gigantic proportions by the same fellow Shelley used up at Top Ryde for the cardboard Khans. And they could probably be hung, too, either side of the altar, flanking poor Jesus on the crucifix. How had no one thought of it before? Leslie was completely preoccupied with her revelation, until she spotted a young floosy with a dangerous cleavage sidling up to Wallace and realised at that very moment that the main reason she'd stayed married all these long years was that she'd be damned if she was going to end up divorced and be the flabby first wife at any of her children's weddings.

Later that night, back home in bed while Wallace was snoring, wobbling his head, dreaming of Bollywood – draped in his favourite position on his side, trapping Leslie beneath his thigh – she managed to squeeze out from beneath him and reach into her bedside drawer to retrieve her notebook and scribble down a couple of her own vows – or, rather, stays.

Will you stay when your dopey husband is flirting with girls old enough to be his own daughters?

Will you stay when one of them you never knew existed from a previous marriage, he also failed to mention, fronts up to your back door at the age of eighteen, wearing your husband's stupid face on her obese body, asking to speak to her daddy?

Will you stay when you realise in, say, sixteen thousand, four hundred and twenty-five days, that the same duplicitous perjurer hasn't said a single word in forty-five years about the baby you both lost together?

(I tell a lie. He did say 'Who?', once, the only time I ever mentioned his name.)

Leslie popped her notebook beneath her pillow and prodded Wallace to move off her. She nudged him as hard as she could, but couldn't raise more than a grumble from his soft but firm slumbering form. Oh, how she envied and despised how deeply he slept. She concluded that depth must be commensurate with density, with dumbness, just as rudeness was with thick skin. She shoved him again, and when he finally rolled away her thoughts pitched from repulsion to wheels of Gloucester cheese tumbling down English hillsides, to bewilderment, to sadness – to her first-born.

~

Leslie had named him Anthony. Patron saint of lost things. And he resided in her heart and limbo until Pope Benedict XVI opened the gates of heaven to aeons of original sinners. In her dreams she saw them ascending, centuries of soft babies with apple-shaped birthmarks, tiny fingers gripping tiny toes in a baby daisy chain, slithering beneath the heavenly bar and emerging stain-free for all eternity, wherein the yellowed hospital bracelet she'd worn during her confinement was joined by the papal dispensation. Printed in *the Catholic Weekly*, she cut it out and folded it carefully into quarters, tucking it away in her pocket alongside her graphite powder, the two going everywhere she did, as Anthony did, growing in her mind into a quiet, neat and tidy child who got straight A's, did as he was told, duxed the novitiate and, most importantly, never left her.

Anthony grew to be the perfect gentleman, with thick auburn hair like Leslie. If you saw them side by side, follicles mingling, you might think it were the same head and rightly so, as he was in her head; scientists had discovered that fetal DNA could live for years inside the mother's heart and brain, possibly preventing Alzheimer's. Leslie copied from the piece in the newspaper into her little Book of Facts, just beneath *Ninety-four was the age of the oldest cadaver harbouring her son in her hippocampus*, which sounded to Leslie like one of those foreign supermarkets setting up in the outer suburbs of Sydney. Science called it microchimerism, what Leslie knew innately as a feeling of being tenanted for life from the moment she conceived. And what Leslie also knew was that little ones who never inhaled were more precious than their living siblings, who reminded you of their autonomy by standing in front of you tattooed, fat and receding, unlike her Anthony, whom Leslie pictured perched on a stool, a Dave Allen minus the disregard for religious authority, blue jokes and whisky. A man with a twinkle in his eye and a 'Goodnight, good luck, and may your God go with you,' who could sort out the Foxtel, stroll arm in arm and companion her in old age. No tattoos or piercings; no foreign, queer, dark or dead partners; no acronym-ed drugged kids, amputees, AVOs, foul mouths, half-castes, cardboard cut-outs, dopey poems, vulgar paintings, small yappy dogs or spare tyres. The child she'd always wanted. Anthony. Suited, sipping ginger ale. Shoes polished. Beloved. Dead nigh on fifty years.

Holy work it was, keeping Anthony's spirit alive, divinely rewarded one day in the laundry in 2004, when (coincidentally only a week after the Virgin Mary on cheese toast appeared on eBay), Leslie was loading the washing machine, sorting coloureds from whites, emptying the pocket of her jersey jacket, when she found that despite its lid being screwed tight, her bottle of graphite powder had leaked onto the papal paper, leaving a sign on the heavenly ticket; a ghostly smudge, two concentric circles, one large, one small – the halos of St Anthony cradling her infant son. Clearly, enough to make you go mad.

And maybe mad is what it means to be human.

These are the Facts

God knows (or maybe he doesn't) maybe motherhood is a myth. Leslie Bird considered the most agonising part of it – motherhood – was neither birth nor death but the separation of selves. The wordless moment a soul finds its skin and enters the world through you. This person once part of you, now outside of you, suckling on your undivided love, body and attention in order to thrive and grow and learn to live without you. To replace you. To leave you alone with your ferocious love and no takers. Just a maze of old cardboard boxes in the boot of your car in the garage. And a pocketful of consolations. But no words.

~

There wasn't a word for the parent of a child who had died – to replace Leslie's struggle to say, to explain that she'd had, that there was . . . a baby, mine – Anthony. Nothing to announce to the world who and what I am without him, and this absence of language made Leslie feel further punished; stirred to search obsessively for a word through Missing Persons, Lost and Found portals and columns; finding and corresponding for a time with Mary Anne Holloway, a loquacious high school English teacher who'd placed an advertisement for 'A Missing Word for the Parent of a Deceased Child' in the *Sunday Telegraph.*

Leslie responded immediately, writing of her Anthony, and expressing how moved she was by Mary Anne's description 'of an abiding loss made worse by the world's not knowing'.

Mary Anne replied almost overnight that she'd lost a baby too, eighteen months before – Bridget, three months old – to SIDS, according to the police officer who'd arrived at the scene to find the young mother sitting on the side of the bed weeping, clutching her lifeless baby. She told him she'd woken up and found the baby buried beneath her. *Not breathing or moving. Clammy. Hot and cold. As if beneath her tiny pink grow suit, she was frozen inside, like a bombe Alaska*, she wrote to Leslie, who'd never heard such hysteria.

> Her eyes were open. White. She had no pupils. They'd rolled backwards, I think. Is that where they go? I don't know. I wanted to smack her, tell her to wake up and look at me. I did. I shook her. I shook her with all my might. Her head lolled about sickeningly. My husband ran outside. She spluttered. So, I shook her again, thinking maybe she was pretending, like her father – don't get me started on *his* deceptions. I thought maybe she was holding her breath. I screamed at her: *Breathe, baby girl.* I pleaded with her to come back to me. But she didn't. She was gone.

Long gone was the officer's first thought.

Gone was the word that enlisted Leslie's empathy, as gone felt more accurate to her than when someone had said to her of her own Anthony, 'He's dead,' which placed the deceased in the present tense, which he never was, so it didn't make sense; she never saw him – never met him. *Can you imagine?* she would say to her very self who it had happened to, and her answer was always, *No, I cannot possibly imagine or forget.* But when Mary Anne wrote '*she's gone*', Leslie understood what she felt – that her Anthony was not here anymore, nowhere to be seen . . . but, most importantly, he who was here, in the past – in her womb – had left . . . and was now elsewhere. Gone.

Gone gave Anthony a past and a future. Made him eternal. Enduring. Undying. Immortal.

And *gone* allowed Leslie to move momentarily past her incredulity that any woman blessed with the birth of a healthy baby would be so stupid and lazy as to sleep with it in the same bed and then be crazy enough to squash it, shake it and then admit it all to strangers, herself and the police officer, to whom Mary Anne said she confessed: *I suffocated her. It's all my fault. The last I remember she was crying. Reaching over, picking her up. I was so tired, I couldn't get out of bed. Had to lie down to feed, so she didn't drown. I had so much milk, she had to suck uphill.*

Holy Mary Mother of God. Leslie took a moment, then read on. The police office asked after the nappy pin fastened to the right side of Mary Anne's stained nightie . . . Oh, why would you mention that, a stain, of all things? Leslie wondered, knowing nothing at all of the bright yellow mystery that appeared at chest level across Mary Anne's nighties in her first weeks home from hospital, causing her to consider it was most likely another emittance, for which she was somehow responsible, having lost count of the strange new things that had come from her body. However, oddly, this one only appeared on the outside of her clothing, as if her body itself was summoning the stains. And why not? Mary Anne thought anything at all seemed possible, after the blessed miracle of the baby in her arms, until one day she sneezed and noticed a puff of powdery yellow lifting off her person and realised it was pollen: yellow pollen from the fuchsia Oriental lilies people kindly sent to celebrate Bridget's birth. The place was full of them, and greeting cards and shiny foil balloons, bobbing about saying *Welcome* and *Girl*, until they collapsed in on themselves at much the same rate as her womb. In her sleep-deprived stupor, Mary Anne had no memory whatsoever of stooping to smell the lilies, one of her least favourite flowers, linked in her mind to something showy or funereal, but there they were – the bright yellow stains across her chest, evidence of another thing happening while she was unaware. And one day that was all she'd have left: stains and memories. Same thing, really. Though only one is visible. Leslie thought, *Soak it in bicarb, you silly woman.*

Mary Anne explained to the poor police officer how she normally fastened the nappy pin to her bra strap on the baby nurse's advice, to remind her which side to start the next feed. Sister Voss had no children of her own, but opinions on everything, from the benefits of sun baths for episiotomies to the perils of ham – 'the cause of most colic in babies,' she exclaimed to her overcrowded waiting room after Christmas. 'Ham is to babies what fireworks are to dogs: it sets them off.' Sister Voss said she had a good mind to march over to the Five Star Deli and tell them to stop selling smallgoods to nursing mothers immediately. Oh, it was too ghastly to recall what Sister Voss had done to her breasts. (But somehow Mary Anne did manage to report it all, much to Leslie's horror – first to the police officer and now to her.) When Mary Anne had first met the baby nurse, she was so engorged her breasts had stretched and flattened like water balloons. With one hand Sister Voss had gathered and pinched her areola (*Hail Mary, full of grace*), while the other hand cupped Bridget's head and guided her mouth until it latched onto the nipple and she sucked with force and the milk flowed. It would have been an intimate moment between mother and daughter but for Sister Voss's callused finger stuck in there between them, making an awful popping noise when extracted.

Mary Anne was telling the police officer all this, supposedly, as she lay Bridget down on the bed, re-swaddled her, then clutched her to her chest, rubbing her back, as if she'd just had the feed Mary Anne had described and wasn't dead at all.

'It's Sister Voss who insists on nappy pins and keeping a diary to ensure alternating sides, regulating milk supply,' Mary Anne said, pointing to her notes open on the bedside table, a page divided into three columns: *Time – Side – Miscellaneous.*

The officer told her of how his wife had used hair elastics around her wrists for the same reason, but could never remember why she'd put them there, and more often than not she'd take them off and tie her hair back. They were strewn all over the house, looped around unopened mail, keeping bags of muesli fresh in the pantry. 'We lived on muesli in those early weeks,' he said. 'Not with milk. Dry. We ate it out of coffee cups. Like popcorn at the movies. We were forever brushing crumbs from the sheets and finding oats in our underpants. Once my wife took the baby to the doctor, fearing she had the measles or chicken pox, but the little marks on her back turned out to be fossilised Uncle Toby's.'

What on earth's wrong with these people? Leslie wondered.

After asking Mary Anne's permission, the officer sat down beside her on the bed, picked up the diary and read her last entry.

1.41 am. Left.

The notes column beside it was blank, unlike the entry above, where she'd scribbled:

11.10 pm. Right. 20 mins. Gagged. Wet. Changed.

After a long silence, the officer gently lifted the baby from her arms and placed her face down in the crib. Then he acted as if he were seeing Bridget for the first time and urged Mary Anne to pick her up while he left the room to call the station and report finding a baby deceased in her cot. He requested an ambulance, while Mary Anne's mute husband paced and smoked in the garden, pulling the heads off dead gardenias. Only later did he wonder if it was his wife's screaming that caused him to call 000 and request the police instead of an ambulance and not mention the baby.

Who knows why one does what one does in such dire circumstances?

The police officer, Wayne, weary from fifteen years of service and injustice – recently divorced, missing his kids, who were off living barefoot in Bali, with their mother and her new boyfriend – decided the second he saw Mary Anne weeping, leaking and holding her dead baby that she'd already suffered enough. He filed his findings then resigned from the force later the same week and took up a plumbing apprenticeship the following year, the only mature-aged apprentice at Hornsby TAFE. 'At least this shit doesn't talk back,' became his go-to refrain over the years, when explaining to clients with blocked sewer pipes what inspired his change of career.

Leslie didn't dare ask, but was dying to know about the bombe Alaska, whether Mary Anne had thought of it then or later, guessing that she may, like herself, have lost her senses and become another person altogether in her grief. 'You're not your thoughts,' a counsellor had once said to her, encouraging Leslie to write her thoughts down on scraps of paper that would be tossed into a fire and incinerated later.

Poppycock, I most definitely am my thoughts, Leslie countered silently, as one by one her truths blazed. *And what's more, the whole world would ignite if it knew what women were really thinking.*

It was not nothing that Leslie had found a penfriend – albeit, she conceded, a bit of a crazy, lazy one – who shared her quest for a word to name her loss, and after much discussion the two women agreed on a new version of Mary Anne's advertisement, titled: 'A Missing Word to Name the Pain of Losing a Child.'

> A request to those who think about language, words and their sounds to consider this assignment; to craft a word to name parents who have lost a child ['parents' at Mary Anne's insistence; Leslie thought it should just read 'mothers']. Someone who

reads and considers cultures, meanings and words, who lingers over poetry and prose and knows how to parse a sentence and its meaning.

Please consider this an urgent request. Our numbers grow daily. With drive-bys and carelessness, accidents, illnesses, suicide, war and murder, the ways in which our children die multiply. And since we have found no word to bring those horrors to their conclusion, we petition instead for a word that encompasses the grief we represent. Send it care of the PO boxes listed below. All contributions will be gratefully acknowledged by Mary Anne Holloway and Leslie Bird.

One person responded to the ad, informing them that the word *empty* had its origins in Sanskrit. Three nominated *saudade*, a Portuguese word to explain the feeling of missing something or someone; specifically, 'the love that remains after someone is gone'. This gave Leslie goosebumps, but left Mary Anne cold, saying it couldn't be verified. Another correspondent wrote of the Hebrew word *sh'khol*, for bereavement, used to describe parents who lost children in war-related incidents. Mary Anne was enthusiastic about this one, but Leslie vetoed it on the basis that their loss wasn't that, and it was too foreign and she couldn't pronounce it. And even if she could, she said, she couldn't call herself something that sounded so orthopaedic. All other correspondents were grieving mothers with gruesome stories who, likewise, craved a word for their lost children but had no viable suggestions. Many sent photos of their babies or themselves pregnant, which Leslie couldn't fathom: the way women displayed themselves these days. In hers, it would've been seen as unthinkably immodest. And she wrote as much back to a few of them; one in particular, who'd sent in graphic pictures showing her husband embracing her bare stomach, his lips pursed near her protruding belly button. Leslie advised them to seek help.

Because she lived in fear that more photos would be sent (and, on top of that, the advertisement was costing them a small fortune), Leslie approached Mary Anne about retiring it. Mary Anne, relieved, agreed; she was utterly exhausted from consoling the many whom Leslie offended. They promised to stay in touch, but when the ad expired so did Mary Anne, via a car accident on the Bells Line of Road, where she'd swerved to miss a head on, hit a sandstone wall and rolled three times before hitting a spotted gum, teetering, and plunging down the Western Escarpment into Coxs River where she died before she hit the water – or so people told themselves, to avoid the image of her drowning, which she did, slowly, agonisingly . . . unbeknownst to Leslie, who kept writing to her associate of her findings as she continued the search. Scrutinising dictionaries, thesauruses, crosswords, Scrabble boards, anywhere words might be lurking, including Caroline's unusual collection of poetry books, which Mary Anne had initially urged her to consider as a source. Leslie hoped they'd been heavily discounted, given the ratio of words to page. Surely poets would have figured it out, she thought. It seemed she was finally on to something when she came across this dog-eared text by a Paul Mitchell:

. . . I read once that Rilke started writing in French just before his death, because there was no equivalent in his native German for the word *absence.*

Caroline had circled the words in a heart-shaped bubble and scribbled beside it: *I understand the dedication to transform longing and aloneness into something more; something so close to truth it seduces feeling into form.*

Well, la-di-da. Shame her handwriting wasn't as elegant as her ideas, Leslie scoffed. Though appalled by Caroline's scrawl, and Germans in general, Leslie thought that this Rilke fellow might be worth pursuing, until discovering he was a petty, pampered philanderer who not only neglected his dying father and abandoned his wife but stole from his own daughter to pay for first-class hotel rooms; a man 'so tenderly sensitive, a delicate blossom easily punished by a passing breeze or sudden frost'. Wallace would say Rilke was a wanker.

Onwards Leslie rummaged, through multiple languages and -ologies, and despite becoming quite the authority on etymology, she never found a word like *widow, widower* or *orphan* for the parent of a child who was – Leslie couldn't say dead, so in its place in her head she simply said 'the d word'. It was as if language itself refused to name the inexpressible grief.

One morning, months later, without notice, she woke up with the word *orom* repeating itself over and over in her mind. *Orom. Orom. Orom.* As it looped, she wondered if it were an incantation, an invitation or evidence she was losing her marbles. Where it came from and what it meant were anyone's guess, so she dismissed it and kept on with the business of waking up, showering, making the bed, smoothing and tucking in sheets and flesh, as she dressed, before breakfast; spreading lemon butter on toast (*just a taste*, she told herself, slathering it on), followed by a few penitent spoonfuls of Yoplait, that Caroline insisted would help keep osteoporosis at bay.

Sighing deeply, pressing in with her thumb on the foil lid of the yoghurt pot, Leslie surprised herself by saying it aloud – 'Orom' – and as she did the long low o's and m's seemed not only to surface independently but to summon feelings buried so deep inside her she knew she'd found something that belonged to her. She licked her fingers and wrote the word down on the back of a Woolworths docket, realising as she did that her coupon for four cents off fuel was due to expire and that *orom* spelled backwards was *moro* – the reflex for life. Reversed. Leslie Bird had found her word. And would never share it.

Except for once, when she was filling out an insurance form and wrote *orom* in response to: *What is your usual occupation?* But then crossed it out.

Oh, and one other time, which she would really rather forget: the last time she ever wrote a little note to Mary Anne, inquiring after her welfare and explaining the extraordinary circumstances of waking up with her special word and how it emerged the moment, she pressed on the yoghurt lid, *which I guess in my mind has come to represent a fontanelle*, Leslie wrote.

Did you watch Bridget's? I was obsessed with my babies' soft spots and had to resist the urge to press them. Not to harm them, of course. Goodness no. I don't know – maybe to touch bones that had grown inside me, still fusing, now here in my hands pulsing. Did Bridget's pulse? It's just the strangest thing to see a tiny heart beating on top of a head. When I was feeding, their little fontanelles held my attention almost more than their tiny fingernails, which I nibbled as if they were my own. Sounds morbid, doesn't it, but I kid you not, Mary Anne. I fed off my dead mother the same way. Not her fingernails – her hair. I took a comb and a pair of nail scissors into the nursing home after she died. But she wasn't there. The nurse at the front desk said, 'Oh, I'm sorry, she's gone,' and I thought: Where? *She wasn't in her room, where Caroline and Shelley had left her after spending the night, honouring some silly promise they'd made to their grandmother that they'd ensure she died with her dentures firmly in place – unlike my father, who was rendered all gargoyle by rigor mortis. Just hideous. And only three days, mind you, after Caroline insisted on moving him from the general ward at Bankstown Hospital to a hospice, on one of the coldest August days Sydney's ever recorded.*

I said to my sister, who couldn't make it to the hospital – busy soaking fruit for her Christmas cake – that I didn't mind other people's visitors rolling kebabs on the floor, spreading hummus and prayer mats. 'Who would?' she said. 'It's a sign of the times.' I told her I didn't mind that nobody in the place seemed to speak English or clean the bathrooms. 'Go at home before visiting,' Martha said to me. And we both agreed, she should halve the glacé cherries but double the brandy and that it wasn't anyone's business or place to make a fuss, and that at least our father was alive, until Caroline butted in. I'm not saying she killed him, Mary Anne, but you do the maths. He was alive in hospital and dead at the hospice, just seventy-two hours after Caroline flounced in, insisting he be transferred after chatting with his doctor, who couldn't recall either his patient's name or prognosis but managed to give her his business card and the name of his favourite cafe and florist.

'Oh, please. I mean doctors are busy – really busy. Men don't buy flowers for their wives,' my sister Martha said, and then took a deep breath and exhaled down the phone. 'Grace Leslie Maloney – that girl of yours is really something. She's always done up, with that stupid flicky hair. Those handbags. Lipstick. I don't know how you can stand it. Why you don't say something?'

I have, of course, but what else can I do other than put up with it, Mary Anne? I said to Martha, 'Caroline's been trying to make people [by 'people' Leslie meant 'men'] look at her for as long as I can remember.'

Martha said, 'They buy them for mistresses. Roses. Always roses. So unimaginative. Pay cash to avoid the paper trail. And roses have zero scent since flooding in from Colombia.'

Zero, I agreed.

Martha asked if Caroline had taken us to the doctor's favourite cafe, so I described the crazy little place she dragged us to opposite the railway station, right at the traffic lights. It was so busy, Mary Anne, people were flying everywhere. And noisy! My goodness, you couldn't hear yourself think, what with the call to prayer from the mosque nearby and the lights changing. Wallace despises the walk signal, the beeping, he hates it and started carrying on, so I told him to be quiet and for the umpteenth time explained that the beeping was for blind people, and he said, 'Lucky them,' right when a big Muslim girl tripped over while crossing and her burqa ended up around her armpits. Wallace said he wished he was one of them – blind, that is, not Muslim. Not what I was expecting to see, mind you: muffin top, jeans and singlet beneath the burqa, sprawled across the pedestrian crossing. Bit like seeing good old-fashioned sausage rolls right next to falafels in the bain marie, confusing, if you know what I mean? It was all too much for Wallace, who lost it, shouting he had a right to his opinions and that he just wanted to get going, right when Caroline jumped up to help the girl. You should have seen her, all over the poor thing. She probably got her phone number as well, and is no doubt praising Allah as we speak, I said to Wallace later, in light of the dreadful things Caroline called us: bigots, bogans and racists. I'm just so sick of her PC rubbish, Mary Anne. If she cared to listen for just one second, she'd have learned that I like burqas. A lot. I think more people should wear them. And cover up. I even mentioned to Wallace that maybe his Lana could do us all a favour and get one.

Anyway, after that awful business we traipsed off to see my father at the hospice, where the parking's a nightmare. Boom gates and tickets. And you can never find the machines. And when you do, they're broken or don't take cash. Wallace was furious. We don't do cards. Never have. And he hates those places. We both do. When a friend called to say her elderly father had died and I asked her where, she said, 'The veggie patch.' I thought how lovely to pass peacefully, among your lettuce and rhubarb, and how Wallace would probably like that, until she added: 'You know – those hospitals you go into and never come out of; veggie patches, we call them.'

'They pump you full of morphine, then sayonara,' Martha reckons.

Or it's the procession of body bags that kills you. You never know who's inside them until Mr So-and-So isn't shoving his walker into you anymore or drooling across the table from you at dinner. What could be more depressing than lying around on the conveyor belt of life, soiling your pants, waiting to get zipped up?

Wallace says those places stink of wee and tuna mornay, and that's why he's never stepped inside a nursing home – beyond the canteen, that is. He doesn't mind a cappuccino and caramel slice, but he refuses to go near the wards. Flat out refuses. As if he's above it. Raises his hand in a stop signal and shakes his head. Prides himself, as if he's discerning not cowardly. Wouldn't we all like to give them a miss, Mary Anne?

He was happy enough to drive me to visit my mother. He'd park and sit in the car. Wouldn't come inside and visit her – not once in eighteen months. Her room was on the ground floor with a view to the garden. It was a selling point when they fleeced her of my inheritance. 'Would you look at the garden?' they gushed. A few dead azaleas, that's about all. She was incontinent. Talking to her umbrella. We had no choice but a shared room. You should have seen her neighbour, a whiskery ex-principal from one of those Anglican schools where girls have unbelievably good skin and orthodontics. There were photos of her at assemblies, dressed up in funny robes with a rainbow of sashes, shaking hands with parents and dignitaries, beaming in the playground, high-kicking in a flash mob, arm in arm with Nepalese beneath the Himalayas. You wonder why you'd bother. Caroline said the robes are symbolic of academic achievement, and the different-coloured sashes identify fields of study. Still odd-looking, if you ask me.

I said to her, 'I've never needed to flaunt my education.'

'But you left school at fifteen,' she said to me, as if it were a crime and not a badge of honour.

'And so did your father,' I reminded her. Wallace boasts he left school, had all of his teeth pulled out and started smoking on the same day. That's just what people did, I explained to Caroline – though not the teeth bit, that was a stupid Bird thing. I told her I skipped the third grade, jumped straight to fourth, and that there were only six girls in my class in Bathurst and it was probably the same for her father in Grenfell. You left school, got a job and started paying your own way – no parading around at university getting brainwashed and collecting sashes, like they do these days.

Not that Caroline was listening, she went on talking right over the top of me: '. . . and the only education you two have had since is from the Daily Telegraph *and* A Current Affair.*'*

Shows how little she knows, Mary Anne. We also watch Today Tonight. *Depending what's on, of course, and who's got the remote, we'll sometimes flick between them. Watch both.*

There was a poster above the ex-principal's bedside drawer that said, Hi, my name is Joan. I like the outdoors, Scrabble, and someone to talk to. *She'd had a stroke a few months earlier and all that was left of her were four words repeated every three minutes:* What time is it? *For the first six months we told her. Caroline even bought her a digital clock. It made no difference. She didn't want the answer. So we drew the curtains around her bed and wore earplugs. My mother wasn't talking to me anyway. Never forgave me for putting her in there. Though technically it wasn't me; it was Caroline and Shelley. Wallace and I were on holidays in Rockhampton when my mother fell over at home. When the ambulance officers arrived they refused to take her. They said a hundred-year-old woman with a suspected urinary tract infection (apparently the delirium and her 'scent', shall we say, gave it away) living alone on a diet of mouldy bread and condensed milk wasn't an emergency hospital admission but neglect. Personally, I've wondered how they knew about the mould. A bit of mould never killed anyone. I've read people pay good money for blue cheese. Anyway, for some reason the neighbours called Caroline. Martha said they probably knew that Wallace and I were away and that she'd be run off her feet, not lying about the place, like Caroline, who was actually off in Balmain eating sushi with Bernadette when they called. One minute she's ordering tuna and avocado rolls, the next she's wrestling her grandmother into the front seat, stretching the seatbelt across her lap, packing her clothes, walker and commode into the boot of her car, and taking her home via Bernadette's house, after her sister said she'd love to stay and help but thought she'd get in the way, too many cooks blah blah blah . . . I told her to just let it go, but of course Caroline still hasn't forgiven her for switching so quickly, as she said, from sushi to shirking any responsibility for their grandmother – and on top of that asking for a lift to the other side of town when their grandmother was reeking, soaking the front seat, and wielding her talking umbrella about dangerously. Bernadette has her own ideas, of course, about the real reason her sister's cranky with her. She thinks it's because the smell in the car was so bad, she had to ride with the back windows down and it messed up Caroline's hair. And we all know how precious Caroline is about that hair.*

Eventually, she got my mother home and wanted to clean her up a bit before taking her to the doctors, so she took her to the bathroom and got down on the floor beneath her skirt to change her sodden underpants. My mother called her perverted and demanded that she look up at her when speaking. And when she did – explaining that she was only trying to help – my mother wee-d straight into Caroline's mouth.

Wallace was furious when Caroline called later that night – furious my mother had outlived him being a good son-in-law ('cunning as a shithouse rat only twice as smelly,' he said of her), and furious that his holiday was ruined by knowing what was going on back at home, after Caroline insisted on calling to give us the blow by blow of the medical appointments and nursing home visits, waiting lists and so on. To be honest, there was that much detail and so many acronyms, I switched off and did the crossword while she talked.

'This is killing your mother, CB,' Wallace said. 'Can't you look after it?'

And Caroline said she would. So you can imagine our shock, Mary Anne, when we arrived home six weeks later to find her and Shelley sitting in the nursing home canteen, eating coconut slices and on a first-name basis with the volunteers. Caroline – whose weight gain had to be seen to be believed – flew into one of her rages about how she and Shelley were fed up with assuming other people's responsibilities, how after weeks of negotiating and currying favour, they'd got my mother bumped to the top of the waiting list, until their prayers were answered and a Sister Jude died and freed up a bed, which they moved my mother into, lock stock and barrel, from her home of seventy years.

It was my home too once, *I wanted to shout, but I didn't of course, keeping the peace – and all Wallace said was, 'What have you two got the shits about?'*

And I know he shouldn't swear, Mary Anne, but you should have seen the looks on their faces. Caroline accused us of neglecting my mother and turning up the colour of tea – tanned but strained – which is probably why Wallace said what he shouldn't: 'Fair go, love. We looked after her for forty years. And so much for finding her a good spot. Couldn't you have found her something closer to the main road, in case she wanders?'

He was joking, of course; rooms at the front of the hospice were far too expensive. I can't tell you how I felt, Mary Anne, caught in the middle of it all, the girls fighting with their father and my mother holed up inside a place that had a legless man in a wheelchair rolling his own cigarettes on the verandah right near the entrance, so that the first thing you saw as you arrived was a smoking stump. So off-putting. Wouldn't you think they could have found a spot for him around the back? Or thrown a blanket over his lap? Martha said she visited once and couldn't go back. Who could blame her?

When I asked her why she didn't return my girls' calls when our mother had her fall, she flew off the deep end and said she'd told Caroline that there'd been a time when she could have helped out, made plans, sandwiches, whatever, but that time had been and gone and she no longer had the capacity. Fair enough, I thought, never imagining how that word 'capacity' would come to haunt us. Martha said to me she thought that our mother had had a good life and then changed the subject to Caroline's weight gain.

'Can you believe the great big shape of her? You wouldn't think it was possible, given the tiny little thing she once was. Remember how Wallace used to say her bottom fit in the palm of his hand? I reckon it's karma.'

'Possibly,' I said, but for what I wasn't sure. 'Wallace says it's why she swims in the dark; she goes at dawn, so no one can see her.'

'Makes sense,' Martha said, before sharing that Bernadette told her Caroline had given up laps due to some problem with her back, that she'd hurt it lifting our mother or some silly thing. Honestly, Mary Anne, if I've said it once, I've said it a thousand times – if I believed for a moment those kids were as affected as they say they are, I could never have lived with myself. Martha went on to say that Caroline really ought to watch herself, blowing out like this, and that it was high time she learned to cook something other than roast chicken and potatoes if she was to have a chance in hell of holding on to that handsome husband of hers.

'It takes more than shoes to hold a marriage together,' Martha said, which just blew me away – I just could not believe she remembered that . . . or anything that's ever happened and hasn't happened in our family. Wallace says it's because she hasn't got kids of her own; she adopts our memories. And never the happy ones, only the bad, he says, because she's jealous.

'Of what?' I asked him, knowing full well what he meant but needing to hear him say it.

'Your thing with the girls – Caroline especially. The way she tells you everything.' (She does, Mary Anne. I can't shut her up.) 'What I wouldn't give to have Michael talk to me like that, man to man – or even one of the girls. If, just once, someone took the time to tell me

something, instead of me finding out every damn thing through you second-hand,' Wallace said, without giving a moment's thought as to why that is. They tell me things because I ask questions and listen to the answers. Even when I don't give a damn! That's parenting, Mary Anne. You put up with it all.

'But what Martha's most jealous of,' Wallace said, 'is this.' Puffing up his chest, he put his left hand on his hip and pointed with his right thumb at himself.

Oh, please. Are you kidding me? Martha thinks he's a bigger fool than I do.

When she said it took more than shoes to hold a marriage together, she was referring to this incident on Caroline's wedding day. She was a nervous wreck. Had been since Toby proposed a year earlier while they were watching TV. He was on one couch, she was on another, when he muted the ad break and said, 'So, do you want to marry me?' And she said yes, because she didn't know how to say otherwise, and she couldn't possibly have imagined that he'd then go out and buy himself new stereo speakers instead of an engagement ring. Oh, it was high drama, Mary Anne, but from my perspective, it seemed more ignorance than malice on Toby's part. They broke up and he wooed her back. But before she could make it down the aisle at St Charles, she stood frozen on her father's arm, until her good friend Salim walked in, this Palestinian used car salesman-cum-philosopher who resembles Omar Sharif, and whose kids she used to babysit. They'd met via his wife Fatima, this tiny little thing, also exiled from Gaza, who could barely see over the steering wheel of the used hearse that she drove, full of kids bouncing around holding the coffin rails. She'd volunteered to host an Yves Rocher party after Caroline knocked on her door and introduced herself as one of their beauty consultants, a job that entailed demonstrating and selling enough products – foot cream, foundation and the like – to scale the human pyramid to become an area manager and drive away in one of their botanically festooned white Falcons. Though Caroline said it was mostly squeezing people's pimples and conning guests into signing up for parties with the promise of a hostess gift. She was far too embarrassed to ever sign anyone else up as a consultant, so that they too could spend every cent they didn't earn on products for their beauty case. (All these years later there are still unopened boxes up in her bedroom.) So gullible, that girl, though we were so thankful it was Yves Rocher and not Herbalife she signed up for. Goodness me. She was all set to receive one of their Lose Weight Now Ask Me How badges, after answering a Be Your Own Boss ad in the paper, which led to her being sized up and lectured in a warehouse in a laneway in Leichhardt on how to approach fat people sensitively and offer to help them. The roller shutter went up at lunchtime, so she binned the pamphlets and bolted home, where it took her hours to settle. She drew the curtains but kept peering out the windows, thinking she'd been followed. Wouldn't let her father answer the phone. When he asked what the hell was going on, I said to Wallace, 'Doesn't it remind you of Shelley and the Jehovah's Witnesses after she broke up with that Paul?'

'The electrician?'

'Who else?

'What about him?'

'He was one of the faithful.'

'Not to Shelley.'

Oh, Mary Anne, I don't know why I bother. Or why I said before that 'we' were thankful it was Yves Rocher, because Wallace wouldn't have had a clue what Caroline or any of the kids were up to. Ever. He seems to still see them as infants; he's incapable of relating to them as adults. And they respond in kind, of course, treating him with kid gloves – Daddy this and Daddy that. It makes me sick. He gets off scot-free. And when they're not whingeing to me about how he hasn't a clue who they are, they seem grateful he doesn't. There's no past. Nothing to forgive. They force me to know them then resent my knowing. Call me a busybody. I can't win.

It infuriates me how oblivious he is, but then there's this tiny bit of me that envies his singularity; his inability to be hurt by what he doesn't know. It's as if he doesn't have children at all until they're standing right there in front of him, when he rubs his eyes, takes his glasses off and says, 'Well I'll be buggered.' Like the day Caroline marched in, grabbed his recliner remote and lowered him until his big stupid face could be slapped with the masks and moisturisers she was trialling. He even let her deface him with lipstick and mascara, practise smoky and cat eyes, and then sat up at the table for lunch sporting one of each, without blinking or ever asking Caroline what she was up to, or where all this Yves Rocher stuff came from.

Needless to say she got nowhere near the white Falcon, Mary Anne, but she managed to spin herself out as a make-up artist, until she got trapped inside a bride's house in Dundas with a cranky Jack Russell, Dexter, after the wedding party she'd made up posed for photos on the front lawn, deadlocked the doors and left for the church while she was still in their bathroom washing her brushes. The dog went crazy. Barking and baring its little teeth. Caroline was terrified. Jumped up onto their kitchen bench. There were no mobile phones in those days, so she used the telephone mounted on the wall by the refrigerator to call her father, who drove straight over, after first stuffing his pockets with Nabisco's Chicken in a Biskit crackers. When he got there, he rang the doorbell and Caroline yelled for him to come around the side, where he talked to her through the security shutter on the kitchen window. Wallace managed to convince her to put on a pair of oven gloves, climb down off the bench and give Dexter some of the biscuits he was able to slip through a gap he created by lifting the shutter. They were able to slide the dog out the same way, though it was a tight squeeze, they said. 'There wasn't a damn thing I could do to get Caroline out, though,' Wallace said, so the two of them decided their best bet was for Caroline to find the dog's lead and pass it out to Wallace, so he and Dexter could head off to the wedding reception at Oatlands House and explain the situation to the newlyweds. Caroline ended up falling asleep on the couch, dreaming of Ann-Margret shimmying in an orange sweater after watching Elvis in Viva Las Vegas, *because Wallace didn't return until much later. Someone at the reception had offered him a beer or seven. I still can't believe he put that dog in our car, Mary Anne. On my seat! I guess that was about the time Caroline swapped make-up for babysitting for the Palestinians.*

The three of them used to stay up all night after Fatima and Salim got home, drinking coffee 'so thick your spoon would stand up', Caroline said, they smoked shishas and ate upside-down cauliflower in their cinnamon-smelling kitchen with its cold tiled floors and shy skirting boards.

Wallace said she always talked funny when she came home from their place. 'She's a mimic,' I said, but the Arabic accent wasn't what he meant. He said, 'It's probably all that eating upside down that makes her give feelings to skirting boards.'

The house backed onto a sheer rock wall and was still being built. Nothing fitted or was finished. Balcony doors opened into voids. One whole floor was just a bare concrete slab with no walls or windows, just a few plastic chairs where people stood around, night and day. The rain blew in, but no one cared. There were far more important things at hand – like Salim holding both of Caroline's. After Fatima checked in on the kids, she'd often go to bed and leave the two of them alone for hours, 'talking directly and indirectly until the sun came up'. Caroline said, 'He knows things.'

'What things?' I asked her, alarmed by the loiterers and his hand-holding.

She said I wouldn't understand and explained that he only ever held her fingers, as this was all a woman should ever give a man in a relationship. He never held her thumbs, because thumbs represent your own interests, things you should keep for yourself. The thumbs give balance, she said. Salim had told her that 'hands without thumbs are rudderless'.

She was right: I didn't understand, Mary Anne. And what's more, when she said she thought he was 'teaching her through her body what to keep and give away', I thought he sounded downright creepy.

But, weirdly, when Wallace went off about him, I defended him. 'Caroline says he's the wisest person she's ever known.'

'Then she mustn't know many,' Wallace said, 'Mark my words, that little wog's up to something.'

Anyway, on the day of Caroline's wedding, after their silent trip to the church, Wallace was far too concerned for my whereabouts to make small talk with his daughter. I was travelling behind them in my car and he was fiddling with his bow tie, trying to loosen his collar. He was turned, looking out the back windscreen, willing me to keep up in traffic. I wanted to shout at him, Don't worry about me! Undo your top button, turn around and talk to her. Tell your daughter she looks nice. Say something.

After getting out of the car and having a quick smoke, they stood arm in arm in the church vestibule waiting to make their entrance. But when the Wedding March started, Caroline was unable to move forwards – because, she said, her 'natural orientation is backwards', whatever that means. She's explained it to me a million times, Mary Anne, but I still don't get it; she's such an unusual girl. (But I must say, you'll never see a better parallel parker.) Anyway, all she wanted to do on her wedding day, she said, was reverse, until she saw Salim walk in. She reached out and grabbed his arm. 'What am I doing?' she implored him. Salim let go of Fatima and took both of Caroline's hands in his and, as Wallace stepped outside for some fresh air, he asked her to tell him what she loved about Toby. And the only thing that came to her mind was that Toby drank wine and wore trousers as opposed to her father's beer and white baking overalls. But she didn't tell Salim any of this; she just shrugged, and said, 'I don't know. Everything I guess.' So Salim grabbed both of her thumbs, positioned them vertically and said, 'See? You're doing the right thing.' Still not convinced, she said, 'But how do you know *Toby's the one?'*

'It's the shoes,' Salim said. And they looked at one another. She didn't have a clue what he meant, but it was something, better than

the nothing in her head, so she called to her father, who stubbed out his cigarette, took her by the arm and led her down the aisle to give her away to his opposite. To say 'I do' to the shoes.

In the early years of their marriage, when things were so strained – goodness only knows what was going on Mary Anne, she's never explained – Caroline said she could barely look at Toby and slept with the wardrobe doors open so she could see his shoes and remember Salim's words. 'I guess it's no different from praying to a statue of Jesus or Mary,' she said to me. She didn't understand the shoes' significance (and clearly blasphemy) but somehow the mystery and the fact that Salim had said it convinced her there was a higher purpose to her marriage. But then, ten years later, on the eve of a long-awaited dinner, Salim called to postpone, saying he was sick with the flu and indigestion. She asked him if he'd been to the doctor and he said he had and would do as instructed: lay off the shakshuka, take some Mylanta and head to bed. As they were saying their goodbyes, Caroline surprised herself by blurting that she was struggling in her marriage.

'Can I ask you something, Salim?' she said.

'Of course,' he replied.

'On my wedding day, you gave me some advice. You said the reason I should marry Toby was the shoes, and I've held on to that all these years and done my best to live by it. But I've always wondered what it was you meant?'

'He was the only one who wore shoes,' Salim explained. 'The rest of the boyfriends were bums who wore thongs or went barefoot.'

Salim died later that same night. Heartburn in the bathroom one minute, heart attack in the bedroom the next. Gone in seconds,

Fatima said. He collapsed on top of her and made a terrible noise. Death rattles, according to Martha. He had the same lazy doctor as Wallace, so maybe that's why she remembered the shoe thing. Who knows with my sister?

I guess we all have our crosses to bear, don't we, Mary Anne? Excuse a lady for babbling on like this. I've been meaning to ask you how your gardenias are faring, and to say they'd probably love a good drenching of Epsom salts. Keeps the leaves green. And don't be frightened to cut them right back after they flower. People are so scared of pruning these days, but if you don't cut back some of the dead wood, your buds won't bloom the following year.

The star jasmine growing outside my mother's window at the nursing home was so poorly pruned, you could see straight through it to Wallace's grille. You could read his numberplate: BB 001. Hear the radio. Talkback. 2GB. Alan Jones. He'd flash the lights whenever Alan gave someone a pasting, and when he was fed up with waiting, he'd blast the horn. Not just once or twice – he'd really lay on it, and people would race around wondering what on earth was going on. An alarm? An evacuation? In this day and age, there's no telling what a racket like that might mean, Mary Anne. I didn't dare tell them it was my husband honking me.

One awful, awful day, when I was trying to sort out what happened in the shower between my mother and a male nurse – all perfectly innocent, I'm sure; she was probably just exaggerating when she accused him of something grubby. I mean really, what a load of fuss. Why anyone in their right mind would want to 'have a go' at my mother is beyond me. She should be grateful those nurses do what they do. I wouldn't want to. Would you? Anyway, Wallace was steaming, furious with me for ignoring his horn, so he lowered his window and bellowed my name. My mother knew it was him but never said a word. Neither did I. She just bit her bottom lip, looked the other way and asked me what I had planned for dinner. Fish fingers, I said. It was Friday, you see. It was as if they'd made this silent pact, him and her, and I was piggy in the middle. He only ever came in to see her once: the morning she died, when he kissed her corpse. What kind of man does that, Mary Anne? Seriously, what kind?

I'll tell you what kind: the same kind of man who also stayed in the car blasting his horn when I asked him to take me to Caroline's to drop off a little gift for her before the funeral – a can of tuna spread, two news clippings and a list I'd written on one of Wallace's mustard-coloured Darling Flour Mill ordering pads. I titled it: 'These Are the Facts: Things She Would Have Said Herself' *– my mother, I meant, if she wasn't dead.* (If Caroline hadn't killed her, *I can still hear Martha harping in my head.) I wanted Caroline to include these few facts in the eulogy I'd asked her to write and deliver at the service the next day. Being the show-off she is, I knew she couldn't resist, would revel in being up there at the altar speaking down to the congregation, so I thought I'd help her out with the wording by including a few things my mother would have wanted people to remember her for.*

Like that she was the first to rise in the mornings and get her bedsheets out on the clothesline. Every Monday without fail. Even in the dead of winter, in Bathurst, with frost all over the grass, she'd rise at dawn to beat our neighbour Mrs Dignam to the Hills hoist. And what a line! I think this was my second point: that my mother had the most amazing clothesline you were ever likely to see, with the peg colours matching the colour of the clothes; the sheets hung just so perfectly they barely needed ironing. No mismatched hodgepodge in her *backyard or laundry – the latter being where she performed number three on my list: handwashing all of her life. No machine for her, if you please. She was neat to a fault. And hardworking. And excellent at budgeting. I think that was the last on my list.*

I didn't get to discuss it with Caroline, what with Wallace blasting away, I just rang the doorbell and left the list on the doormat with the clippings, beneath the tuna spread, hoping it wouldn't blow away. Martha said she had only one thing she wanted added to the list: 'Tell them she lived a life of leisure.' I left that off, of course, thinking Martha could do her bidding.

When my mother was visiting my father on his deathbed, the nurses told her that hearing is the last of the senses to go and they encouraged her to keep talking to her husband. So she moved – not closer to him but to the edge of her seat – and shouted into the room, as if we were all deaf, 'You know Robin Williams had the same thing – but he hung himself.' Then she tied an imaginary noose around her neck, tilted her head and made a choking noise. Caroline and I were staring at her, horrified, when she stopped abruptly and asked me if I'd seen the orderly's shoes. 'I'm sure they're your father's,' she said. 'You'd think they wait.' You'd think they would, wouldn't you, Mary Anne?

Anyway, she closed her eyes and refused to move closer to the bed and hold my father's hand before his last breath. When I asked why, she said, 'I don't want to remember him like this.' And then she took out an emery board and began filing her nails. Tidy until the end, my mother Agnes.

'And vain. Like Caroline.' Martha said I should have put that on the list.

I can't say I wasn't tempted, Mary Anne, but far be it from me to make judgements like that about people – loved ones especially.

'A bitch of a woman,' were my father's last words, whispered in Caroline's ear, apparently, just after she finished mauling him. You should have seen her – trimming his eyebrows, ears and nose hairs with these ten-inch paper scissors my mother produced from her handbag. 'She'll pierce his eardrums with those,' I said. She shrugged and said, 'Oh well.' So Caroline clipped and combed and recited his favourite poems and rubbed lanolin into his arms and legs, as if she was getting him ready to go somewhere; she couldn't keep her hands off him, never could. He was barely conscious, in one of those awful hospital gowns with no pants on and a plastic tube coming out from between his legs. Well, Caroline just ignored all that and kept on talking to him, massaging his scalp, reinserting his dentures after scrubbing them in the sink. And come to think of it, I did see him open his eyes and mutter something to her moments before he died. At the time I just presumed it was drivel, or that he might be saying what we were all thinking: 'Shut up and leave me alone.'

But I didn't ask. And she didn't say.

We were sitting side by side in cubicles at Dooley's Catholic Club, when Shelley told me what those awful last words were. I was tearing off sheets of toilet paper, aghast, struggling for the life of me to imagine my father swearing like that. I'd gone in there for a minute's peace, just to sit and relieve myself. My father had been in the ground less than an hour, when Shelley told me – and she said Caroline still wasn't sure if he'd meant me or my mother.

'You mean which bitch he meant?' Martha called out. I was mortified, Mary Anne. I'd had no idea she was in there. Should have guessed, though, when I heard someone weeing like a horse. Enormous bladder, my sister. No children, you see, so she can hold it. Can you believe I had to listen to all that then freshen myself up and go back out there to the wake and make small talk with the rabble? There was my mother, fleecing the table of paper napkins, dirty as well as clean, all woe is me, telling the waiters my father had gone off and left her, as if his dying was a choice. My neighbour's sulky Russian mail order bride, in a miniskirt, stuffing her handbag with egg-and-lettuce sandwiches while Wallace chatted to her bosoms. I was about to lose it when Martha stopped me. 'It's the Gulag,' Martha said. Nasty business.

Never mind.

When it was my mother's turn to die at a hundred and one, with a gangrene tide rising up her legs, thanks to Olivia Newton-John falling onto her – well, not Olivia in person, but an issue of the Women's Weekly *with Olivia all Xanadu-ed on the cover – a long story, all Caroline's doing, of course. Oh, she's a good girl, that one, bringing in bumper magazines and pastries to finish off my mother. What do they call it in bingo? Two from two. Two-two. Bishop Desmond. Killing one hundred per cent of my parents. But before she died, my mother still thought everyone in the nursing home was keen on her. Made the nurses tell this ancient little Chinese man down the corridor that he could only be her 'waving' friend. What else did she think he wanted to be? He could hardly shuffle. Doesn't bear thinking about, does it, Mary Anne?*

Despite her body's valiant efforts to rid itself of all foreign matter, Caroline and Shelley stayed by her side, following the nurses' instructions to 'keep her mouth moist' and 'give her something to eat', which seemed not only contradictory to the girls, but ridiculous, given how close my mother was to the end. But who were they to argue? They did as they were told and fed her mashed potato and broccoli and swabbed her mouth with a sponge-tipped paddle-pop stick soaked in lemon cordial until the end, then laid their heads either side of hers on the pillow, which grew damp with their tears. Not from weeping, like you might expect, but from laughter. I'll never understand that pair, Mary Anne. Doubled over, they were, when she died at dawn with the little Chinese man standing at the end of her bed, the sheets rolled back, holding both of my mother's feet, blessing her with an ancient Chinese prayer. I could barely make out what they were saying when they called.

And I was quite taken back when I arrived to see her bed already stripped and being prepared for the next victim. The nursing home chaplain – a woman, it turns out, though at first I thought it was a stout little man – did her best to comfort me. She took me down the hallway to what looked like a linen cupboard to see my mother's body. I guess you have to put them somewhere, don't you, as you wouldn't want bodies left around for visitors to see. It had shelves, like for luggage on trains. Luckily, she was the only one on board that day. And it was dimly lit. Nice. As nice as a cupboard for the dead can be, I suppose. There was a crucifix and flowers. Plastic, but still.

There she was, laid out on this little shelf, and I had an overwhelming urge to shake her and take something from her before the undertakers arrived. I reached inside her pink nightie and ran my fingertips over her flesh. Where Nelly and Kate used to be before they hid out in her armpits. Her bosoms, I mean. Don't ask me why she named them. Or which was which. I think Nelly, was the one on the left? I dug my fingers in a little. Thought about DNA beneath a victim's nails. Her body was still warm, but her face was cold. Like your Bridget's, I suspect? My mother would have died if she knew what I was doing. I didn't know what I was doing, what to take, so I reached inside my handbag and, without thinking, grabbed a comb and pair of nail scissors and teased her hair into a little white halo and then cut off a puff. It looked like fairy floss. I rolled it into a ball, pulled off a strand. Ate it. Took the rest home and stuffed it inside a locket that Shelley had once given me, filled with red dirt she'd scraped up from the Simpson Desert, until I tipped it out.

Why on earth you'd give someone dirt, I wouldn't know – that's Shelley for you. I wore the locket around my neck until one day a strand poked out and tickled me and I screamed as if my mother herself had reached out from the grave. I threw the hair in the bin. By then it was pink. But then I thought of the magpies nesting and retrieved it and placed it beneath Wallace's tomatoes. And it disappeared in no time. Wallace thought it was a hoot and said it was high time my old mother comforted her flock. Rude, isn't he, Mary-Anne? She was never anything but cordial to him.

Leslie also went on to introduce her special new word and explain that *orom* spelled backwards was *moro.*

Can you believe it? Saying it felt like my body speaking.

She finished the letter by sharing a favourite quote by an author whose name she couldn't remember.

'There are connections between words and feelings, and when they meet, there is a resonance that goes beyond the literal, that strikes a chord in the heart and mind that enables transformation.'

I may not be transformed Mary Anne, but I'm struck, now I can name my grief.

I'm an orom. We both are. Try saying it for yourself. Orom.

I leave you with my word and my sincere hope that it strikes you too.

Kind regards,

Leslie Bird

~

When the letter came back marked 'Return to sender', Leslie wondered aloud, 'What kind of person does that?'

'Does what?' Wallace asked, looking up from his paper.

'Nothing. I wasn't talking to you. Who receives a letter like that and doesn't respond?'

'A letter like what?'

'Like the one I sent. It was . . . I was . . . I poured my heart out, trying to help her.'

'Who?'

'Never mind. Mary Anne.'

'The one who squashed her baby?'

'Don't say that!'

'You told me she did.'

'I did not.'

'You did. You said she squashed it and the police covered it up.'

'Shh. Shut up.'

'You shut up. There's no one else here, Les. Maybe she hasn't answered you because she's got enough problems of her own?'

'I didn't give her any problems – I did the opposite!' Leslie raged. 'I consoled her . . . I gave her my word.'

'That you wouldn't tell?'

'What? No. For goodness sake, just forget about it. Oh, that's right, you already did.'

'What?'

'Nothing. Just your son.'

'What's Michael got to do with it?'

'Not Michael. Anthony.'

'Who?'

Wallace turned to the form guide; Fiesta in race five at Rosehill looked like a sure thing.

No wonder he died, Leslie thought, storming out of the room. *Probably wrapped the umbilical cord around his own neck when he realised you were his father.*

Wallace called after her, 'You need your head read, love. Hey, what's for dinner?'

~

When Leslie Bird first heard that her daughter Bernadette had made her husband a poo sandwich, she couldn't possibly imagine how anyone even remotely related to her could commit such a despicable act. But now she wanted the recipe.

Martha

On Parramatta Road, on the bus going home from the inaugural book club meeting at Jo-Dee and Alex's apartment in 2011, Leslie Bird sat devouring the gifts she'd been given: her first-ever doner kebab and a novel that Alex had rocked rapturously against her brand-new bosoms before clearing her throat and pressing it into both of Leslie's hands with both of hers – in a gesture that seemed to say so much more than, 'You must must read this, it's my favourite book ever: *Olive Kitteridge*.'

Leslie Bird had had the following thoughts: *Clothes may maketh the man, but voice maketh the woman. More gargling and modulation, Alex. Less Bea Arthur and hairspray. But my what magnificent bosoms you have. Yum! Why haven't I had one of these before? The kebab, not the book or boob job. Wallace, that's why. Damn him!*

Leslie's associations between hummus and Wallace, stemmed from her skimpily skirted second-born's ghastly after-school job at Abdul's milk bar. 'Is it lamb?' Leslie had demanded. 'It can't be lamb.

Your father said he saw them pasting gunk onto a vertical rotisserie that looked like a giant paddle-pop of Pal.' Unbeknownst to Leslie, that hadn't deterred Wallace from devouring a kebab with the lot every time he'd fetched Caroline from work, wiping his face of evidence afterwards, with a hankie he stuffed back into his pocket, which went some way to explaining the origin of the odours that perfumed Leslie's laundry basket – meaty, garlic, hummus and lemony sumac, which Caroline explained was the delicious purple spice they sprinkled on raw onions. The heady smells caught Leslie Bird off guard while turning down the sheets at night or putting away her undergarments. She'd catch a whiff and try to resist the urge to sniff her own armpits, thinking how extraordinary (but not unexpected) it was that the Middle East had invaded her white things. Eventually Wallace put an end to Caroline working for 'wog bastard perves' after arriving at the kebab shop one Thursday night to pick up his sixteen-year-old daughter, who was, he said, 'Nowhere and everywhere to be seen – up a ladder scrubbing grease from the ceiling while Abdul and his swarthy posse crowded beneath, pointing out where the dirty spots where.'

How very Caroline, Leslie mused, until the memories receded with every delicious mouthful and page turned.

Oh, Olive! she exalted, after reading the words: 'No one's cute who can't stand up straight.' By the end of Norton Street, Leslie Bird was so overwhelmed with feelings that she had to stop reading and clutch her lapels. She turned and looked around. But there was no one seated behind her. Funny. She could have sworn someone was looking over her shoulder.

Leslie resumed reading about Olive Kitteridge's husband Henry: 'Inwardly, he suffered the quiet trepidations of a man who had witnessed twice in childhood the nervous breakdowns of a mother, who had otherwise cared for him with stridency.'

And there it was again, this sense of someone looking not just at her, but *through* her. Leslie couldn't explain what she was feeling as her mind ricocheted between wanting to hug Henry and punch her older sister Martha, and settled on thoughts of her own horrible hip pain – from the time she was strapped inside an MRI machine, hyperventilating, clutching the soft little ball the cranky ultrasound man had said she could squeeze if claustrophobia overcame her. Which it did. And why wouldn't it? It was like being in a white coffin with curved walls and was so narrow that it squished her hips. Caroline had warned her mother it would be a tight squeeze. Scared her with stories about a zoo in Texas that had its plans to mate the last white rhinos in captivity interrupted, because they had to scan a 600-pound man who got sick at an all you-can-cat buffet. Leslie clenched her buttocks firmly at the memory, then turned and looked around the bus again. Nothing. No. No one there. No CCT cameras. No one looking. *How unusual,* Leslie thought, *to feel so seen and yet not judged.* She held *Olive Kitteridge* to her chest and rocked back and forth. 'As perfect a novel as you will ever read,' went the quote on the cover, and Leslie Bird had to agree, feeling that, at almost seventy-six she might finally have found her soul mate in Olive Kitteridge, a big brave woman as perfectly normal and nice as herself, a type who was never ever found in fiction: serving an unwanted dinner guest, *an object of her husband's affection*, baked beans and one scoop of vanilla ice cream, speaking the plain and simple truth. 'Not keen on it.' Flexing plump wrists, shooting straight from the hip. 'We're going to hell like the Romans.' Olive's words lit Leslie Bird from within, making her nod, clap, laugh and poke her tongue out at a snotty-nosed brat bawling two rows in front of her. Leslie Bird suddenly felt less alone in the world; almost as if she'd found a twin sister in dear Olive Kitteridge.

Well, not a sister exactly. Leslie shuddered, and gripped the book even tighter, thinking of her only sibling, Martha, three years her senior, the omniscient hand that rocked her cradle. Well, rocked is putting it mildly. Martha was more of the push and shove, turn the dishes over, pinch when no one was looking, Chinese burn variety. Quietly furious at her stained newborn sibling after her arrival robbed them both of their mother Agnes – who spent the next few years in a fog, inert in her nightgown in the daytime, sitting for hours on end, unmoving, holding a compact mirror and a pair of tweezers as if poised to pluck a stray eyebrow or herself from oblivion, as she receded into what was now known as postpartum psychosis (back then, it was simply referred to as 'not being quite oneself'). This lasted until Agnes walked into the kitchen one morning with no eyebrows at all and demanded that Martha relinquish the tea towel. After a little tug of war, Agnes said, 'Thank you, Martha, that will be all,' and resumed her maternal duties, opening and closing cupboard doors, cleaning the pantry from top to bottom, dusting and restacking copious tins of condensed milk and bags of flour and sugar, scrubbing surfaces with Sunlight soap – marking her territory – in a seething stupor that never left her nor dispelled her daughters' deepest sense that their mother's scouring, hoarding, absent presence revealed some awful dirty truth about themselves. And future famines.

~

Martha, a spinster and district nurse with chronic bilateral lymphedema and bulbous ankles, had hovered like a blimp, head bowed low with seemingly unsupportable feeling, leaking lymphatic fluid and advice and fussing over Leslie her entire life. Never more so than in the years after their parents had passed, when Martha adopted their father's habit of saying, 'Keep yourself nice,' and their mother Agnes's constant refrain of, 'Thank you, thank you,' emanating not from a place of gratitude but from a location of rote piety, sarcasm and shaming. 'Whatever you've done to the least of my brethren, ye have done it unto me.' As old Agnes neared her end, her thank yous increased, which made her seem other than what she was – polite. Martha visited the nursing home as little as she could and watched as Agnes thanked the weather, the windows, the doors. Anyone who walked in the room was thanked for coming, for going and for leaving her there dying with her dinner going cold on the lunch tray always positioned just out of reach. Mind you, if anyone ever bothered to move it so she might be able to retrieve her curried egg sandwiches and the little gifts Shelley and Caroline deposited when they were picking up and returning her washing (since Agnes wouldn't allow 'foreigners' anywhere near her underwear), she would have been terribly grateful and said, 'I don't know how to thank you,' as she did to the cleaner, Lolita, who said, 'Of course, ma'am, no mention it.'

Lolita put down her mop and bucket and positioned Agnes's lunch tray as instructed, snuggly in over her lap so, later, Agnes could lean forwards to help herself to just a taste of vanilla slice, knocking a *Women's Weekly* off the lunch tray and onto the bed, where it landed on her calf, causing an ulceration that grew gangrenous, and a decision by the geriatrician that Agnes would not survive an amputation. the best course of action, the doctor said, was to start her on morphine – which they did, until her muffled *thank yous* sounded like *fuck you*, perhaps what she'd meant all along. Agnes died on a blustery night, beneath a full moon and open skylight, with the venetian blinds and Caroline and Shelley clattering, sitting either side of her bed, administering her last supper and pushing her dentures back in when they ejected, as per their grandmother's last wish: that she should die with her teeth firmly in place.

When Caroline and Shelley called to say Agnes was gone, Leslie's first thought was: *Where?* Her second was to call Martha. It was early Monday. Martha's washing day. Martha said 'shame,' and that she might pop over to the nursing home after mopping, but she couldn't guarantee she'd get through her ironing and lunch before the undertakers carted Agnes away. *Fair enough*, Leslie thought. *I wonder if I can get a load on too?* And she wondered why the girls sounded hysterical and couldn't think of anything nice to say about her mother, except that her teeth were still in.

When Leslie arrived at Agnes's death bed, she felt angry, not sad. Angry that she'd been left. And then she felt an overwhelmingly sense of deja vu, and it occurred to her that perhaps this might not even be her mother, as she'd never seen Agnes looking so . . . helpless. Lying there. Not since . . . Leslie's glasses fogged. She wiped her eyes and left the room, not wanting her mother to see her – mother still there, but not there.

Somehow, death made Agnes Maloney look like a beautiful stranger – glimpsed once, by a Grace Leslie. A little girl who had lost her mother . . . long before.

~

The opposite of a fair-weather friend, Martha Maloney approached wherever storms gathered. With the air of one accustomed to doors being flung open – 'Oh look, the nurse is here!' – Martha descended in a warm sour draught to the tune of latex thighs chafing: a sound that conveyed her long dutiful life, and her and her mother's tutting and rubbing everyone the wrong way, making you feel guilty, for whatever ailed you, paled in comparison to their sacrifices, such as the cost and discomfort of Martha's custom-made compression stockings, which could only be yanked on first thing in the morning immediately after showering with the aid of donning and doffing devices – in particular, Martha's trusty Medi Travel Butler.

With its folding frame and step-in structure, catering to larger leg circumferences often associated with limited mobility, the Medi contraption was sold to Martha as the ideal companion. Collapsible to the size of a stroller, elegant and easy to use and dismantle with its inclusive spanner, Martha was rather taken with the idea of travelling with her own personal butler. And named him Don. Don Draper. And the two were inseparable for years, until Don was taken from her and thrown in the cargo hold after his spanner set off alarms at airport security, causing Martha no end of distress, as flying alone was not her intent when she finally booked – or, rather, asked Caroline to book – her first-ever flight, at the age of seventy-nine.

Fear had kept Martha from the air: a fear so intense she'd assumed it to be (before meeting Don and, later, a Captain Tom) incurable – after Pan Am Flight 103 exploded thirty-eight minutes after take-off, at thirty-one thousand feet, catapulting two hundred and fifty-nine bodies across Lockerbie and Martha's psyche.

In fact, the horrific news reports seared so deeply into Martha Maloney's brain that she couldn't tell where her memories stopped and Bunty Galloway's started.

~

Wednesday, 21 December 1988. Bunty Galloway had just sat down in front of the TV to watch *This is Your Life*. It was 7.03 pm. Cold and windy. No one was outside on the narrow street in front of her house. Many of Bunty's neighbours were also inside watching TV and others were wrapping Christmas gifts.

Suddenly, Bunty noticed a strange noise. She had never heard anything like it in her life. It was coming rapidly closer with a rising groan and howl, as if at any moment the noise would make the house explode – like a kettle under pressure. When she got to the door, the roar had abruptly stopped. It was dark and quiet. The electricity had gone out.

When she opened the door and looked outside, the scene was as horrific and bizarre as a Hieronymus Bosch version of hell. Down the hill, about six hundred metres away, a wall of flames was bathing the town in orange light – incinerating all in its path. 'It smelled of kerosene,' she would recall later.

What Bunty saw next is what Martha's seen ever since, whenever she hears the word *aeroplane*: a young woman still strapped into her seat, on a roof, propped against the chimney. Sitting so upright that Bunty Galloway thought she might still be alive, until she reached her.

There were other bodies, too. A baby boy snagged in a tree. Another slumped over a low garden wall. Two women on the asphalt. Others lay in groups of five or ten or twenty in fields and car parks, in gardens and on pavements, next to telephone booths. Many seemed to be sleeping. Bunty counted eighteen in her own backyard, strewn and stripped of their clothes. Many still in their seats, like the young woman. But the detail that will remain forever in her mind and Martha's was how 'most of them had crossed their fingers and died that way'.

~

'Focus on the facts,' were Captain Tom's parting words to Martha. Meaning his facts, not hers – that the artificial knee of eighty-one-year-old Mary Lancaster was all that remained of the eleven people who died on the ground when two hundred and ninety tons of wreckage and two hundred and fifty-nine people fell from the sky in thirty-six seconds. Which doesn't sound like long until you're in bed, counting; trying to get to sleep before or after a nightmare in which you're one of the sixty per cent of passengers seated in the middle of the plane, who descended to levels of air rich enough in oxygen to ensure they were conscious as they plummeted. Thirty-six seconds is eternal hell, Martha decided.

'The facts,' Captain Tom said, 'are the statistics. When you get on board, recite them over and over, just as we practised. Breathe. Sit back. Relax. Enjoy it, Martha. You've done so well. You've waited so very long to fly. And remember: you've got more chance of getting gored by a bull than you have of dying in another Lockerbie.'

'As long as I steer clear of Pamplona!' Martha said.

She guessed she was as ready as she was ever going to be, and with dear Don by her side and the Queen on her mind – *jumping out of a helicopter with James Bond at the London Olympics so recently* – and after studying eleven DVDs and enduring sixteen hours of specialised counselling with Captain Tom and scoring ninety-three per cent in her SOAR fear of flying test, to finally visit the only place on her bucket list – Rudyard Kipling's 'eighth wonder of the world', Milford Sound, New Zealand – for the occasion of her eightieth birthday.

No small gesture, given Martha also feared birthdays. Despised them. Thought they reeked of boiled cocktail frankfurts, fuss, excess and vanity. Not to mention cruelty – as the vast deficit of self-esteem required to pull off the great 'look at me' was regifted annually, only reinforcing the cause of it: the hypocrisy she'd sensed since childhood that her presence should be celebrated only one day of the year, when the remaining three hundred and sixty-four she felt she was merely tolerated. Less than tolerated. Unloved. Worse, over time, undeserving of it. Love, it seemed, was something other people did. Like flying.

Martha told herself and others that a creeping sense of her own mortality, rising like a tide since she was four or thereabouts, was the reason she booked the flight. 'It's a case of now or never.'

Leslie didn't believe her. Thought the whole thing unnecessary. Selfish, even. And as for Martha's thing for David Attenborough, who gushed about Milford Sound and set her dreaming of fjords in the first place – well, the less said about that the better. It was stupid and embarrassing. And it was just plain infuriating that Caroline, as Martha's secret Santa, had bought her the *Planet Earth* DVD box set.

Once on board the aeroplane, Martha tried to employ Captain Tom's strategies, but with Don discarded to the bowels of the plane and her compression hose dissecting her midriff, when the crew closed the aircraft doors and cross-checked, she felt her fate was sealed too, and she abandoned statistics for prayer for the remainder of the flight. Except for time she spent gazing out of the window or watching back-to-back episodes of *The Golden Girls*, or chatting with the woman beside her. Barbara turned out to be a charming companion, a retired nurse like herself, and terribly interested – in a way no one had ever been before – in Don, whom Martha didn't quite get around to mentioning wasn't exactly a person. Never mind, at thirty-seven thousand feet everything seemed transmutable – the pillowy clouds, the green fields, the white caps out at sea . . . *even me.* Martha thought of her own great weight on the earth below, now floating above it, and wondered if seeing things from a new perspective might be a kind of prayer too? If flying itself was not the very definition of faith?

She nattered with Barbara over quiche and salad, and before she knew it her seat was being returned to its upright position and she was collecting and cleaning cutlery and miniature salt and pepper shakers, and stowing them in her handbag, which she placed, reluctantly, back beneath the seat in front for landing.

Poor Don was never the same after the flight. Martha's heart leaped when she saw him at the baggage claim. He was wearing an awful fluoro Fragile tag, but was otherwise unharmed as he rode the conveyor belt, waiting for Martha to retrieve him – as soon as she got rid of Barbara, who was not only looking less like her lovely in-flight self by the second, in the bustle and cold light of Queenstown's arrivals hall, but making a nuisance of herself by insisting on waiting by Martha's side to meet this charming Don of hers.

Martha swore she didn't let Don out of her sight as he orbited the carousel, jostled by all manner of suitcases. All she could think to do, given the unusual circumstances, was fake a loud phone call to him, and sigh and explain to Barbara that, as Don was running late, she had best be on her way. The two women exchanged details and Martha bid Barbara goodbye.

When she turned back to collect Don, he was being crushed under the weight of a Delsey. When Martha retrieved him, Don was in pieces.

A shame, as his support had been vital to Martha. It was hard to explain just what he meant to her. It wasn't only that she thought of him as a beloved friend, perhaps her one and only, who assisted her to dress to compress; he was also a silent witness to her suffering. Unjudging, as she stretched her stockings over his powder-coated frame. Dusted cornflour onto her towel-dried legs, before pulling on a pair of pink rubber gloves to grapple and wrestle the bastard stockings on, having first stepped a leg at a time into his frame – a requirement even for the revolutionary open-toed summer stockings, which promised not to cut in or bunch behind her knees, but did both mercilessly, leaving Martha's powdered toes exposed, looking like ten little cured sausages – often wriggling up in the air when she overbalanced and fell backwards with Don onto her bed, in a teary tangled cloud of latex, flesh, powder and metal.

Every day began with this taming and trussing of flesh. Since being diagnosed with primary lymphedema (as opposed to 'secondary' when cancer destroys nodes and glands) Martha had been compressed, dredged, lasered and catheterised, injected, bandaged (from toe to groin, making her look and feel like a Michelin man) butchered and swindled by numerous quacks and treatments; including the purchase of a $600 Chi Machine that promised to save you, 'In the comfort of your own home,' from drowning in your own lymphatic fluid by vigorously vibrating your legs, but all it did was make her dizzy, 'Like being spun around before pin the tail on the donkey,' she told Leslie. She suspected she'd done her hard-earned dollars on the machine. But who could blame her buying in humid February when stockings were un-put-on-able. Shoes two sizes bigger than ones she wore in winter couldn't be taken off and put on again when her toes begged to wiggle free, less she be left to waddle from the cinema to the car barefooted in Hornsby Westfield – like some crazy woman from Darlinghurst.

A life of moo moos and flip flops beckoned.

People without the affliction – including and especially doctors and nurses – had no idea, Martha thought, how hard it was to live with, let alone leave the house looking even part way normal. People presumed you were a slob. Someone who cried thyroid from the drive through at McDonalds. Someone who just needed 'to roll' according to Dr Liz, Martha's GP, who'd recommended rolling as a cure. One thirty-eight-degree day, when Martha had sat in her rooms feeling as if she might explode – Dr Liz held up a rolled towel and asked, 'Have you ever used one of these?'

'My father taught my sister and I how to roll one over our legs into a cape with a crown. When we were little, we wore them after swimming. And felt all fancy.'

Doctor Liz carried on as though she hadn't heard a word Martha had said, hitching up her skirt, placing the towel beneath her shapely thigh – *no doubt whittled by all that squatting in third world countries where she volunteered for Médecins Sans Frontiers*, Martha thought, as Dr Liz rolled back and forth. Back and forth, staring at Martha, as if more rolling would elicit a better response.

Martha didn't know what to say or where to look.

'You can use it sitting or standing,' Doctor Liz said, lifting and lowering her leg. Flexing her toes and ankles. 'Give yourself a lovely stretch. They sell foam ones at the chemist or pool shops.' Or you can just buy one from out at reception for a discounted $59.95.

The truth was Martha wished she could shield her own eyes from her hideous form.

And her shame wasn't only confined to her swelling, but to a crazy patchwork of scars from surgery in her late thirties that the surgeon described, as he scribbled over both of her legs with blue texta in the pre-op area, as akin to diverting traffic from the freeways onto the back streets. What he failed to mention were the roadworks – the deep potholes he gouged in Martha's groin, destroying her nodes, and the fifty-seven angry red keloid scars etched on her legs, that aged to look as if a caterpillar had left a shimmering trail of whatever it is caterpillars excrete. Doctor Liz joked about Snakes and Ladders.

Martha hid all of it religiously, vigilantly, beneath trousers or maxis, as she strode out the door each morning for thirty-five years to minister to the sick and elderly in her job as a district nurse for the Hornsby Shire. The latter part of her career saw her caring for a spate of old men with prostate cancer from Beecroft to Brooklyn, with testicles swollen from the size of squash through to butternut pumpkins. Martha prided herself on her empathy and her ability to estimate vegetables commensurate with testicles, and so designed a range of slings and padded contraptions in cahoots with dear old Mr Pattison, her chemist, to alleviate her patients' distress.

Martha lost count of the genitals she'd comforted. Ironic, given her virginal state. But she was never aroused, not once. When Leslie was flouncing about in her teens, it occurred to Martha that perhaps something vital and fundamental was missing from her own life by way of desire. As if by hosting a disfiguring disease and caring for her younger sibling she had forsaken it and gone straight to bitter, bossy, barren aunthood.

It wasn't until years later that Martha considered the matter more deeply, when on weekends she'd let herself go, take a shower and pad about the house bare-legged, in her powder blue terry-towelling kaftan, wobbling from the pantry to the lounge room eating her favourite chocolate (Darrell Lea Rocklea Road), watching TV, napping and reading (Susan Duncan, Di Morrissey). She tried *Olive Kitteridge* but didn't get past page five – too many pine trees and flowers for Martha's liking, and as for that stupid husband of Olive's . . . 'Inwardly, he suffered the quiet trepidations of a man who had witnessed twice in childhood the nervous breakdowns of a mother who had otherwise cared for him with stridency.' *Oh, spare me*, Martha thought. *Grow a pair, Henry.* And went back to her rocky road and her remote: *Mad Men*, *The Good Wife.* Martha hated the main character, Alicia. Her wigs and her tolerance of Mr Big. 'Go back to Carrie,' she shouted at the TV. Once when she mentioned this in front of Leslie, who kindly informed her sister she had the wrong series. 'Not that I've ever watched *Sex and the City*,' Leslie hastened to add. 'I only know what I read at the checkout. Don't I, Wal? . . . Wal?' she yelled. 'What are you doing?'

Wallace was reading the newspaper and pretending not to hear Leslie, who grew even more cantankerous in her sister's company.

'Can't you just put it away when Martha's visiting?'

Wallace looked down to check his fly.

'The paper, stupid.'

'I love what's-his-name,' Martha interjected, shaking her head and widening her eyes at Leslie, as if to say, *It's okay – just leave it. Leave poor Wallace alone.* 'You know the one, Lesy – the little fellow . . . the Jew. What's his name? The campaign manager.

With the floppy hair. Dopey daughter. In love with the Mexican. I thought he was gay.'

'He is,' Leslie said. She'd never seen Eli Gold either, but had heard Caroline say that you weren't supposed to call someone a Jew unless you were one too.

'Caroline's an idiot – a PC Nazi,' Martha said. 'It's all piffle. People have lost their minds when it comes to free speech in this country. What are you meant to do? Resign yourself to say nothing at all ever again except, *Yes, sir, no, sir, three colostomy bags full, sir. Goodbye?*'

'Hello, how was your weekend?' patients had always asked Martha on Mondays, and she would sigh and say, 'Oh, flat out.' Which wasn't entirely untrue. The procurement of her favourite chocolate was an exhausting business. It used to be sold exclusively in Darrell Lea stores but then these closed down, so Martha stockpiled supplies when they began popping up in supermarkets and now, of all places, her local chemist, just a tempting two-minute walk from her own front room. Or one hundred and sixty-nine steps and fourteen beeps. On a quiet day she could hear the pedestrian signal beeping at the traffic lights – her own call to prayer, which led directly into the front door of Mr Pattison's, where the Rocklea Road was displayed to the right of the counter, alongside essential oils and tubes of Lucas' Pawpaw Ointment. Somehow, buying chocolate from the chemist made Martha feel less guilty about it, until she was home alone watching TV and a few bites in, when the guilt would surface and spoil her enjoyment. Then she hit upon a 'recycling' method, chewing then spitting out mouthfuls into a paper towel. But because she feared dying alone and being found out, like Agnes and her dentures and poor Wendy down the road, who expired in front of the TV, and all anyone at her funeral could talk about was how surprised they were to hear she'd been watching a twenty-four-hour Kardashian marathon. Martha wore a path in the carpet trekking back and forth to the garbage bin to deposit the moist mounds, as she feared leaving stains on her side tables (which, incidentally, do not come out with mayonnaise). She also discarded the Rocklea Road packaging, keeping only the festive ribbons tied around limited-edition Easter and Christmas varieties. The ribbons that reminded her of the glory days when Darrell Lea's staff were once festooned the same way – wearing giant bows at the collars of their artist's smocks. They were too pretty to throw away, so she wound up the ribbons and kept them in her bedside drawer, thinking they might come in handy one day.

Martha wondered if the flux of feelings aroused in her when she heard the walk signal might be akin to what people felt when they are attracted to one another; if not being able to stop yourself was desire. Who knew? Occasionally she'd asked her patients what it felt like for them. One fellow said he felt love in his lobes (brain or ears, she didn't know). Another said his joints were calibrated by barometric pressure, which Martha thought had nothing to do with desire but was somehow connected to what a diabetic patient once told her as she dressed and numbered his ulcers: that he knew unequivocally his wife was having an affair when he could no longer walk upstairs.

Patients confessed all sorts of things when Martha was ministering to them. One of her favourites ever was a special patient (SPs she called them in private) called Peter, a handsome sixty-seven-year-old confirmed bachelor with nasty excoriation from prostate radiation. He had told her, as he lay face down, bare bottom winking up at her, that he felt the deepest desire in his Wernicke when he met a lovely Penelope on the bus. 'One glance at her ample curves, Martha, and I was reminded of Gaudi's maxim: "Straight lines belong to men, and curves to God." It was so unlike me, but when she sat down next to me, I heard myself cry out, *Amen!*'

'Oh, I bet you did,' Martha said, filled with the envy that flooded her whenever one of her SPs talked about their lives. Lives that excluded her. Lives they couldn't possibly carry on without her tender care of their most intimate bits.

Slipping on a pair of disposable gloves, Martha thought that the world really was made up of two kinds of people: benders and wipers. And she'd never met one person who was both. If you had to ask which one you were, or the difference between them, then you were definitely a bender: someone happy enough to bend on over and let someone else wipe up their mess – and, more often than not, point out the bits you've missed.

Wipers, on the other hand, set aside their own needs in order to attend to the needs of others, and would rather suffer than draw attention to themselves. They made the best nurses and teachers, but the worst patients; they often wound up dead because they didn't ask for help and no one gave a hoot about the work they did. Wipers got depressed. *And why wouldn't we?* Martha thought that if she had her way, there'd be ticker-tape parades – a sea of gracious wipers seated on the back of flatbed trucks as benders lined the streets, cheering in gratitude for their caring. The kind of caring that keeps the world going.

Martha often wondered what to do with what she saw and felt every day – when, say, a Peter was lying face down in front of her, going on and on about some Penelope.

'So, what did this Penelope have to say for herself?' Martha had probed, squeezing saline solution into a kidney dish.

Peter turned his head a little further to the left. 'Oh, she was delighted. In fact, it turns out she's a Gaudi devotee, like me – or like us, I should say.' Peter believed that Martha was a Gaudi fan too, after the discussion they'd had about the biography he'd given her last Christmas. In truth, she'd regifted it after skimming a few pages and the back-cover blurb. Which apparently was enough to fool an old fella face down with his pants off.

'Well, you certainly wouldn't read about it, would you?' Martha said, taking a deep breath.

'I know. What are the chances? She studied art history and majored in Catalan modernism. We were so engrossed in our conversation on Gaudi's oeuvre we missed both our stops. We've been inseparable ever since. And guess what?'

'What?' Martha rolled her eyes and then her shoulders, trying to loosen a crick in her neck.

'She's never been to Barcelona.'

'Oh, poor thing.' Martha bit her lip.

'I want to take her to see the Sagrada Familia. Not just to pay our respects to Gaudi's genius – but to mourn his death, which Penelope said "stubbed her heart". I tell you, Martha, it was love at first word.'

His Wernicke went wild, Peter said, when he heard the word *stubbed*, as it so accurately expressed the pain he, too, felt upon learning that Gaudi had died anonymously.

'They thought he was a bum, didn't they, a *culo*?' Martha said, dabbing at Peter's wounds, an inch at most away from her face.

'Yes. Can you imagine that?'

'Hmmm, let me see . . .' Martha looked up and made inquisitive noises, as if she wasn't wishing Ms Stubbed an early death or thinking that Gaudi's architecture was nothing but soft serve and gaudy, and who the hell she'd regifted the damn book to. Caroline probably.

'Taxis wouldn't transport his body,' Peter said, choking up. 'The poor man, in the midst of creating such glory, lived alone and unloved.'

'On lettuce dipped in milk,' Martha added, remembering that when she'd read that line she'd thought it would have made a good title.

She picked up her tweezers.

'Oh yes,' Peter said. 'And before he was run over by a tram one morning on his way to his daily confession, he'd slept for years in the darkest corner of a room as though already laid in a crypt – his eternal single bed, with a chequered blanket and a view of nothing.'

Martha hadn't read the single bed bit. 'How tragic,' she gulped, swallowing a sudden lump in her throat, as the thought rose in her that as soon as she got home, she must look into how to get herself airborne.

'Stay still, please, Peter,' she said. 'He must have been one hell of a sinner, though, if he had to confess daily.'

'Oh, Martha, you're hilarious. Don't make me – ooooh, that's so tender. Go easy there, please.' Peter flinched as Martha tweezed the last little bits from between his cheeks and got out her ointment.

'I want to propose to Penelope in the basilica – but do you think I can trust my gut to know I've found true love, Martha?'

'Yes, I think you can,' she replied, slapping on a thick layer of salve. 'I certainly have.'

Martha took off her gloves, turned them inside out and cleared her throat. 'It might sting for a while. But I think we're done here, Peter.'

On her way home from work, she stopped off at Mr Pattison's and bought all of his Rocklea Road. When she got home, she scoffed the lot, without spitting out.

~

Long before Darrell Lea, Don Draper and benders with excoriated anuses, few things had roused Martha Maloney's ire the way Lana O'Sullivan's arrival had back in 1976.

Martha had bellowed at Leslie, 'Oh, darlin' girl, I came as soon as I heard!'

Initially Martha roared out of habit, to be heard over the Birds' squabbling and to accommodate Wallace's hearing, *'All but buggered by combine harvesters by the time I was in me early twenties,'* but then Martha roared regardless of whether Wallace was present or not at her sister's house up on Quarry Road,

Ryde; which he wasn't on this particular occasion of her visiting, bestowing her benevolence.

Leslie was sitting at the kitchen table, slumped over in her grief after finding out about Wallace's Lana the previous week.

'It must be a dreadful shock, Les. I can't believe it. I haven't slept a wink since I heard. I don't think I'll ever sleep again. Are you sleeping? How could you sleep at a time like this? I'm so tired I might have to lie down myself. Do you mind?'

'Of course not.'

'Thank you. My legs are killing me.'

Martha lay down on Leslie's couch, then sat up suddenly. 'You didn't answer me, Les. Are you shocked?'

'No, Martha – your legs are always killing you.'

'Not my legs, silly – the girl. Lana! Look at me, I said her name. I didn't think I could say it. Oh dear. I thought not saying it might make her disappear. I hate her. Shall we kill her? I'll do it! Oh, I don't know how you're coping, Les. Seriously, I'm not coping. Lana, Lana, Lana – oh god, I feel like I need to wash my mouth out. Excuse a lady.'

Martha got up and went to the kitchen, where she spat in the sink. Then turned on the tap. It gushed and water sprayed off dishes soaking in the sink, wetting the bench, and her chest. Leslie jumped up to clean the mess. Martha ordered her to sit back down, 'Now you just relax there, Les, I'll take care of this. I mean who wouldn't be surprised to know you've let yourself go, least of all clean up at a time like this, but good to see you're still cooking, keeping yourself busy.' She turned off the tap, but not all the way. The faucet continued to drip. She picked up the tea towel and dabbed at tears that weren't there. 'I can't believe *you're* not in tears, Lesy,' she said, sniffling. 'My brave little sister. I'm just so shocked. Aren't you shocked?'

'Of course. Of course, I'm shocked. It's horrific.' Leslie trembled. It was *all* horrific: her marriage, Lana (what the hell was she supposed to tell the kids about Wallace's deception?), her stupid sister with her spitting and hijacking Leslie's suffering, suggesting murder, moaning, making it all about herself, feeding off Leslie's misery.

'How old is she again? I was only saying to Mrs O'Rourke – remember her? She's married to Keith, the revolting plumber – the one with the filthy fingernails and his bottom crack always showing. That man makes me shudder; I don't know how she puts up with him. They couldn't have kids and adopted that brat who was always bawling about wanting to find its "real mother" remember? Anyway, I bumped into her at Coles just this morning, standing by the fruit and veg, and I said to her that just when you think you know someone – I mean, I've known Wallace for what? Forever. I've known him forever and then he goes and does something like this and you think . . . well, you don't think, you just don't know what to think. I can't think. And yet you know what everyone else is thinking. Oh, Lesy, I feel sick for you. I need to lie down again. Wait. Do you want me to call Keith for your tap? Have you noticed it's dripping? She said to send her best regards by the way, Mrs O'Rourke, and that I should tell you she's thinking of you. Isn't that nice? Shame she can't sew.'

'What?'

'Keith's shorts. If you were her, you'd stitch some elastic in that waistband, wouldn't you? Or maybe *you* wouldn't, not in your current state.'

Leslie got up, and turned off the tap, took the tea towel from her sister, shook it before flapping it at her, to shoo her from the kitchen. 'Please sit down, Martha,' she begged.

'It's unbelievable, Les. I can't believe you're not more upset about it. Your husband marches in here with some twenty-year-old, and –'

'Eighteen, Martha. She's eighteen.'

'Thank you. Exactly. Old enough to be –'

'And he didn't march in with her; she knocked on the door. Marched in and introduced herself.'

'Eighteen? Knocked on the door? And you had no idea?'

'How could I? He's never said a word. Can you please sit down, Martha?'

'What did the kids say?'

'We haven't discussed it yet.'

'Creepers. What does she look like?'

'I don't know. I couldn't look at her. Freckly.'

'Freckly, really? I don't blame you. I wouldn't look at her either. And fat? Is she fat? I'll bet she's fat. She sounds fat. He always liked fatties.'

'Gee, thanks.'

'Now don't go getting all paranoid on me, Les. Her being fat isn't about you.'

'I didn't say she was fat.'

'Is she as fat as me?'

Leslie, speechless, failed to answer Martha, who was peeling down the gusset of her compression stockings to reveal a dappled, corrugated stomach. The bruises from her daily anticoagulant injections reminded Leslie of deceased flesh she'd seen on crime shows, pulled from rivers or car boots, bloated blackish mauve – 'plum preserve' they called it on paint charts.

'Look at me, Les, I'm huge. I'm enormous. I told you I was. I'm an elephant. Look at me.' Martha made a trunk of her left arm and a trumpeting sound while grabbing rolls of flesh with her right hand, offering them up to Leslie, who averted her eyes, quite taken aback, for the two had kept themselves completely covered up for as long as both of them could remember. They had even made a pact back at Martha's twenty-first that the body of whoever went first (Leslie prayed it would be her) would be shepherded through death with the greatest dignity, as quietly and privately as possible. Or, rather, as 'privatey' as possible – privatey being a special word coined by the sisters for the purpose of their pact, which promised modest, clean-pressed clothing, a requiem mass and white hydrangeas. Leslie's haemangioma, Martha's swollen legs and any other nasties that might blight their visage in time were to be wholly hidden – inside closed coffins, it went without saying.

There was to be no hoopla and no gawkers at the church. But there should be beautiful organ music. And discreet undertakers. Australian owned. Women only – even those awful burgundy-hatted ones would be better than men. That was what Martha and Leslie wanted, they agreed, and they shook hands on it, knowing that what each had guarded so vigilantly through life would be honoured in death with the utmost privatey by the other.

So, when Martha pummelled her stomach and offered her rolls up for a feel, Leslie felt violated, and certain that her sister had lost her mind.

'Have you seen those ads?' Martha asked. 'Grabbable gut, they call it, making a mouth of her belly button. Remember Ma's bread and dripping? It's going to kill me.'

Leslie, looking out the window, wishing Lana was dead or at least had never been born, reassured her sister, 'You're not fat, Martha. It's the fluid.' Leslie can't believe her always-compressed sister has exposed herself like this in the midst of her sorrow and knew she would never be able to think of her sister again without picturing her grabbable gut, bread and dripping.

'I know. It *is* fluid, isn't it?' Martha tucked herself back in and headed back to the kitchen, to make little sandwiches out of two arrowroot biscuits and slabs of butter; she offered to make her sister a cup of tea, 'But no one else knows that, Les, just you and me. The rest of the world just thinks I'm a nice girl with fat legs.'

'Well then, the rest of the world is wrong,' Leslie declared, thinking Martha was neither nice nor a girl. She walked into the kitchen to put on the kettle and rubbed her big sister's back.

'There, there, Martha.'

Martha moaned. 'Ohhh, that's lovely, Lesy. Can you go a bit lower?'

When Martha died suddenly on a Greyhound coach en route to Milford Sound, the cause of death was initially reported to be an asthma attack, due to the great gasping and wheezing witnessed by helpless bystanders. Two of these were Jack and Val Donovan, recent retirees from Wellington who'd been seated in the row behind Martha and became Leslie's penfriends, after the police put them in touch. They shared Martha's last moments and that they were privy to her last words, which Val and Jack still argued about. Val, who had cradled Martha's 'handsome', is how she referred to Martha's head in her lap – on the floor of the bus; claimed there weren't any words at all, just great big sighs, *as if all the air inside her was leaving.* Whereas Jack, an experienced first aider who had straddled Martha to unsuccessfully administer CPR, swore Martha's last words were 'fingers crossed' – *as she gazed not at me, but through me, if you get what I mean.*

'I'd go with him, since his ear was so close to the old cow's mouth, it doesn't bear thinking about what that man did to try and save ya' sister's life –' Wallace said, when Leslie read him the Donovans' account.

Then, later, as if answering a question no one had asked, Wallace added, 'You know, I thought about visiting her once – after that big operation she had, when you said she was miserable. But I worried how it would look, what people might say.'

'Oh, she was miserable alright,' Leslie replied. 'I'd never seen Martha so low. She was sobbing in pain.'

The autopsy ruled it was an anaphylactic response to a routine insecticide sprayed throughout the coach.

Mrs O'Rourke said at the funeral that she knew someone who knew a Rosemary whose mother had died the same way but on an aeroplane and, as a consequence, even though she never flew, she now carried a little mask, made fashionable by the Asians during bird flu, in case she's ever proximate to the killer spray. And now the little mask would always remind her of Martha. She brought two to the funeral and offered one to Leslie, who took it and used it later to strain gravy.

Leslie was thankful it was spring. At least Martha died with her tummy and legs fully covered.

She tried to feel sad. First hovering by Martha's open coffin, doing up her top button, licking her finger and dabbing at a little brown stain on her blouse, whispering, 'Happy birthday, Martha.' And later, at home in front of the mirror, her face contorted, she waited for tears. But in the first days after her sister's death, all Leslie Bird could think about was soda water – Lana's suggestion for stubborn chocolate stains – and how awfully smug Martha looked, lying there in her coffin. Even when old Keith O'Rourke leaned in and touched her cheek, she seemed without a worry in the world, almost as if she didn't mind leaving it, and Leslie, alone at all.

Hate and Liar

'It only seems fitting we begin with both.

'Hate and *liar.*

'Just two little words, but the first my mother forbade my siblings and me from saying. Growing up, she insisted we replace them. Dubbed us, with "dislike intensely" and "lie person", because lie persons are what Leslie Bird dislikes intensely the most apart from our father, who, despite Florence and Lana, is neither a liar nor hater, but reminds her she might be both.

'The third word is *poo*,' Caroline said.

'Leslie changed it to *pain* and claimed hers arrives every day, first thing in the morning, after a mug of boiling Nescafé and sitting in the bathroom, atop her Cush'n Soft 2000 throne, waiting. My mother desires regular pain.'

'Your mother's insane. And you Birds are obsessed with eliminating.' Toby shook his head.

Caroline informed her husband he'd do well to mind his own business and was completely wrong-headed in thinking that she, of all people, was obsessed with pooing, when the real culprit was Leslie.

'And what's more,' she stressed, 'by six I was constipated, down on my knees doing as I was told, parting my cheeks, biting the pillow; while Shelley, in the bed next to me, laughed hysterically, as Mum inserted Preparation H, via a sharp cold plastic applicator. The memory still makes me clench.'

'Okay, enough already.' Toby called time out with his hands.

'Too much detail for you, darling?' Caroline teased, knowing full well her husband's delicate constitution. That he'd never been good with anatomy or ailing bodies. Or suffering in general.

About the only things Toby Reid didn't excel at. Making him prey for know-all Birds with big chips on their round shoulders and a penchant for swooping in and pecking at any poor soul who might confuse a tumour with a catheter as Toby once did, when he mentioned, during a rare lull at the Birds' dining table, that his beloved father had just been diagnosed with a stage-three catheter. The table cracked up. Wallace leaped to Toby's defence. 'I've had one of them meself, up me clacker, and I can tell you lot, it's no laughing matter. You can't possibly imagine . . .' He paused, and Caroline wondered if her father realised what he was about to say, and might be trying to figure out how to put it more delicately – but he wasn't, he was just swallowing a great lump in his throat rising up from the great depths of 'sympathising with himself,' before pointing at each of his girls in turn. 'You can't possibly imagine what it's like having someone stick something up your hoohaa.'

The girls erupted. Tears streamed down their cheeks. Shelley snorted, then jumped up to put the kettle on and threw Caroline a tea towel. Leslie gasped, 'Don't you dare,' and asked what a hoohaa was, just as Bernadette grabbed her crutch and burst into song: '*Hoohaa, I lost my bra, left my knickers in my boyfriend's car.*' They roared laughing. Caroline wiped her face on the tea towel, rolled it into a ball and tossed it back to Shelley – over the head of Leslie, yelping and reaching, all piggy in the middle. Shelley threw it down on the kitchen floor and stomped on it with her smelly feet, swishing it across the lino, wiping up the milk she'd spilled while making tea. Wallace said they were all mad. Mad as cut snakes. And asked Toby how the hell he put up with Caroline. Leslie cried. Not for her girls or their hoohaas, but for her tea towel. Which Shelley said wasn't a tea towel at all, but an old cloth nappy, 'probably Bernadette's'.

Wallace loves Toby. Thinks he might look a bit better with more hair and less ears, but he's just so happy that such a good bloke had married his daughter and makes a point of telling Caroline all the time.

Avoiding ill health – via luck, not virtue – is key, she believes, to her husband retaining not only a childlike naivety when it comes to corporeal affairs, but a 'pristine colon', according to his doctor after a colonoscopy, which is when Caroline took to calling him Christine, Christine Polon, as a way of taming the fury she felt towards his genetic good fortune as opposed to her bad.

Not that she wished polyps and clogged arteries on him as he gorged on key lime pie and she grazed on spinach. She just wanted him to stop asking her if he should have ice cream, cream or both. And besides, she only called him 'Christine' to herself, or so she thought, until others said, 'I beg your pardon?' and she'd realised she'd called him Christine aloud. Puerile, perhaps, but less provocative than calling your husband a prick in public, for the contempt he expresses in private for those he deems less pristine than himself.

Grunters at the gym and shit parkers, for example. The former were asked to keep it down, lower their weights, improve their technique and/or stay at home. The latter were left notes on their windscreens.

Customers waiting in line at the Twelve Items or Less Express Checkout quivered, clutching their groceries as Toby counted their items, then broadcast and removed what he deemed unnecessary.

'Who does that?' Caroline had pleaded with him, trying to get to the source of his rage after watching him win a tug of war with a little old lady and an eight pack of Sorbent toilet paper.

Toby insisted it wasn't rage. 'I want fairness, that's all.'

'And . . . ?' Caroline let her question hang in the air.

'And my side of the footpath.'

'Your side?'

'Haven't you noticed that no one watches where they're going anymore?'

'You mean people on their phones?'

'Correct. And others oblivious to etiquette. Strayers in general.'

Toby told her he was going to start tripping them over. 'I'm sick of moving out of their way.' He said he was going to hold his ground against stragglers too, 'slowcoaches clogging up roads and airports. And queue-jumpers. Dwarves especially! Someone needs to tell them it's rude.'

'Someone not rude like you?' Caroline cringed, remembering the dozen or so little people that Toby accused of pushing-in, at the reception desk of a Christchurch hotel, where he'd paced, waiting to settle his bill before his free parking permit expired. 'They just swarmed in right in front of me, then stood on tippy toes, arguing over their mini bars,' he said, before he blasted them and four times as many again with his horn in the car park, as they climbed into a convoy of Taragos and did their darndest to exit the car park.

'They were on their way to play golf,' the convenor of the vertically challenged convention told Caroline later that night, when they exchanged insurance details for the damage Toby did to one of their vehicles when he 'sought justice' – cutting in, tailgating through the boom gate.

Toby just laughed. 'Let's hope it was a Mini.'

'It wasn't a Mini, it was a Tarago,' Caroline fumed, furious at his insensitivity and that he'd forgotten their vehicles already.

'Not the car – the golf course. Don't you go getting all Grumpy on me, Caro.'

Mortified, she refused to speak as they drove across the billiard green Canterbury plains – until her anger with him turned into something else . . . Disgust? No. Something worse. Something that made her want to open the car door and hurl herself from their rental. But she discovered Toby had set the car to central locking – 'to save us from being carjacked,' he explained. Caroline exploded. 'By who? Sheep?' She rattled the doorhandle and yelled all the way to the Hermitage Hotel in Mount Cook, where an unseen valet opened her door and she elbowed him right in the groin.

Toby laughed and told Caroline that she was psycho and that he'd never seen her move so fast. *Really?* she thought, *you try walking through this world as a woman and see what sort of reflexes you develop.* Then she called him Christine to his face for the very first time and continued to do so for the rest of their trip through the pristine South Island. When people commented on what an unusual name he had and asked after its origin (which, they did in droves), she took a deep breath and said, 'Go on, darling, you tell them.'

'Shame. That's what it was. The thing that made me go berserk.' Caroline confided to Shelley sometime later. 'When will I ever learn that shame is always the kindling for that kind of unhinging, that rage? Directed not at Toby but myself. I was ashamed I'd married such an impatient callous man. And what doing so said of me. For what is marriage, if not a mirror of our own depravities?' Shelley shrugged. 'Well, mine is, at least.' Caroline continued. 'But I didn't know that then. I just knew I had to get the fuck out of the car. And not kill anyone. Myself, the valet. My husband.

'That said, I shouldn't have been surprised by Toby's inclinations. The way he just says whatever's on his mind. For me, raised in our family – no, raised isn't right, as that implies a conscious act, some cultivation, some awareness of the needs of children, as opposed to the unconscious composting that took place in our house, where everyone talked all the time but no one said anything, apart from the occasional "What the fuck?" when a weed sprouted instead of a rose. Or we ate continuously, stuffing ourselves, to stop from spilling the beans, as Mum was big on manners. Big on not speaking with your mouth full. So, when we weren't eating silently or speaking shit, we talked about who or what we'd devour next. So, when Toby turned up with his thing, of just "saying the thing", that was the bullseye, the arrow that fit my wound: my lifelong desire to hear someone speak their truth. Toby Reid was everything I couldn't say. And that was the thing I loved and hated about him the most. That and his hair, which was scruffy in a Sting way when I met him. Remember?'

'Kind of.' Shelley yawned.

'God love him, he's been incorrigibly himself since we met, most grievously and indelibly over breakfast on Boxing Day 2004, while we were watching live coverage of the tsunami and a pregnant woman, on the verge of drowning in the raging waters, tried to save herself by grabbing on to a man clinging to a branch. And Toby shouted, "Get off, fatty!"

'I decided then and there I'd have to leave him. Toby pleaded, "It was a joke. Come on. Try saying it with a Scottish accent. Git orff, Futty." Which only made him sound more callous. I didn't speak to him for a week until he wrote me a letter illustrated with *Karma Sutra* stick figures and bought me a book of Khalil Gibran poems, and we both pretended that Toby liked the cowgirl position and that he would no longer call poets "wizards" and that his indifference towards anything but hi-fi, Weimaraners, Depeche Mode, parrots, Natalie Portman and flora was a thing of the past. That his icy heart was thawing. And that I believed him and forgave him.'

~

'You still haven't answered me.' Caroline said to Toby.

Toby shook his head.

So, she asked him again. 'Is that too much detail for you, Christine?'

'No, it's not the detail, it's just that you've already told me about Leslie inserting the . . .'

'Good,' she interrupted. 'Now, where was I?'

'On your knees clenching.'

'Oh, that's right – then I farted accidently on purpose, in Mum's face and she smacked me on the back bottom and stormed out, slamming the bedroom door.'

'Then you begged Shelley not to tell a soul. But the next day Michael and Bernadette nicknamed you Gomer, right? Gomer Piles? Hey, Gomey!' Toby reached over and poked her.

She poked him back. 'Don't call me that.'

'Don't call me Christine.'

'Deal.'

They shook hands, and she apologised for having told him the story a hundred times before.

'Thousands actually,' Toby corrected. 'But what's with back bottom? I've never understood that bit.'

'Where else could it go?' Caroline said indignantly.

'Not where – *why*. Why did you call your bum a "back bottom"?'

'It's another one of Mum's euphemisms. Same as we had to call' – she pointed between her legs – 'our "front bottom". Leslie Bird thinks naming things makes them real. So, if we don't mention it, it doesn't exist.'

'Wow. Makes you wonder who was more constipated.'

'Exactly.'

'Did she ever take you to the doctor?'

'Yep – after weeks of tummy aches, fever and vomiting. He was this big Norwegian guy who wore a white coat and looked like Lurch. Smoked at his desk. Flicked ashes on to the floor and his stub into a sink before washing his hands in lemonade. He told me to hop up onto his examination table. "Roll onto your side, face the wall and hug your knees," he said, before giving me the fright of my life and a diagnosis that I was full of faeces. I remember thinking, *It's not me, bucko – it's you.*'

'Me?' Toby looked shocked.

'No, not you – or the Viking with his finger up my bottom, inserting, what I didn't know then was a suppository; but my bloody mother, sitting in the corner of the room nodding.'

'Nodding? Jesus.' Toby assured Caroline he needed no convincing that Leslie was full of shit.

'"See, I told you it was just a pain in the stomach," she said as we left the doctor's office and got in the car. The doctor said I'd be fine, but I wasn't. The closer we got to home the worse I felt. Mum told me to hold on and think about something else, but I couldn't think of anything but exploding all over her Datsun. When I told her, she yelled, "Not on your life" and threw her arm across in front of me to try and stop me headbutting Saint Christopher . . .'

'Saint Christopher?'

'Patron saint of travellers, shimmering on a magnet on her glovebox – when we swerved and pulled over into a Golden Fleece, where I did my pain – much to her horror, as Mum is of the view that service station toilets are the domain of filthy men like my father, carrying the big communal key, dumping smoky beer bogs, staggering out into the sunlight, spitting tobacco, buckling up their overalls, sniffing their fingers, groaning, "Jesus Christ, that was like trying to pull a nail out of a boot."

'The longest I ever went without a pain was two and a half weeks.'

~

Well, not *ever*.

Leslie Bird's desire to disconnect words from their meaning impacted not just her children's bowels but their brain matter. Like an errant switchboard operator, she rewired their limbic systems, so that it would take the lucky ones decades to reconnect what their bodies knew back then but tried to forget, while the unlucky ones would pass on the same crap to their unfortunate broods, unaware that their wiring is faulty.

Caroline's *ever* was more like thirty-five years later, on the seventh of September 2013, ironically the day Tony Abbot became prime minister, three weeks and one day after Bernadette strangled her at their nephew Sage's tenth birthday party.

The icing was grass green on the soccer cake Lana made him. Piped vanilla frosting marked out the field, decorated with tiny plastic men with newsreader hair wearing red or blue jerseys, two goalies in black falling backwards with their hands in the air, a ball, two nets and a chocolate bullet fence. It was kind of amazing. Not so much Lana's baking prowess as what set Dette raging: her insistence that Caroline was enabling their sister Shelley's maybe/maybe not breast cancer by not calling her out as a liar. Not because she wasn't, clearly she was. But Caroline wasn't keen on shaming her without proof. And perhaps a little doubt left a little hope for Shelley's sanity? Caroline desperately wanted her sister to have cancer – not so she'd die, but so she couldn't be proven insane, alongside the rest of the family sitting out on Lana's verandah, stuffing themselves and watching as Bernadette shoved Caroline up against the pool fence and strangled her, screaming, 'Fuck off, Caroline,' over and over. Caroline finally yelped and her sister released her. Leslie called out to offer Bernadette a sausage roll – 'Quick, before they go cold' – and Wallace asked, 'How's your mortgage, love?' through a mouthful of party pie, tomato sauce dribbling down his chin.

Bernadette shrugged, said she wasn't hungry, then walked over to the table and grabbed a fistful of birthday cake, as Caroline clutched her throat, coughing and spluttering, making a show of her shock and wondering why the fuck no one was saying anything at all to her. Not a word of concern. Surely Shelley, leaping up to scratch their father's dandruff, would pause to see if she was okay? Maybe not. Or Michael? Are you kidding? He was busy on his phone, editing photos of his sisters wrestling. Later, he would lie, they all would, and say they didn't see or hear a thing. Then the lies would morph into murmurs that Caroline probably made the whole thing up. 'Given that imagination of hers, anything's possible,' Leslie would have said to Martha. 'Who knows who strangled who? And what's the difference anyway between strangling and hugging?' And this from Shelley: 'What cancer?'

Remarkable, really, that leap from Shelley. From cause to affected. From sitting to scratching; particularly for one so excoriated, still weeping from the ravages of the radiation treatment she claimed she'd undergone, and confided to Caroline; who not only believed her beloved sister but raced to Coles to buy icy poles to place beneath Shelley's armpits as she leaned against her sister and sang KC and the Sunshine Band's 'Please Don't Go' to her bosoms between fielding calls and texts from George and Mark, Shelley's ex.

George wanted to know what the hell was going on since his mother had hinted at calamity then ignored him, a Shelley speciality. Mark insisted in late-night whispers that Caroline should 'take care of things, for god's sake,' as Jilly, his new girlfriend, just a few years older than George, was newly pregnant and this was the last thing any of them needed. 'Of course,' Caroline, the big ninny, agreed, and then promised not to say a word about any of it – they all did. Everyone promised Shelley they'd keep the secrets she entrusted them with from Leslie and Wallace, as selfless Shelley didn't want to distress anyone, least of all her poor old parents.

Cruelly, Shelley's 'cancer' had appeared on Mother's Day – or, rather, late on the evening of: right after George didn't visit or call her. So, Shelley rang him in tears.

It was George's first year of university, living away from home on campus. And the Mother's Day call was the first time they'd spoken in the three months since the Armidale Horror, when Shelley had driven six hours to visit him, only to be told when she called on arrival to ask where they should meet for lunch, 'No – I'm good thanks.'

'What do you mean, no, you're good thanks?' Shelley had screamed. 'I've just driven six hours to see you.'

'Well, no one asked you to,' George pointed out, and he hung up.

On the long trip home, Shelley called her aunt from the car and wept while Martha talked over the top of her, telling her not to waste another minute on the imbecile. 'Twenty-four, thirty-five and eighty-six,' she said. 'Keep your eyes on the road.'

Shelley was confused. 'What's with the numbers?'

'Not what, *when*,' Martha said. 'It's the ages when men soften or not. In between, just go about your business. Expect nothing and you won't be disappointed. Like the bakery at Walcha. Drive straight on through to Gloucester and get yourself a decent custard tart and view of the suspension bridge.'

Pacing up and down her dimly lit hallway on the first Sunday in May, waiting for George to answer his phone, Shelley was wishing she'd taken her aunt's advice and just sent herself a Mother's Day card like she usually did. She wished, too, that she'd never volunteered at a single damn Mother's Day stall back when he was little.

All those years of boring craft mornings, acting like she cared about what Mrs So-and-So said about Mrs Whatsie. Queuing at Spotlight, like she had nothing better to do than cross-stitch *Best Mother in the World* on thin tea towels and give George money to buy her one. *You think you're teaching them to be thoughtful, but all you're doing is thinking for them. Delaying the inevitable realisation that most of your offspring won't give a shit about you in the long run.* Shelley thought no matter how many times she'd said to George, 'No, I'm good thanks' when he asked if she'd like another candle for Mother's Day – he always, always bought her another one. She wondered why fathers didn't organise the stalls for Mother's Day the way mothers did for Father's Day. *World's best dad* and all that shit. *I guess we've only got ourselves to blame*, she was thinking, when George finally picked up his phone and said, 'Hey.'

Shelley brightened. 'George! You're home!'

'Gee, thanks for telling me. What's up?'

He sounded distracted, Shelley thought. As if he was holding his breath – in the midst of playing *Call of Duty* or with himself. 'Have I caught you at a bad time?' she asked. 'Am I on speaker?'

'What? No. Why?' George exhaled. 'What do you want? And why are you panting?'

'I'm not. Am I? You just sound so far away, Georgie.'

'Not far enough,' George muttered. There was the sound of rapid-fire clicking, a chair creaking, then a 'fuck' and the sound of something hitting a wall and then more 'fucks' and a 'fucking hell'.

Shelley heaved a big sigh and walked into his old bedroom, where she stood before his bookcase. *Lord of the Rings. Harry Potter.*

Brian Jacques – a whole series of books he'd adored about woodland creatures. She'd thought her son exquisitely sensitive for caring about the little lives of moles and badgers. Harry, not Voldemort.

'Are you crying?' George sounded angry.

'No – why?' Shelley sniffed.

'Just spit it out. Why did you call? What do you want?'

"I don't want anything. I'm just . . . I'm old, George. I'm tired. Okay? I just thought – I don't know. I just thought you might have, you know, called. Since . . . since it's Mother's Day and all.'

'And all?' George laughed. 'You know I don't do Hallmarks.'

'Hallmarks?'

'Isn't it Mother's Day every day when you have a kid?'

Kid sounded so crude. 'I guess it is,' Shelley said, imagining them both as billy goats, hoofing it up the side of some mountain, George on higher ground kicking rubble back into her path.

'Then *you* should be visiting *me* and thanking *me*,' George said, taking a bite of something – an apple? – and chewing loudly in Shelley's ear.

She wondered when he'd started eating fruit, given that he'd spat out every mouthful she ever peeled, stewed and spooned him . . . and why in God's name should *she* be thanking *him*? *You're an ungrateful goat*, is what she wanted to say, but knowing he'd have some biting comeback, or find a way to make 'goat' a compliment, she said instead, 'Is that an invitation, George?'

'Settle down, Smelly. Don't get ahead of yourself.'

There was no chance of that.

Shelley followed George's lead and turned her phone to speaker and threw it down beside her on his bed, then she lay down and stared up at the glow-in-the-dark galaxy she had painstakingly stuck on his ceiling with both legs shaking, as her toes gripped the rungs as she'd straddled her fear of heights and Mark's stupid ladder. Most people had hollow ones, but not Mark who insisted on buying solid aluminium so he could show off in front of the woman with the big bosoms at the Bunnings sausage sizzle. Now he wasn't around to carry it in and out of the house light bulbs weren't replaced. Shelley lived in the dark. 'What are you, a mushroom?' George had said last time he was home, flicking the light switches, off and on, 'Lucky you've got a cupboard full of candles.'

When he was little, George recited the names of planets and stars as he and Shelley lay on his bed together. He used to like me then, she thought, remembering how he would reach out and grab her arm to prevent her leaving when she'd thought he was asleep and tried to slip out of the room. Or maybe he was just scared of the dark?

The only other time she recalled him needing her was when he'd faked an upset stomach to leave school camp on day two of five.

Mr Grieves, his year eight teacher, had called and said, 'Your son is vomiting and has a temperature of forty degrees.'

(She later learned George had eaten soap and held his breath to induce this state.)

So, she left work at Camperdown and drove all the way out to Mulgoa. She was more excited than alarmed. *He needs me,* she thought, flipping through her street directory, thinking the camp site had to be on the map – but it wasn't and she got lost. Ended up in an industrial estate full of cul-de-sacs and yuk trucks, tooting their stupid musical horns. She couldn't resist buying herself a ham and salad roll.

When she finally arrived, George was sitting inside the camp leader's office, clutching his tightly rolled sleeping bag with a look of fury on his face. He didn't look up or say hello or hug her or anything. When she bent to kiss him on the head, he just pulled away and said, 'You're late. Are they crumbs on your face?'

~

'So, I guess a visit home is out of the question?'

George didn't answer.

Shelley picked up the phone and held it close to her ear. 'George? Are you still there?'

George took another bite and chewed even louder. 'I'd better get going.'

'But what if your poor mother was ill, George? Would you visit her then?' It was out of Shelley's mouth before she could take it back.

George's chewing slowed. 'What do you mean? Are you sick?'

Shelley leaned in closer to the phone, heard him breathing and herself say, 'No, no. Of course, not. It's nothing. Nothing. Really. Well, nothing for you to worry about, Georgie. The oncologist says I should be fine.'

~

When the Birds were fledglings, Leslie told them to always tell the truth. 'If you tell lies, you'll get caught,' she said. 'I'll always know. Tell one lie and you have to tell another. Lies are like feathers in the wind. Once they fly off, you can never get them back.'

News of Shelley's cancer spread like wildfire.

George called his father. Mark called Caroline. Caroline called Shelley, who managed to confirm the rumours were true without actually saying in so many words that she had cancer. She pleaded with her sister not to make a fuss and to give her the privacy she needed to deal with this – and then asked her if she could keep an eye on George and, when the time came, take him to any support sessions the Cancer Council offered. 'Just in case some of them fall on the days I have treatment,' she said, explaining that she'd decided to go to Nepean Hospital rather than her own, so her colleagues didn't make a fuss. 'I'm not sure if you've heard, but George has decided to take the rest of the semester off and move home. I tried to dissuade him, but you know George – he's just an old softie who loves his mummy. Oh, and please don't tell Mum and Dad or any of the others about my condition; I don't want to worry them. But let's just say I wouldn't be upset if Mark and his bitch shit their pants.'

'Okay.' Caroline agreed to keep her sister's illness a secret, then promptly called her siblings.

They met up over Thai to discuss the situation. Lana and Michael cried. Dette called it a crock of shit. They took a vote. Two maybes. One maybe not. One definitely not. They did agree, though, that the fish cakes were outstanding, that the 'situation' would screw up George either way, and that Caroline should step in/up, since she'd volunteered.

'Great idea, seeing as you're a gullible rich bitch with too much time on your hands and no kids,' Dette said. Then, when no one laughed, 'It's a joke, people. Lighten up!'

Back at the pool fence, when Dette's hands were around her sister's neck and Caroline finally yelped, Dette said to Caroline quite calmly, 'Why the fuck you believe her when everything Shelley says is a lie is what really gets me.' And Caroline squeaked, 'Maybe you're not angry with me; maybe you're angry with yourself, because you don't have the capacity to care for anyone else – at the moment, I mean, what with the divorce and the girls and your studies and your job at Jamberry.'

Dette loosened her grip. Held out her hands and admired her fingernails. Gold with black spots. Roar. A bestselling set from the Jungle Collection. *Empower the women around you* went the marketing spiel.

Caroline coughed. 'And if Shelley hasn't got cancer, then she's got a mental illness and still needs our help, don't you reckon? Hey, great nails, by the way. Can you get me a set?'

'They've sold out,' Dette said, then she headed up to snatch some birthday cake as Caroline, clutching her throat, looked at her family on the verandah, stuffing themselves.

She reeled off down the driveway. No one but Sage, the demi-orphaned birthday boy, came after her to see if she was okay.

'I'm fine,' Caroline lied, unfurling his clammy fingers, shaking her head from side to side, hoping some part of Sage would remember in time her incongruent gestures and interpret them as what she couldn't say – that she was certainly not okay after being strangled by her sister in front of their silent family. This was the day on which the part of her that always saw the Birds for who she hoped they'd be saw them for who they were. And died.

'Not to worry, Sagey, I'm fine,' she repeated. 'Now you'd better hurry back to the party and blow out your candles. Off you go – and don't forget to make a wish.' She said, making a wish herself for him in her head. *Dear god, let this precious little boy survive this insane family.*

She watched as Sage – unable to walk in straight lines since his father Viktor's departure had slumped his skinny shoulders – zigzagged back up to the verandah, where Lana lit the candles on his gouged cake and the Birds began singing – loudly at first but then fizzling without Caroline to lead. 'For he's a jolly good fellooooooow . . .' they droned, as she listened, wanting to scream, just like Sage had back when he was five.

~

Oh, how clearly Caroline remembered him, full of fire, screaming out at his cousin George's confirmation; as he'd sat thrashing on his mother's lap in the upper chapel, as Lana did her best to restrain him from kamikazeing onto the congregation entering the church below. His aunties, uncles, cousins and grandparents, dipping their middle fingers into holy water, making signs of the cross and genuflecting, shuffling into pews ahead of the bishop in his Ku Klux Klannish vestments, processing behind two lines of candle-carrying altar boys, pimply pubescent confirmands and their sponsors; dressed in a wide range of Sunday best and worst, all of them intoning, Oh Come Holy Spirit – when dear little Sage screamed out above them all – 'You're all fucking idiots.'

Ah, Sage indeed, a prophet – one who names what he sees right in front of him, Caroline had thought, beaming, as she looked up at him. *A wise man has finally been born into the Bird family.*

She had to stop herself from clapping and cheering as Lana put her hand over Sage's mouth and wrestled him back from peering dangerously over the wooden banister, straining to watch his younger sister Paris, trailed by Viktor, running straight through the middle of the holy procession, with Paris shrieking that she needed to go to the toilet. Stepping out of her underpants and Viktor's grip, she fled the church and ran through the car park towards a tree, which she climbed effortlessly. Then, perched on a branch, hiked up her skirt and defecated.

Dear Viktor, who would process himself from this very same church in a year's time, was accustomed to people shitting on him, aka his daughter's bizarre inability (which Lana spun as an 'eccentricity') to empty her bowels anywhere other than from a great height, preferably up a tree, with her father waiting below for her to finish, pacing around, all moribund Eeyore, mumbling to himself, before pulling a plastic bag from up his sleeve and bagging Paris's poo much like he would a dog's.

Viktor left Paris's business by the back wheel of his car, to be retrieved after the confirmation morning tea taking place over in the church hall, thanks to Caroline's ascension to the parish council, in a church she neither believed in nor frequented. But wanted to. Kind of. Not really. Actually, the closest she'd ever come to recognising her faith, or lack thereof, was in a line written by Julian Barnes: 'I don't believe in God, but I miss Him.' Caroline missed believing in something. Anything. Santa Claus. The Easter Bunny. A mother's love.

~

Her connection to the parish came about through a Brian or Allen Murray; Bernadette's recently widowed, lilting old Irish neighbour, a retired accountant, with dreadful psoriasis and a first name no one could agree upon.

Just before she died, his lovely wife Maureen had asked Bernadette for help, over their shared side fence – when she was bald and dripping wet; her swimmers gaping over her mastectomied chest. She'd been playing with her grandchildren in the pool, when she heard Bernadette screaming, again, at Amir and the girls, she hopped out and called to Bernadette to join her at the fence and casually explained, like her azaleas had aphids, that her cancer had spread to her bones and liver, and as such, she wouldn't be able to keep up her catechist classes at the local school (where Dette's girls were booked in) so was there any way Bernadette could help her out?

When Bernadette said she couldn't possibly, because she didn't believe in God, Maureen laughed and said, 'Who? Just go in there and love those kids, darlin'. And believe in yourself.' Then she shouted 'Polo' and dived back into the pool.

Bernadette introduced Caroline to Brian slash Allen and in no time, Caroline agreed to take Maureen's classes and assist him with a crazy scheme he'd devised 'to save' a parish councillor, *also a widow*, named Julie, that he suspected was being taken advantage of by their parish priest. Brian slash Allen didn't have the hard evidence he needed. What he needed, he said, was someone on the inside. Someone like Caroline.

She should have seen the train wreck coming, but was a complete succour for an old bastard with a sob story and a cinnamon swirl.

'It's nothing, they're just perks,' Brian slash Allen said of the plentiful pastries he brought to Bernadette's when the three of them met for morning tea. He explained that he had a son, who brought leftovers home each night from the Vietnamese Bakery in Carlingford Court, where he worked, when he wasn't shooting heroin.

Caroline said it was hard to hear the horror in heroin, in the soft sing-songy way Brian slash Allen said it. 'It put you in mind of Old Danny Boy, and the Emerald Isle.' Even three months later, when his son overdosed and was found dead by the side of his bed. After which their morning teas turned weekly.

Caroline relished sitting in Bernadette's kitchen, demonstrating compassion to a sister who thought she was a gullible fool, a first-class idiot. And visiting Dette to check in on the girls, who were becoming weirder by the week, was somehow easier with Brian slash Allen sitting there too. When he left, the sisters had something to talk about other than their husbands and parents.

They talked about how weird Brian slash Allen was and whether or not he wanted Julie for himself. Dette was sure he did.

Caroline told herself it was the memory of Maureen swimming with her grandkids – bald with no bosoms, but still laughing and calling Dette *darlin'*, urging her to go in and love someone – that made her agree to accompany Brian slash Allen to an Agape dinner/mass thingy on Holy Thursday. She arrived with a bottle of sauvignon blanc and was met by Father John, who took one look at her bottle and gravely told her they only used consecrated wine. 'Oh, but it's Houghton's, Father,' Caroline retorted, as he swiped it from her and pointed to a basin and wash cloth, and told her to grab herself a set and make her way up to the altar and stand next to Julie. Julie! The two women nodded at one another, then knelt with their heads bowed, in front of a row of old clergy sitting with their pant legs rolled up – waiting to have their ugly, smelly old tinea-ed, toe-jammed feet washed and dried. The drying was important Father John said, 'take all the time you need.'

Caroline would have run off there and then, if Brian slash Allen wasn't sitting behind her, in the front pew, with his flaky forehead and unimaginable grief. She should have said no, categorically, to Father John's invitation to join the parish council, 'unelected' he whispered, as she towelled between his toes, if she'd not been completely stupid and raised by misogynists – including Leslie, whom she often accused of being worse than Wallace.

Months later, she was standing in her kitchen stirring Bolognaise, talking on speaker phone to Father John's secretary, when Toby walked in from work and asked who the creep was on the phone and what the fuck was going on?

Caroline hung up and tried explaining some of it – Maureen's lack of bosoms, Julie's abundance, Brian slash Allen's poor son and theory about Father John and 'Paul from the Parish', his sweaty little secretary; a recovering alcoholic who'd taken a shine to her and the minutes at their parish council meetings, between sips of vodka from his Mount Franklin water bottle.

'It's okay – it's under control,' she assured Toby, that it would all be over soon now that Brian slash Allen had his evidence.

'What evidence?'

Caroline clarified that Paul from the Parish had left a photograph under their door mat.

'Our front door mat?' Toby looked stunned.

Caroline nodded. 'At first glance, it isn't apparent what you're looking at. Who's who and what's what. You have to turn it this way and that,' she said, 'but then you realise – Chessus – that what you're looking at is a photo of Father John and Julie in the bath.'

Caroline told Toby how she'd already shown her parents the photo and how Wallace wasn't surprised and said he'd never known a priest who wasn't rotten. 'Mum defended him.'

'Your dad?'

'No, Father John. She said she'd heard that he wasn't a priest at all – only a Brother.'

'So that makes it okay he bathes with widows and takes selfies?'

'Of course not.'

Caroline didn't tell Toby it wasn't a selfie.

It makes you wonder then, four years down the track, if Caroline tolerated Bernadette's hands around her neck – which would trigger bulging discs, migraines, a short prissy bow-tied neurologist and a Chinese masseuse named Norman – because some part of her thought she deserved the fuck offs. (Maybe not seven. Maybe one or two.) Not just for believing Shelley's probably-not-cancer, but for all of the bullshitters past and present. Maybe the strangling was Caroline's penance?

Or maybe she was still feeling sorry for Bernadette over the mirror thing – the compact mirrors that Dette gifted all of her sisters at the height of her divorce as a way of thanking them for their support.

Caroline thought that Bernadette engraving *Sisterhood* on the mirrors was an ingenious way to remind you of your sisters when seeking your own reflection (as if the Birds' thin lips and weak chin wasn't enough) and was blown away by the gesture; she could barely imagine her sister coming up with the idea, let alone buying the mirrors, finding an engraver, and choosing such a pretty font. Caroline held hers to her chest and told Bernadette she'd cherish it forever . . . only to lose it two months later down the side of her seat on a BA flight from Sydney to Singapore in the middle of the night. She pressed the button to summon a flight attendant and the hostess came and tetchily turned it off, flashing her torch about wildly and waking up everyone in the vicinity, before ordering several passengers to stand in the aisle while she crouched down and tried to retrieve it. When she couldn't reach it she asked Caroline if it was valuable, and Caroline said it was priceless. The hostess told her that the best chance of getting it back was if ground staff took the whole seat apart when they landed, and she suggested that Caroline should jot down her name and address, along with a brief description of the mirror and what it meant to her. Caroline put pen to paper immediately, and handed it to the hostess two and a half hours later.

'That's quite the novel,' the hostess smirked, when Caroline disembarked at Changi Airport.

Too distressed to tell anyone that she'd lost Dette's precious mirror, and convinced she'd never see it again, Caroline was overjoyed when it arrived a month later, tucked inside a tiny padded post pack. She called Shelley to share the good news.

'Hang on. Back up. What mirror?' Shelley sounded confused.

'The one Bernadette gave us. How could you forget? She got it engraved with *Sisterhood*. It's the nicest thing she's ever given us.'

'It's the *only* thing she's ever given us. I regifted mine the next day.'

'You did what? I can't believe you gave it away!'

'I can't believe you didn't know that Witchery were fundraising for Breast Cancer and handing them out as a free gift with every purchase over a hundred bucks. All she did was go on a bender and palm off the freebies.'

Or maybe Caroline didn't fight back because she still felt guilty about the little matter of Bernadette's big jealousy over how close Caroline and Lana had become in the wake of Viktor's death?

On the day he died, Caroline and Lana had gone shopping together at David Jones. They were lying down in the bedding department, testing a Medium Sealy Posturepedic when Lana told Caroline that she'd left Viktor hanging at home. Caroline didn't know what else to do but hold her half-sister firmly, for the longest time, before they wolfed down Valium and returned to Lana's house with three sets of Sheridan Supersoft sheets and called the police.

Bernadette had decided, along with Leslie, that Viktor's suicide was all Lana's fault. How could it not be? She said, 'What kind of psycho goes shopping for sheets and gets stoned at a time like that?'

'Exactly,' Leslie said. 'It's hard to imagine a more selfish deed.'

Viktor

Caroline had explained incessantly to Leslie and her sisters that she'd had no way of knowing that when Lana called 'that morning' that Viktor was already dead. And that of course, she'd thought it was weird that Lana needed to buy sheets so early in the day and that she sounded strange: 'Kind of whispering really loud and fast . . . and hey, who wouldn't sound strange and take Valium after waking up and finding their husband dangling above the toilet half naked, sporting a Bulldogs jersey and boner, foaming, his tongue bulging, reeking and *dead*?'

Viktor's big toe had landed on the full flush button, where it stuck, hissing, as shit ran down his legs and pooled on the floor. All Lana could think to do – not think – do – was watch where she stepped and elbow his foot to release the button.

Viktor was swaying and chunks of ceiling plaster were falling onto the floor when Lana locked the bathroom door and got the kids up and off to school, none the wiser – though in time Paris would connect Bacon & Egg McMuffins with the day her father died – before calling Caroline.

'It wasn't at all like it is in the movies,' Caroline said. Where hands are tied behind backs and calves are strapped together and the executor causes a couple of Houdini-type jerks, before the hooded figure goes still. The body seems heavy but not messy, when the drop is calculated correctly and the spinal cord snaps, as opposed to an agonising death by suffocation, as in Viktor's case. The evidence of his struggle was writ monstrously, making him look more of a grotesquely clawed purple piñata than person, when Caroline saw him. He was an exemplar of why seventy per cent of (mostly beautiful) young men – *God love them and save them* – can't be viewed in an open coffin, despite the mortician's best efforts, and Caroline's too, after she and Lana hauled a ladder into the bathroom and Caroline climbed it and followed Lana's instructions to tidy up Viktor's hair, raise his collar and try to close his eyes, feeling for his pulse, despite how clearly dead he was. Caroline attempted CPR, prising Viktor's jaw open with a fork, thinking, *it's not going to be easy blowing into a dead's man's mouth with his wife watching.* And it wasn't.

When there's a suicide, everyone asks if the deceased left a note.

After descending, vomiting and gargling, Lana asked Caroline to have a scout about to see if she could find one, whilst she called triple zero. So Caroline told her feet to move and started to search, thinking how surreal it was to be snooping around her half-sister's house – looking for something so intensely intimate that might – what? Speak louder than Viktor's actions (the sight, smell, sound, touch and taste of which would stay with her until her own dying day)?

There was no note. No envelope. No paper or pen that Caroline could see, but on a desk in the living room was an open laptop. So, she sat down in front of it, moved the mouse, and up on screen flashed one word:

Sorry

Jesus, was that it? Not one loving word? Would it really hurt to add more . . . Caroline wondered; as her fingers floated over the keyboard, time suspended, until there was a loud knock on the front door, then police in heavy boots coming down the hallway. She could almost hear their height. Men to the rescue. She wiped the mouse on her shirt, got up and joined them. Introduced herself. Made tea.

Lana told the police that the second she woke up and heard the cistern gurgling, she knew that Viktor had done it. Knew he was dead and ran down the hallway to their beloved back bathroom – frequented she said, 'when someone wanted a little privacy.' Lana knocked and opened the door, which was unlocked – and why wouldn't it be? Viktor had all the privacy he needed now, pants-less, soiled, *Jesus,* hanging from their recessed light fitting, fixed to a wooden beam inside the ceiling.

It turns out, once the police tape was finally removed and Wallace inspected the damage and made repairs, that the ceiling not entirely collapsing would show up in Lana's 'fors' column a year later, when Bernadette urged her to get both her shit and a list together. The fors and againsts of why she should continue living and not merely existing as a widow with two small children in the very house in which their maker had hanged himself. Maker too in the sense that in marriage Viktor made Lana a wife and in death made her a widow, presiding over this mess.

Yes, quality of construction had put the fors one point ahead of the againsts and bolstered Lana's resolve to stay put and tackle the mortgage on her own. She listened to Wallace when he suggested she take no notice of what Leslie was saying and to leave the kids with her a little longer, whilst he continued to sleep over, whip up a bit of dinner and whack up a bit of gyprock, 'if that's alright with you, love?'

Lana nodded and buried her head in Wallace's shoulder.

Little house of horrors, yes, but hers nonetheless.

~

'I still don't get why she thought he was dead when she heard the toilet flushing,' Bernadette said to Leslie, who nodded then looked to Caroline.

'It wasn't flushing; it was hissing, not filling. There's a huge difference. Lana had been living in a heightened state of emergency, attuned to the minutest of details, calibrated like a weathervane, listening and watching every which way the wind blew. When Viktor was still driving, she'd listen out for his car at night, and could tell you from which direction he was approaching and how long it would be until the garage door lifted and closed. The tone, too, of his key turning in the door, the door shutting, his steps – eleven to the lounge room, eighteen to the bedroom.

Lana counted them, ever vigilant. The whirring of his toothbrush making twelve rounds of his mouth; the way it hovered for about fifteen seconds over his dodgy back molar. The change jingling in his pocket when his trousers crumpled to the floor. The noise of a fifty-cent piece rolling as distinct from a twenty-cent piece – Lana knew it all. Could write a book about the sounds of the living. What to listen for. Viktor sliding between the bedsheets and sighing deeply before eventually slipping into sleep, which was when Lana could finally breathe, knowing he'd survived another day. That they'd all survived another day. The sigh was what she waited for. His sigh brought her relief. Can you imagine that?' Caroline asked Leslie and Bernadette. 'And by *you*, I mean *we*. How can any of us ever know what it's like to live in constant fear for one's partner, children or themselves? To wake one morning and hear a hissing and think for a split-second it's a sigh, and reach out with your eyes still closed, relieved, to touch your beloved, only to realise . . . he's not there.'

'Yeah, nah . . . it's still insane she left him hanging there to go shopping,' Bernadette said, adding that 'people' were convinced Lana drove Viktor to it, watching over him like a magpie the way she did.

'And don't forget how she left him alone every day to go to work,' Leslie tutted. 'Like she couldn't wait to get away from him. So selfish.'

'Selfish! You "people" haven't got a clue what it's like to live with someone suffering from severe depression who threatens and tries and fails and then tries again to kill himself, for years on end,' Caroline said. 'Not a friggin' clue what it means to keep someone alive. To hold the fort financially, emotionally. Sidestep. Thwart. Keep up appearances at work. At school. Protect kids, whose "normal" it is, living in a dark house with a sad, sleepy dad and mum with a crunchy bra – stuffed with diazepam. Lana did her very best, given the circumstances her life must have felt like one long *Noooo.*' Caroline said. 'Imagine what it's like never knowing what you'll find at home. How it must change you. Living with your shoulders frozen up around your ears. Always on the alert. Sleeping with one eye open on a bare mattress topped with blueys.'

'Blueys?' Bernadette screwed up her nose.

'The slippery things the hospital gave Lana after Viktor's last attempt, which no amount of Napisan would make their mattress forget.' Caroline said, 'You "people" say stuff like, *It must be like walking on eggshells* – but you're the friggin fragile eggshells. Lana's been walking around with her shoes flapping against the ground, ever since Viktor's doctor told her to get rid of her shoelaces, and anything else that could be tied; including bedsheets, towels, skipping ropes and electrical cords. Anything at all at home that Viktor could use – pills, knives, garden tools, hoses, matches, the car. He even recommended disconnecting the gas, as it was near impossible to prevent Viktor's death. After years of failed therapy, treatments and medication, he said, there was nothing more that Lana or anyone could do but protect themselves.

'When we think of severe depression, he said, we think of utter despair and apathy, and yet killing oneself, requires the exact opposite: it takes immense energy and determination. To be suicidal, is to be seized simultaneously by these conflicting forces. The why and how align, and eclipse the soul.'

And Lana's soles, Leslie thought, she'd listened to as much of Caroline's claptrap as she could endure, and was surer than ever that she'd lost the plot and that Lana was guilty, particularly after hearing that the doctor also claimed that people like Viktor don't kill themselves because they are selfish, but because they were trying to stop some unimaginable inner torture.

The eggshells associate imagination with weakness and whimsy, and they neither understand inners nor really cared about Lana or Victor's suffering, as they are too concerned with their own – and with what they suppose those Viktor left behind are hiding. They speculated rather than asked, saying they didn't want to intrude. 'But gee,' Leslie had said, 'Lana should think herself lucky she found him in one piece, as opposed to that poor chap in the paper the other day, who jumped in front of a train. The police reported that his body was located from Town Hall to Central. And what makes Caroline think she's the expert, anyway? Busybody, more like it.'

The eggshells didn't know that Lana dearly loved her husband and the kids adored their father. That Viktor cherished his wife and his kids more than life itself – and that it wasn't about love or not loving, or what he did or didn't do to stop it. God knows Viktor tried to save himself, before illness left him lying on the couch at home in the dark, eclipsed a little more each day.

Too busy bitching from the bleachers, Bernadette and Leslie never visited – 'It's none of our business,' they'd said – so they would never be able to grasp that, when Lana heard the hissing and found Viktor hanging and locked the bathroom door and woke the kids and took them to McDonald's as a treat on their way to school before calling the only person she could think of who might understand and arranged to meet her in bedding at David Jones; that she had been waiting for this day for almost a decade. That she was in shock. But not surprised. She was repulsed. Relieved. Talking gibberish. Traumatised. She thought she might be dreaming. She was awake in a nightmare – needing sheets.

⁓

In the end, it was tea towels that Viktor used as a noose.

Tea towels that Sage and Paris had decorated with portraits of themselves, along with the rest of the kids in their KU and first grade classes, as a fundraiser to employ a food allergy officer in the school canteen. Little stick figures with startled arms and legs. Lana thought, *Bless their funny little drawings – all dots for eyes, half-moon mouths, big bellies and hair squiggles. I'll get the P&C peanut Nazis off my back and order a dozen for the family and hide them away as Christmas presents.*

Linen, Lana would learn, was one of the strongest fibres in the world. Threaded through banknotes. Woven into armour in the eighteenth century.

How could she ever share with anyone her knowledge of flax and of tensile ratings and why she couldn't cry when she didn't know herself – but suspected it might be because she too was tied up in constriction knots, focused on the children, who mustn't, she decided, ever know that their father took his own life. More than anything, Lana feared what it would do to them to find out that Viktor had hanged himself just down the hall from where they slept. She would tell them he died in his sleep. A heart attack.

Something that needed no explaining. Tell everyone to keep their mouths shut. One day she might show the kids the little note that he left them all. Brief though it was, she gives thanks for his beautiful words – but for now, she prayed, *God, give me the strength to attend my husband's funeral. Bury my children's father. And cry.*

~

'Did you see the way they huddled together by the hearse?' Bernadette said to Leslie.

'I did. It was weird.'

'The way their shoulders moved up and down as Caro held Lana's face in her hands.'

'Laughing?' Leslie asked Bernadette.

'Or kissing – who knows with those two?'

'Exactly. I just don't understand why everything with them has to be such a big secret.'

Lana had asked Caroline to blow in her eyes before she walked into the church so she looked at least a little teary in front of the congregation baying to see a grieving widow. Lana could feel their hungry eyes on her back as she took her seat behind Viktor's coffin.

She clasped her hands together, locked her knuckles, then turned them over and wiggled her fingers, mumbling, 'Here is the church, there is the steeple, open up the door and here are all the people.' *Yes, all the bloody people,* Caroline thought, *guarding their own secrets, holy orders and rituals; their own ways of keeping things together.* She resisted turning around and telling Leslie to shut the fuck up and stop with the tutting and reached out to hold Lana's hand instead, as Lana muttered, 'I'm a grieving widow.'

In the same way, in this very same church, she'd told herself she was a happy bride on her wedding day. And when Paris was born: *I'm a mother.* And way back, before all that, when she was eighteen years old and met Wallace for the first time: *He is my father. I am a daughter. A sister. Fancy that.*

It takes time for words to find feelings. And vice versa. And sometimes they don't. Lana knew this much to be true – and that no one tells you what grief feels like, or that the closest she'd come to sharing the tiniest truth of it was when an old friend squeezed her forearms in the vestibule and whispered, 'Hello. Sad.' And when Caroline held her fingers at the service – not to stop them from wiggling, but to join them in trembling.

~

There's something so *I told you so* about the Birds gathering for a funeral, taking their pews.

Between church availability and the autopsy, Viktor had been at the morgue for ten days when Wallace, fed up with the waiting, stood with his hands tucked into his armpits rocking back and forth by the hearse, as Leslie strode down the aisle, wondering why Catholics couldn't get themselves organised like the Jews, who always seemed to have a rabbi and plot on standby.

Leslie Bird felt most herself on this holy stage and had to stop herself from walking towards the organ, to the left of the altar, flexing her fingers and ankles, assuming the position, and leading the congregation. She knew the choreography of the mass by heart. The mass was as much a part of her as her elbows and knees, and she knew she'd be right once it's rhythms swept her away; but for now she was feeling all out of sorts, wondering where to seat herself and why mourners didn't just sit on separate sides of the church, like they did at weddings. Us and them. Leslie wanted to sit with the groom's people to get a good look at them. *They're so unusual. Tall and waxy-looking.* It was only when Caroline grabbed her by the elbow and guided her to sit down next to Wallace in the row behind herself and Lana that Leslie realised she'd been waiting for this, a death in the family, and was quietly relieved that it wasn't one of their own but an in-law. And a German at that.

Viktor's mother and brother, fresh off the plane from Lübeck, were inconsolable. The mother wore a clingy purple and yellow dress, patterned with pansies, which Leslie Bird thought explained everything. The brother, a coffin kisser, had the same roll of pock-marked fat at the base of his head that Viktor had. Kissing the coffin wasn't enough for the neck-fat twin; he had to hug it, too, causing it to wobble on its silver stand, until its front legs curtsied, almost collapsing, and Amir of all people – *hello* – jumped up to straighten it. Then he put his fingers to his lips and kissed them before rubbing them on the lid. *Where he imagines Viktor's head is,* Leslie surmised. *Thank goodness the coffin didn't fall and the body roll out. Who on earth could live with themselves after glimpsing his corpse?* Leslie was sure it would be the death of her and that Shelley was right, Caroline had always been a mauler.

Sitting behind her, watching her play thumb wars with Lana and stroke her limp hair – *dyed at the hairdressers, so they say, but honestly, who could tell, given the way the ghastly raspberry starts a third of the way down from her part?* – was almost more than

Leslie could bear. There was talk, too, of the molesting Caroline gave Viktor while he was still hanging. It beggared belief. *It's a wonder the girl's never been arrested*, Leslie thought, trying but failing to push it to the back of her mind. Thinking she was going to be sick, she reached for her hanky and prayed for her tummy to settle – then woe and betide, three Hail Marys in, she found herself restored to the benevolent mother she was, praying for Caroline's odd tendencies, wanting only the best for the world. Really, she did. *Oh, and for people to just keep their hands to themselves, touch up their roots and avoid colouring their hair that Cottee's cordial red which gets blamed for everything from ADD to curing Bali belly.*

Speaking of which: 'When did Garuda start flying direct from Kuta? And isn't it about time you taught that girl of yours some manners?' Leslie whined to Wallace, elbowing him as they left the church, skirting around the rabble milling around Lana in their scrappy attire, shaking their heads, lighting cigarettes, speaking to their thongs or the sky, saying how sorry they were for her loss and how she must be feeling this or that . . . while Lana all but ignored them.

~

I'm not sure what I am, Lana might have said, if she could have spoken.

That's another thing no one tells you. That you may never be able to cry or speak of the living hell you are left with when a person you love suicides.

That their pain doesn't end – it is just passed on to someone else.

Someone else then, four years after Viktor's death, might reasonably conclude that the sum of all that history is what silenced Caroline through the seven fuck offs before yelping. But that's still not the whole story of that spring day in Sydney when the sun glinted from the bluest of skies and bees flirted with the blossoms blooming in Lana's backyard. Sage, the forlorn, fatherless, birthday boy, was smiling for the first time in years. His soccer cake was a great success. Caroline didn't want to upset him.

If you stood back and squinted at the icing, its texture and colour looked as real as astroturf. Lana had become so good at baking that she placed a little ad in the window of her local IGA and since then had been so busy baking for strangers that she ditched her job at Qantas and bought a Mixmaster, cake boards and the like, and even got herself business cards and a second-hand refrigerated one-tonne van to make deliveries.

The van had Lana's business name – The Magic Pudding – and logo painted on the side. It was Michael's first commission. 'If you can call it that, when cakes not money change hands and it looks like shit,' Wallace had said when Leslie commented on what an uncanny resemblance Michael's pudding bore to Lana.

The van was parked within sight of the strangling.

But it wasn't all or any of this that finally made Caroline yelp. It was hearing her name. Her full name. It was the first time Dette, or anyone other than Leslie, had ever called her that, and she still couldn't grasp what it meant. The extent of what was exchanged.

Dette saying it seemed to confirm to Caroline that she existed – which, she realised as her airways constricted, that perhaps Dette preferred she didn't. And the way she said it, 'breaking it into two syllables, growling, 'Carol – iiiiiine,' awoke the same wild thing that flung their bodies together when they were little – biting, kicking, scratching, pinching, punching.

'I could see the hatred in her eyes as they bore into mine,' Caroline said later. 'And once I saw it, I couldn't unsee it, and I returned the favour from that day forwards. As much as it pains me, I've called her Bernadette ever since and felt us both wince, then wondered whether Mum's dubbing of us, and ours of each other, was not so much to prevent us from hearing a despised word but to save us from feeling it. To stop us from killing each other.'

Feelings are Overrated

Traded to diminish or commemorate, names in the Bird family were nicked as currency. Caroline Reid, nee Bird, had answered to Caro, Gomer, Gomey, CB, 10-4, all of her life apart from the day Bernadette, Berty, Ernie, Dette, strangled her in front of Michelle – Shelley, Smelly – and Michael, who remained Michael, unseen, therefore un-nicknameable to all but Shelley and Caroline, who called him Popeye (*I yam what I yam*) behind his back – as it was with Lana, referred to by all, including Leslie, as Wumpa, derived from 'one point one', as in first child, first marriage – Wallace's never mentioned previous matrimony.

They were twenty-four Wallace and Florence – Wumpa's mother.

Florence was Sammy O' Sullivan's sister. Sammy was Wallace's best friend. And it was the freckles on Florence's nose – the same sun-kissed braille that decorated Sammy's – that Wallace fell in love with. Not that Wallace ever joined the dots; he was too busy feeling and acting to be thinking of all that foreshadowed his union. A 'glitch' was how Leslie referred to it once, while clutching her graphite powder and lubricating every door in sight. Her intolerance and obsession with easing squeaky hinges arrived hot on the heels of Lana, the blubbering miss, who knocked on the Birds' front door one frightful April night and introduced herself.

'Without doubt the most exciting night of my life.' Caroline claimed that Leslie, who kept the house inhospitably tidy for visitors that were never invited, heard the knock and panicked. Set to straightening the rugs and cushions, flushing the toilet and fluffing her hair. Wondering who on earth it could be, she concluded it must be the *Encyclopaedia Britannica* salesmen that Wallace had been stringing along. (He had no intention of ever buying anything from them, mind you; he just revelled in the sight of men in navy suits, in possession of knowledge, standing in his lounge room wanting something from him.) And so, she pushed Wallace towards the door, whispering, 'Hurry up.'

'Why? What the hell's a wife for?' Wallace protested.

'Your fault – you open it,' Leslie said through gritted teeth.

Then, hearing another knock and the sound of weeping, she stepped forward and opened the door herself, and saw this enormous freckly girl (she thought it was a girl) with Wallace's face blubbering on the pebblecrete, shaking – the Birds' very foundations.

Leslie fainted.

'It wasn't only the arrival of an undisclosed older, fatter sister who looked exactly like my father in a dress that was so exciting,'

Caroline said, 'but the fact that she was untainted by my mother's bitterness and dubbing. Lana was living, breathing, undeniable proof of my father's secret suffering which, until then, at the age of ten, I'd had no evidence of but sensed, as if it were my very own.'

No one knows the whole story of what happened back in Central Western New South Wales, but everyone agreed it doesn't get much greener or golder than the legends of Grenfell's wheat, sheep, gold, booze and bushrangers. Ben Hall's booty buried in the Weddin Mountains, overlooking Lawson's birthplace of brooding old bastards, with their bent shearers' backs and bowed legs, getting pissed and poetic in the public bars on the bendy Main Street. '*We bow our heads and we brood and fret, because of the masks we wear . . . We fight it down, and we live it down, or we bear it bravely well, but the best men die of a broken heart for the things they cannot tell.*' Where Wallace and Sammy O'Sullivan grew up and Wallace married Sammy's sister Florence and had a baby, before leaving for Sydney, where he met and married Leslie twenty months later, without breathing a word about any of it, until Lana knocked on their door when she was eighteen.

Since then, it had just been bits and pieces, shared now and then when Wallace had had a skinful, with Bob Savage and Caroline – the only ones who probed the past that Wallace didn't feel judged by.

We was twelve, Sammy and me.

Best mates.

Used to run our rulers along Mr Fletcher's corrugated fence and get chased by his missus; Mrs Hindenburg, we called her, 'cause of the way her big white undies blew up off her Hills hoist.

We played footy together, Sammy and me. He was a beaut little halfback. Afraid of no one.

The old man used to drive us about after a game on the back of his ute. We lay flat as wheat sacks when the coppers drove by, laughing our heads off.

We were always laughin', me and Sammy. Laughin' and skylarkin'. And his dog, Mate, barkin'.

Two little skinny buggers, sucking orange quarters, holding St Joseph's under-thirteen's footy shield, beaming in our last photograph together – the one that ran on the front page of the *Young Witness* in 1946, after Sammy entered local folklore.

Skylarking on the back of a '28 Dodge ute out on Quandong Road. They said we deserved it, the bastards.

If I had me time again, I'd say to 'em: Why wouldn't a boy and his new pup be jiggin' about – after skipping out a school for a day of man's work, fencing with me and me old man, who'd called out to Sammy to jump up and join us, with the promise of a dunking in the local dam at the end of the day – in a world gone mad, still reeling from war. From slaughter and bombin' the bejesus out of each other. The Japs did unspeakable things to our own in the jungles of New Guinea? Five hundred and forty-five of the slants, surfin' on blankets over prison wire, brandishin' baseball bats, breakin' out of Cowra, a stone's throw from town; just two years earlier. Sammy's uncle Ben was the gunner, shootin' 'em, kamikazeing, before removing the firing bolt on the Vickers and the Japs bludgeoned him to death. A bloody hero, he was. Maybe Sammy was cartwheeling or surfin' himself when he was flung off the old man's ute and impaled on a rusty fence post?

Word was, he didn't die immediately.

They reckoned he bled to death on his knees, body convulsing, right where I left him and his little Mate yappin' and runnin' circles through his blood – spurtin' like a broken bloody water main, it was – flooding the road, when the old man hunted me into town to get help, while he stayed and tried to figure out how to shift a boy with a metal splinter through his shoulder and other bits that turned your thoughts to abattoirs.

I ran as fast as I could. I did. But me legs felt like lead. Like I was running into a headwind.

I ran the mile into town and knocked on Dr Wright's door, but he was out doing house calls; at least, I supposed that was why his bike was leaning up against the side of Mrs Hindenburg's house and he was rising and falling above her against the kitchen bench, with his hand covering her mouth and her eyes wild with seeing me when I peered in the window after knocking and no one answering. I didn't understand what I was looking at, so I ran across the road to Father Frank and found him stumbling about the sacristy pissed. Refused to help me, he did – just laughed and threw me a coin. Told me that, as an altar boy, I ought to know better than to be hangin' around dirty Protestants, who wouldn't be going to heaven anyway. The best I could do now, he said, reaching into his pocket, was bugger off and place his stinkin' penny under Sammy's tongue 'to pay off hell's highwaymen, or some shit'.

I pleaded with him to help me. I grabbed his robes. He shoved me off. I'll tell ya, I had to stop meself from stranglin' the stinkin' slob, starting at his collar, and I've never seen a priest since and not thought his collar was a sign saying: *Tear here.* I hate 'em. I hate the bloody bastards.

I put the coin in me pocket and tried to run back up the hill, but me legs took me home. I crawled under the house. Lay face down in the dirt. Waitin'. Prayin'. Even though I knew no one was listening. That no god known to man would've made Father Frank his envoy or Sammy suffer the way he did. I put the coin in me own mouth. It tasted like Sammy's blood. I prayed to the devil to piss off. Dr Wright, too. I stayed there until it got dark and me father come home and found me, told me to man up and gave me a flogging.

He never recovered. The old man. Drank himself to an early grave. And me – well . . . I dunno. Maybe Bob's right when he says I left me emotions under the house.

'Excluded forever from beatific vision,' went the gobbledygook the Sisters of Mercy peddled at school about Sammy being sentenced to 'eternal damnation' – with no thought for his mother, who Grenfell labelled 'the procreator of St Joseph's exemplar of a mortal sinner' – for wagging school and ending up the way he did. Heartless bastards. The lot of them. No one, not a one, spared a thought for old Mrs O'Sullivan or the consequences of their preaching.

People said she went mad with grief.

She wanted Sammy buried at home. In them days you could do that – so long as you had a decent backyard. Me old man dug the hole, with Mate barking by his side clawing at the dirt like he was digging for a bone. He lay out there for weeks by Sammy's grave . . . then shadowed Florence, until Florence and me –

She was the sweetest thing you've ever seen. I tell ya. Deserved more than a shotgun weddin' to a good-for-nothin' Birdbrain baker.

Havin' babies was women's business.

The baby was born at her mother's, where we were livin', and when Florence departed – well, Mrs O suggested I should too.

Who was I to argue? It seemed like the right thing to do.

I tried to – never mind. I mucked that up too.

What right did I have to a child of me own after killing both of hers?

It broke me mother's heart . . .

But leaving town was the least I could do – to bury the past. And in time it was like they never existed. Me too. Like I had no rights to me feelings either. Do you know what I mean? People didn't have feelings back then. You just got on with it – you know.

Feelings are overrated.

Mate come and lived with me, never left me side, until just before I married your mother . . . the most wonderful woman in the world.

Despite Lana's murderous ability and uncanny resemblance to Wallace, all eleven pounds two ounces of her were seized upon by Florence's mother Merle, as Wallace said. Still grieving the loss of her only son and now her daughter, she'd be damned if the Birds were going to take any more of her flesh and blood, and she assumed possession of the baby before Wallace ever laid eyes on her.

Lana, they christened the little fatty, after Lana Turner, though as the years wore on Lana became more Apple Turnover, the human two-seater sofa, who moved as if she were being shoved across floorboards that needed repolishing. It was Lana's size and the extent of Wallace's genes that she carried that proved too much in the end for her great-aunts, sitting around arguing as their sister lay dying in the front room. As soon as Merle O'Sullivan had drawn her last breath, Lana was shown the door whilst she could still fit through it, albeit sideways.

⁓

There's a difference between denying something is true and denying that it exists. The former requires engagement, argument, sides taken, whereas the latter seeks to make suffering simply disappear – abracadabra.

Leslie couldn't deny the truth of the flesh and blood blubbering in front of her. How easily the whole thing could have been erased, she thought, if she'd just not answered the door or if she'd slammed it in the face of the great lump of a lookalike who'd killed her mother in childbirth. *We could have just carried on as before, as if she never existed.* Which was exactly the point Leslie hoped they could all progress to – if only Caroline would just stop bringing it all up. Leslie had reminded her repeatedly that it was none of her business and to stop asking questions and going on and on about how affected everyone was, when 'no one could be more affected than me!'.

'Really?' Caroline asked her. 'Can you even begin to imagine what losing a child has done to Dad?'

Leslie gasped and came as close as she ever would to telling one of her own about Anthony. She stopped just short – remembering the utter devastation of sharing with Mary Anne Holloway and getting zero response. Too caught up in her own misery, Leslie swore there and then she would never tell another soul, least of all her children. No sirree. A pity party wasn't what she wanted. It was bad enough that Martha, Wallace and his mother knew everything and had said nothing but, 'Never mind,' and, 'How can you die if you weren't born alive, dear?'

Leslie discovered that the dismissal of her loss hurt her longer than the loss itself, which over time had become a deep enduring sadness, quite unlike the enduring rage she directed towards her dismissers.

'Let's not forget for a moment that your father is the villain here,' Leslie said for the thousandth time, narrowing her right eye at Caroline. 'And if I believed for a moment you kids were as effected as you say you are, I could never have lived with myself.'

'What does that even mean?' Shelley asked Caroline, when Caroline relayed Leslie's latest.

'It means she's completely incapable of imagining this "you", or this me, or any of our feelings. She'd rather die than believe us. And her not believing us will be her greatest legacy, as being unbelieved and ashamed is what sets you adrift from your body and perception of how the world works. What Leslie Bird will not be able to believe is the lifelong lesson in deception and hypocrisy she has gifted us. She can't even give us *affected*.' Caroline winced. 'She accused us of being *effected*.'

'Hang on there, Oprah. I don't get it. What's the difference?'

'The difference is, *effected* means you cause something to happen, whereas *affected* means something has happened to you. You're so affected by it,' Caroline said, 'you can't even see she's blaming us.'

~

Leslie's fourth word (two words, really) was *shut up*, which she disliked intensely almost more than any other, greeting its use with a shudder and a flick of the feather duster. When the children were little, she chased them around and around the dining table, trying to land the duster's tip on foul-mouthed bottoms, insisting they substitute those awful words with, *Please be quiet.* Or, better still, Leslie said, 'If you can't say anything nice, then say nothing at all.'

So, nothing at all was said until everything that wasn't became the Birds' alma mater and the title of Caroline's first solo exhibition. *Odium, Mendax, Silentium, Stercus.*

Hate, Liar, Shut up, Poo.

Leslie would say Caroline was a lie person and should stop blabbing the Birds' business. Stop blabbing and painting, for Lord knows things would never be the same again after she announced two months after Sage's party that she had an exhibition opening on the first of December at the D. & C. Gray gallery; 'self-portraits', supposedly, but everyone in the family, from forefathers to foreskins were rendered, much to their shock and horror. Even Viktor was to be depicted. 'Apparently alive, thank goodness,' Leslie said. 'But still, I can't for the life of me understand what I've done to deserve any of this.'

Demonstrating a range of techniques, and shifting perspectives so close or far from a subject that perceptions were challenged, Caroline's recent works were reviewed as 'unsettling', 'ambitious', 'lewd', 'provocative' and 'heartbreaking' by critics who variously noted: 'The exhibition invites you to lean in so close to the work, you become one with it; exploring and exposing your own empathies.' 'A rare reward when an artist paints in the first person and the piece takes on a life of your own.' A nightmare for the Birds, but a triumph for Caroline – who learned early in her career that most people, critics and women in particular, reduce you to the level of their own compassion; blaming you for what they don't understand.

To celebrate its fiftieth anniversary, the gallery published a book of its past and impending exhibitions, and chose one of Caroline's brooding portraits for the cover – unbeknownst to her, until she tripped over an open box of promotional flyers at the book's launch and watched her *Adoration of the Bertie* flutter up off the wharf and into the harbour, where the figures in her painting blurred then slipped silently beneath the surface of the dark water.

She desperately wanted to dive in and save them: the flyers, the figures – Bertie, his mother and the others. But it was too late. Omen or not, she hurried home and emailed the gallery director to request that the painting be removed from the exhibition when it opened the following month.

When Bernadette heard about the book, she bought a copy and a two-dollar scratchie and headed over to her parents' place to visit. Leslie and Wallace were overcome to say the least with

Bernadette's gifts, the first either of them had ever received. They decided, after keying the scratchie, that even though they were terribly grateful and would love to stay and chat, they really needed a little air; so, they jumped in the car and went for a little drive – from Sydney to Perth. And back.

Leslie commented upon their return how beautiful the Great Australian Bight was.

'Yeah? Where?' Wallace asked, dumbfounded.

'About sixteen hundred kilometres on your left.'

Wallace hadn't dared look in Leslie's direction. Had kept his eyes on the road, foot on the pedal and mouth closed. Neither of them said a word on the 7800-kilometre round trip – not to each other nor to the booksellers they confronted. By the time they reached Broken Hill, the book's cover had come to look like a Wanted poster to Leslie, as she and Wallace took turns buying up 'Caroline's crap' to fuel the incinerator upon their return.

The silence descended just outside of Dubbo, heading west, when Wallace asked Leslie why the hell had she ever let Caroline paint in the first place when it enraged her so much? Not speaking was almost as hard as not breathing for Leslie. It required every ounce of her concentration.

In her mind it all went back to Caroline's year three teacher, the peroxided ratbag in a tartan mini and knee-high boots, who put a paintbrush in Caroline's hand and encouraged her to keep going, even when what she painted looked like nothing at all to Leslie. But nothing seemed to be applauded. 'Lauded even.' Wallace had said they needed a war.

'Who?'

'The whole damn lot of them. Teach 'em to stop making mountains out of molehills. Get real jobs.'

'So unusual,' was all Leslie could think to say when Caroline won school art prizes and insisted on studying fine art, making painting a 'career'. 'I guess she likes to think of herself as an *ar-teest*,' Wallace said when people praised his daughter. It made Leslie's skin crawl. If it wasn't bad enough that she made people look at her, now Caroline was making people look at *them* – 'not to point the finger, but to part the curtain,' or some such rubbish, according to the stupid book, which Leslie had tossed in the recycle bin after the briefest flick through the pages, declaring she'd never seen anything more repulsive in her life. 'What with the cover painting being blasphemous and unfinished, supposedly an ode to some da Vinci thingy? Da Emperor's New Clothes more like it, the whole art business, if you ask me.'

Caroline took a deep breath and explained how she'd agonised over her selection for the exhibition and only chosen the most ambiguous pieces – and how, out of respect for the family, she had decided not to hang the one painting she'd been working on for decades, off and on. 'So, you don't have to worry, Mum – I've left Bertie out.'

'Now why would you do that?' Leslie sighed and shook her head, before joining with Caroline to recite one of Wallace's ditties: '*Poor Bertie, no mummy, no daddy someone has to play with him . . .*'

Mother and daughter looked at one another aghast.

Leslie remained silent.

What was there to say that wasn't already unsaid about what Wallace had taken to saying to himself, first while lying in bed for weeks weeping after his mother's death, and thereafter whenever he was feeling worried, tired, scared or sorry for himself; which was most of the time really. He'd put his hands in his pockets and say ever so tenderly, '*Poor Bertie – no mummy, no daddy . . . Good Bertie. There, there, Bertie,*' driving Leslie to despair. But Bertie might have been the only word Leslie despised that she didn't dub. Because that would have meant acknowledging whatever Wallace was up to and his stupid mother and her propaganda. And no. Just no. She wasn't about to do that.

From the age of five, whenever Caroline overheard her father chatting to Bertie, she joined with him in her head. '*Poor Bertie, no mummy, no daddy . . .*' and it was the rhythm, the *poor*, that she heard, that lodged in her heart and kept all the King's horses and all the King's men from putting her childhood back together again. From that moment forth, for better or worse, her empathy was born; not just for some unseen member of the family – the only one she'd ever heard comforted – but empathy for all.

'Poor Bertie' seemed such a kind and astonishing thing to say. She'd thought through the years how lovely it must be to have a friend to talk to day or night, so close at hand – with the exception of her teens, when a few less murmurs of '*Who's a big boy, Bertie?*' in front of her friends would have been appreciated. But, even then, she understood something about consolation she'd never be able to articulate.

Whenever she was asked why she started painting, Caroline longed to quote poets and say it began with birdsong, like Whitman, or Pushkin's stomach, as it was for Akhmatova, but it hadn't. It began in childhood, squished between the end of a brown chenille lounge and the radiogram, listening to Johnny Tapp call the trots at Harold Park while her father comforted himself, as she stood behind him scratching his head and Shelley squatted at the foot of the sofa cutting his toenails.

'I can't believe you'd sacrifice your family to amuse a few strangers,' Leslie said to Caroline a week before her exhibition opened, when she shared the news that she'd been invited to exhibit in Iowa the following year.

'Well, I'll be buggered,' Wallace said. 'America, love!'

'Are they still hanging them there?' Leslie asked.

Meaning traitors, not painters.

Caroline's paintings bewildered Wallace. Not that he got a proper look at them at first, what with Leslie binning the book and banning him from gawking. He'd had to duck off on his own and hide up the back of a bookshop.

One of a woman wearing electric blue stilettos, gigantic false eyelashes and spinning a wheel of fortune that had landed on the word *cancer* was . . . bizarre, by his reckoning, while another of a child perched in a tree, baring its bottom and shitting all over a family was so perverse he had to go home and have a lie-down. Not to mention another painting, of a big-bottomed woman bending over to squirt something into a doorjamb, which was so baffling that he turned to Leslie one day and asked if she had any inkling as to where Caroline had got her twisted ideas. Leslie rolled her eyes, adjusted her control tops, made quotation marks with her fingers and said, 'Her im-ag-in-a-tion.' As if to say, *Don't look at me, dummy; haven't you heard of that fairground?*

The painting on the cover, though – the one that enraged Leslie – touched Wallace in a way he couldn't explain. A woman working in the bookshop asked him if he was okay and if he'd like to buy a copy of the book, as she'd seen him looking at it more than once.

Buggered if I know what to make of it, Wallace thought, putting it back on the shelf and heading home.

It wasn't just the way the mother was gazing at the baby in her arms, with the rest of the mob looking on, all religious like – three of them, bearing gifts. *Wise men*, Wallace guessed, *and looking like dead ringers for Bob, Doug and Viktor – and holy smokes – could that be Ron, Amir and Toby all frocked up? And Sammy and Florence and some baby wearing wings?* . . . But it was his old Mate, curled up asleep at the mother's feet, that made his glasses fog and gave him a queer feeling – like he couldn't be sure what he was seeing or imagining, but for dead certain someone had seen him; seen right into him – *and I'll be damned if I can understand why a decent-enough picture of a mother cradling her newborn son could enrage Leslie the way it has, but that's me missus for ya: a bloody near mystery.*

On the morning of the opening, when Bernadette called by to see if they wanted a lift to the exhibition, Wallace thumped the table and yelled, 'What the hell! Cheer up, Les. Come on, love – let's get going.'

So, Leslie grabbed a bag of brown onions, a box of Sultana Bran and books and her André Rieu DVD collection, Wallace his Nu-Lax (the fruit laxatives he'd taken to chewing obsessively), and the two of them jumped in the car and Wallace drove north this time from Sydney, shitting himself quite 'naturally' at rest stops and service stations all along the highway until they reached Far North Queensland. It was a relief to say the least for Wallace to be on the move again, and possibly even losing weight.

Slave to a treasonous liver or twitching sphincter; what did it matter? His body's desires and dark secrets, the fill-me-fuck-me thing itself, was of less significance than the fact that Wallace Bird's body was talking to him again, screaming loud and clear, *Git git, git, git goin', mate*, making him feel alive, not dead or dying as he'd felt in the time before laxatives, after baking and retiring, when he was sure he'd go mad, his mind having nothing better to do than dredging and amplifying all the mess he'd made, drowning him in shite and shame, everything echoing, *Guilty – guilty as charged* within his body until Nu-Lax arrived and anointed flesh dominion over mind. Christ, a man needed to die or get dementia before his damned life flooded back in – or CB disgraced herself, her family and friends with her stupid bloody ideas.

Two and a half thousand kilometres up the coast, in Kuranda, lived Patricia, a dear old friend of Leslie's, suffering cancer and, now, two unexpected visitors. But not for long, for just after they arrived Wallace shook his head and declared that Pat looked real beaut. Despite both of her arms being swollen like watermelons and her wig falling off to reveal that she was as bald as a badger's backside, Wallace suspected Pat was 'bunging it on' and 'right as rain,' so he finished his coffee and fruitcake, while the two women laughed over old times, and gave Leslie the hurry up, then went and sat in the Fairlane, furious that their long trip north had been for nothing. Oblivious to the fact they'd been seeking comfort in someone else's crisis, worse than their own, Wallace revved the engine, reversed and beeped the horn – only once or twice, not continuously, as Leslie would have you believe – then they drove back south, only stopping for Wallace (still chewing Nu-Lax) to empty his bowels, which were exploding with greater frequency, and to fill up the tank and, later, their bellies at Sizzler. He, swerving across unmarked lanes around Queensland's enormous roundabouts, to the sound of André Rieu's enchanted violin-ing, while Leslie sat in the back, with a Howard Spring book in her lap, trying to read, getting giddy, watching the glorious orchestra, the bow ties and ballgowns waltzing, asking Wallace to keep his eyes out for a patch of scorched grass where she'd heard a Pajero and its four passengers (retirees, poor things) were incinerated just last week. There could be worse things than a show-off daughter or losing your hair to cancer, Leslie conceded. The DVD where Rieu, the maestro, was accompanied by the Australian Federal Police Pipe and Drum Band was her favourite, and thus watched thrice by the time Wallace pulled up at the Versace Hotel in Surfers Paradise, where they stayed the night, flouncing about in fluffy robes, gorging on seafood and mangoes.

The next morning, Leslie filled her pockets with tea and coffee sachets and bread rolls from the breakfast buffet, stuffed with the most unusual cheese and processed meat, for the trip back to Sydney, where she eventually alighted not at home, but in emergency with potentially deadly DVTs.

Social Services

'Or maybe she'd got DVDs, from five thousand kilometres of André Rieu!' Shelley said, laughing, when she called Caroline to share the news of their mother's predicament and the number of her hospital room. She assured her sister that she'd told Leslie and Wallace to stop blaming Caroline for their dire dilemma. 'And the others, too. I told them all to calm the hell down, after Bernadette sent us a group message pointing out that the poor old dears had now clocked up 12,670 kilometres trying to escape your exhibition. I said to them, they're only silly paintings; so just ignore them, like the public.'

'Gee thanks.' Caroline seethed.

'Don't mention it. Are you still there?'

'Yeah'

'Good. Because I also wanted to tell you that Bernadette shared that she binned that picture of yours that Gavin bought her, and that your show's closing on Christmas Eve. Jeez, Caro.

Sorry to hear that. But don't worry, we'll be there to cheer you on. Anyway – I guess I'd better let you get on the road. Sorry I can't come with you; I'm just on my way to radiotherapy. Say hi to Mum and Dad for me. And don't forget your date with George this afternoon. George said you have to wear yellow for Cancer Daisy Day and bring a gold donation. Okay, I'd better go – I've just arrived at Nepean. Wish me luck. I should be at yours by five to pick him up. If that's okay of course?'

'Of course. Good luck.' Caroline wasn't sure what else to say without losing it.

She hung up and grabbed the only yellow thing she owned – a fancy silk scarf Toby had once bought her duty-free – and tied it around her neck. She looked in the mirror, thought – *fuck – sallow – girl guides*, then hopped in the car to drive to the hospital, dazed again by Shelley's – *madness* was the first word that came to mind, but she knew it wasn't right from the countless times she'd used it and failed to convey the Birds' particular kind of crazy. Where were her Annes when she needed them? she wondered, thinking of Carson and Enright, the only authors she'd ever met – well, not met, but read – who spoke of crazy families like her own. In one poem, Carson wrote of a mother who accuses her daughter of remembering too much. 'Why hold on to all that?' she asks, and the daughter answers, 'Where can I put it down?' as her father sits in the background talking to a lettuce. *Enright's people could be related to us*, Caroline thinks, gripping the steering wheel, trying to remember the name of Enright's book. How could it escape her? The one where a father's wig is a secret everyone in the family knows – even the cat. She can recite whole passages by heart: 'For years my father's wig felt like an answer. It rode around on his head like an animal. It was a vigorous brown. I was very fond of it as a child. I thought it liked me back.' Caroline laughed, remembering how often she'd quoted that bit . . . and this: 'I could say I am the way I am because my father wears a wig. I could say I am in love with you because I have told you, and no one else, about my father's shameful wig. But this is not true. I have told strangers about my father's wig in discos.' Only, Caroline replaced 'wig' with 'sister's cancer' or 'Bertie' and found her strangers in dress shops, in neighbouring change rooms, where her stories floated up and over the cubicle doors, before she bought the thing she was trying on, whether it looked good or not, and took it home and shoved it in a drawer. There were times, too, when she didn't even try the thing on, but just sat on a chair in the change room holding it, telling stories, getting teary, using it to dab her eyes – turning her head this way and that, gazing into the three-way mirrors, lifting her jowls and trying to tame the cowlick on her crown. The strangers' replies didn't seem to matter. Though it was nice when someone said, 'Oh dear,' or a shop assistant called out, 'Everything okay in there? Do you need another size or colour?' It was only now – crawling along the M4, looking for the Concord exit, that Caroline wondered if consolation stemmed from the telling and if the change rooms were linked to the confessional boxes of her childhood? Saturday afternoons, sitting up the back of church, making up lies to tell the truth, then asking for forgiveness.

After taking the exit, she found herself in the wrong lane and traffic at a standstill. Heading away from the hospital, towards Silverwater, looking to drop a U-ey, she wondered why there'd been nothing on the radio about the congestion and why she could never get her stupid satnav to work properly, like it did for Toby. Every time she tried to use it, the map spun and zoomed in and out. And it never talked to her. So, she'd turn it off and drive by feel, following her own internal compass. And get lost, but enjoy the discovery of people and places she'd never have found otherwise. Toby said it was easy to operate. So easy, a Muppet could do it. Bloody Toby. When he was away for work, Caroline slept with a selection of books arranged in the shape of a man on his side of the bed. Her book husband. One book for the head, two each for his arms and legs. Sometimes it was hard to choose what went where, but Enright's wig book was always there, so she could re-read one bit in particular. The bit where the father is dying and can no longer climb the stairs but sits in his chair in the lounge room while his wife goes about her business. And one day, by accident, she shrinks the wig in the washing machine, but she manages to get it back on her husband's head 'by giving it a tug at the back and a double, symmetrical tug at the sides – all done in dignified silence, whilst husband and wife look elsewhere; before the wife retreats upstairs to hang three bald photographs of the husband in the hallway'. And this bit – Caroline's favourite: 'The wife thinks she's hung them out of sight because she loves him. She says she wants to remember things as they really were. As if she doesn't know, that seeing things as they really are is the greatest possible revenge.'

Caroline re-read that bit often, thinking of the Birds, and Shelley – her bestie, who wouldn't hurt a fly, but was always scheming and most likely pretending to have cancer. She had form in the fib department, Shelley, from years of pretending she was a real doctor, long before attaining her honorary title. No one knew when it started, but they all remembered that when they were little, whenever they'd played schools or doctors, it was always Shelley holding the stethoscope. Caroline the chalk.

'We've all seen the lanyards, the LinkedIn profiles,' Caroline had told Toby, when he asked why no one had ever called Shelley out on her lies.

'You know she's not the only one who's crazy,' he'd said.

And Caroline erupted, saying that what incensed her the most was not so much Shelley pretending to be a doctor as the fact that she was so lazy about it. 'She doesn't even dress up or cover her tracks. She just expects us to believe it. Dares us to believe her, because not believing means dealing with a lie person, and you know how good us Birds are at that! "If you can't say anything nice, then say nothing at all." Who does she think we are, bloody fools? Don't answer that.' Caroline wagged a finger at Toby. 'I've called her out numerous times. We all have.'

'Yeah, sure you have,' Toby said, wondering what he might have done if he'd been privy to this madness before he proposed.

'Well – maybe not Michael. And definitely not Mum and Dad. Or Lana. But George, Dette and I certainly have. Instead of causing embarrassment, though, it only seems to confirm her fantasy. And what about Mum?'

'What about her?' Toby looked confused.

'It's like she's proud of what Shelley pretends, because whenever I bring it up, she sighs and says, "Well it's not as if she's ever operated on anyone."'

Replaying it all, when she finally arrived at Concord Hospital and circled the car park twice, before finding a narrow spot and swinging in too wide, scraping her driver's door on an orange pylon before reversing and straightening up, Caroline thought, *Shrink the wig, and make it fucking fit, and what a shit show shame it is I can't take one of the vacant Doctors Only spots, like Shelley would if she were here, and not off having 'treatment.' How dare they fucking blame me. The fuckers.*

~

'There you are!' she said, walking into Leslie's room.

By a large window overlooking Parramatta River and Silverwater's smoke stacks, Leslie sat propped up in bed, leashed to an IV and fitted with an anticoagulant device, a small machine that regulated blood density and bothered her far less than you might imagine. She was clutching it to her chest like a beloved purse, right in the spot where her bosoms would normally be if they hadn't been freed and flopping over her big belly, also liberated from their usual constrictions. It took Caroline a moment to recognise her mother without all of her armour; sitting there swivelling her hospital bracelet, reading it; as if it might remind her who she really was. Not this vulnerable little old woman with DVTs, a *TV Week*, a deflated bouffant and squishy bit jiggling beneath a skimpy hospital gown, with a cantankerous old man sitting on the end of her bed picking his teeth, jumping out of his skin when Caroline walked in. Wallace turned his back and hissed, 'Have you ordered the ham yet?'

'Hello to you too, Dad. Sure! Eight kilos, just like every year. Hi, Mum.'

'Oh, for goodness sake, Wal, it's still a few days until Christmas – forget about your bloomin' ham, turn around and say hello to your daughter.' Leslie nodded towards Caroline, looking at her over the top of her glasses. 'Yellow's not your colour. Eight kilos sounds like a lot. Did you know Julie has Weimaraners?'

'Julie who?' Caroline kissed Wallace on the back of the head. Wallace flinched. Flinched as if she had hit him. She bent and kissed her mother on the forehead, being careful not to get tangled in her drip. When Leslie raised a hand to wipe away the kiss, Caroline was hit on the back of the head and laughed – relieved to glimpse the old Leslie.

'Look out,' Leslie said, flipping through her magazine, her mouth gaping open as if she were about to take communion. 'Julie thingy. You know the one.'

'Sorry?'

'I doubt it,' Leslie continued flipping pages.

'Pardon?' Caroline knew exactly what Leslie had said but was daring her mother to say it again.

'Never mind. Short. ABC. Lesbian, isn't she?'

'I don't know. How would I know?'

'I thought you knew lesbians.' Leslie tried to fold her arms.

'I do, but how would I –'

'See? I've already dog-eared it for Toby,' Leslie said, finding the page and pointing triumphantly to the Julie, sitting next to another woman with a crew cut and two silvery-looking puppies with piercing blue eyes curled on her lap. 'Says here they're sisters.'

'So they're not lesbians?'

'The dogs, silly. Speaking of which I've got a few more in my handbag.' Leslie gestured to the locked cupboard by her bed, saying if Caroline wouldn't mind fetching it, she'd give her the clippings she'd been saving for Toby since he up and surprised everyone by buying himself a Weimaraner.

'Guess he got over the parrot?' Wallace smirked. 'But why the hell did he call it Kurt?'

Caroline ignored him. Leslie gave her the key, and Caroline unlocked the cupboard and reached for her mother's bag. Looking inside, she spied Leslie's graphite powder and picked it up to take a closer look as Leslie pleaded with her to put it away and pass the bag over. Instead, Caroline held it just out of Leslie's reach and retrieved the clippings herself, not mentioning that Kurt was the name Toby had chosen for the son they'd never have, after multiple miscarriages rendered her infertile. She placed the bag back in the cupboard and made small talk about puppy classes, rawhide, wee pads. The need to crate the puppy on Christmas Day, to save Bernadette's girls going nuts.

'It's not them you'll have to worry about,' Wallace said. 'It's Lana's Paris. Wasn't she bitten on the bum once?'

Leslie wiped her brow. 'Yes, I believe it was the right cheek of her back bottom.'

'Don't forget to make those beaut potatoes of yours,' Wallace added, stressing that the crispy bits were his favourite.

'Of course, it wouldn't be Christmas without your tatties, Dad. Do you want a scratch?'

'Would I what!' Wallace moved over, and as Caroline sat between him and Leslie the bed creaked, and the three of them listed towards one another. Caroline pushed Leslie back up with one hand and reached for Wallace's scalp with the other as Leslie bloused her skimpy hospital gown in the name of modesty and – for the sake of peace – Caroline's exhibition wasn't mentioned. Thank god. And it seemed the longer they didn't talk about it, the further it receded from reality. In a year from now it would be, *What exhibition?* Just another disgrace in the family that no one ever mentioned. But for now, their bodies said what they couldn't. Leslie's clotting. Wallace's flinching. Caroline's scratching.

'*The Wig My Father Wore*!' Caroline shouted suddenly, clapping her hands together.

Leslie and Wallace paid no attention.

'Sorry. It's just the name of a book I love. Not to worry. You should read it, Mum. How was your trip?' she asked as Wallace wobbled his head to coax her fingers to the itchiest bits, his stomach grumbled loudly.

'Jeez, hungry, Dad?'

'Hardly,' Leslie said, shooting Wallace a nervous look. 'The trip was alright, I guess. Your father thinks Pat's pretending, don't you, Wal? Better still' – Leslie said, making a stop sign at him with her right hand – 'why don't you just keep certain *things* to yourself? And while you're at it, take yourself off for a little walk.'

'Are you kidding? And miss this?'

Wallace moved back and forth beneath Caroline's fingers, which were slowing as she considered the irony of someone who really did have cancer not being believed. She wondered what those either side of her would make of Shelley's claims and the insane lengths she and her siblings had gone to to protect them from the maybe/maybe not drama.

And for what? Dette had roared, from the very beginning. *Why shouldn't they bloody know?*

Because they're old, and Shelley asked us not to tell them?

Recalling her feeble answer, Caroline scratched her father's head harder.

'Jesus. Go easy there, love, you'll draw blood!' Wallace said. 'Too right Pat's bunging it on. You should see the great big arms on her.'

'Oh, poor thing. Sounds like she's got lymph trouble, like poor Aunt Martha had,' Caroline said, looking to Leslie, who shrugged as Wallace replied, 'You don't get wrestler's arms like that from lying about with cancer. You can bet your bottom dollar she's been stirring cake batter for the CWA. She looked fit as a fiddle to me, sitting there giggling with your mother for over two hours while I sat out in the car waiting – G'day, love.' Wallace turned to greet a young nurse who'd come in to take Leslie's obs. 'Don't take any notice of what anyone says' – he winked at her – 'you look real beaut in your get-up.'

The nurse ignored him, leading Wallace to wonder if she even spoke English. As he watched her clamping the oxygen meter on Leslie's finger, he thought of the nuns he'd had at school whose faces were framed the same way.

'It wasn't two hours of giggling, Wal,' Leslie objected, blushing.

'You're right. It felt more like four.'

Leslie didn't mind Wallace's lies, if they made it seem more exciting, like she had a life. 'Anyway, not to worry,' she said, raising herself more upright and getting excited. 'We got to see the spot where the people got torched! Just off to the side of one of those big roundabouts outside of Surfers Paradise The ground's still scorched. Awful business.'

'Indeed,' Wallace agreed. 'They must have been going a hell of a speed to come a cropper like that.'

'Or trying to steer clear of the likes of you!' Leslie said, noticing the nurse giving Caroline a wry smile. 'We got beeped every time we entered one of those things. It was absolutely terrifying.' She looked at Caroline and huffed, 'What's so funny?'

Caroline shrugged.

'The concierge at Versace called me sir,' Wallace reminisced. 'And he didn't blink loading yer mother's brown onions onto his gilded trolley. He just hung 'em up and pushed them clean across the marble. Bloody beautiful they were, too, those floors. All cool and soothin' for your mother's poor legs and my arthritis, weren't they, Les?'

Leslie nodded.

'Your lot go in for a bit o' marble too, don't they, love?' Wallace tried again to engage the nurse by slowing his speech and speaking louder. 'Bet there's nothing better than kneeling on cold floors in those stinkin' places. I read somewhere Dubai Airport's got more marble than you can poke a stick at.'

'I wouldn't know,' the nurse responded in a broad Aussie accent. 'I've never been to Dubai.'

'Well, bugger me,' Wallace said, slapping his knees. 'Then save yourself the airfare, love, and go to Versace. There's plenty of other towel heads there. And you should see the beds and the beaut bathrooms; we had a sink each, didn't we, Les? I don't know what it is, but there's just something about the whole joint that makes a man feel real good about himself.'

Wallace's tummy grumbled again – so loudly that everyone turned to look at him. Leslie gasped and placed a fearful hand to her mouth and held her breath as Wallace stood up and stretched. Loosened his belt two notches. Exhaled. Then sharted.

'Jesus. Quick.' Caroline motioned for her mother to pass her the packet of wipes, but Leslie Bird could not for the life of her seem to see one of the only two things on her bedside table. 'Next to the jug.'

Caroline pointed and Leslie reluctantly retrieved the wipes. Carefully lifting the tab, so as not to ruin the seal, she pulled out a wipe, unfolded it and handed it over, as the nurse turned her attention to Wallace.

'That'd be right. It was only a matter of time,' Leslie said, narrowing her eyes and glinting. 'Why don't you tell them what you've been up to, Wal?'

Wallace shrugged as a large bloodied stain spread on the back of his trousers and gushed down his leg onto the floor.

'Never mind, sir,' the nurse consoled him. 'We'll get you cleaned up in no time.'

Wallace winked at Leslie. 'Hear that, Les? Sir!'

Caroline glared at her mother, imploring her to pass the packet and speak up.

'No, no, it's not my place to tell.' Leslie said, stroking her device. 'I'm not in the business of blabbing – not like some people.' She threw the wipes at Caroline then curled a finger towards herself.

Caroline leaned in to listen.

Leslie whispered, 'Make sure you put those back where you found them.'

~

'You know those people who are in their bodies? I'm not one of them. Which is why I'm here, I guess. Here in the first person, back *their* in the third. Accusing *you* in the second. I'm two point two, second marriage, second child of Wallace and Leslie Bird. Caroline Reid, nee Bird. Caro, CB, ten-four. You know those people who are in their bodies? I'm not one of them . . .'

Caroline sat in the hospital car park reciting by rote, over and over, this little thing that she wrote years ago, when a yoga instructor accused her of being outside of her body – because she wouldn't go barefoot in her studio – and suggested it might be best to head home and try to write down who and where she was. And it worked a treat and had done ever since; whenever Caroline found herself disembodied, she recited those few lines and located herself. But it wasn't working today, as she sat holding her car keys, staring at the dashboard, shaking.

She knew she was in a car. A nice car. A comfortable car. Parked at a hospital, where she had just visited her parents. She knew that things went bonkers, right after leaving them.

Maybe even a bit before. Somewhere between Shelley's call (*old dears – escape your exhibition – only silly paintings*), and getting stuck and lost in traffic, touch parking. Seeing Leslie unarmed, lesbian Weimaraners and Wallace calling a Muslim a towel head and sharting. Somewhere just after that, things went skew-whiff. After she scrubbed her hands and got in the lift. Somewhere between the fifth and ground floors, when she started shaking and humming 'Mary Had a Little Lamb'. By the time she got to the parking machine she could no longer read or open her purse. She remembered that: standing before the slots – the card, the cash, the all day, weekly, endless options – her fingers trembling, singing, '*It made the children laugh and play to see a lamb at school*,' before stepping aside to let someone else pay for their parking, so she could copy them.

Finding the car wasn't a problem. Its dinged black door slashed with orange seemed to find her. She remembered she had to get home quickly to feed Kurt, let him out and make up a story about damaging the duco. Something plausible. And orange? She had to grab coins, too, from Toby's cupboard and George from Shelley's and take him to a Cancer Council thing, because Shelley couldn't, because she was off having radiotherapy. *Poor thing.* Caroline knew all this, but the voice inside her that chimed in, *Poor thing*, seemed to belong to someone else. Someone higher-pitched. Someone who knew something she didn't. It was the same voice that sang 'Mary Had a Little Lamb'. She knew this the same way she knew there was a windscreen in front of her, but not what any of it had to do with her at this very moment. She didn't know how to do anything but stare at her shaky hands gripping the steering wheel and think how funny it was that after all these years they were still doing as they'd been told by Hector, a slob of a driving instructor who burped and gargled Mylanta but taught them how to hold the wheel as if their hands were the hands of a clock, set at ten to two, for maximum safety. She wiggled her fingers and had just begun another round – 'You know those people who are in their bodies?' – when her phone rang.

She looked at the screen. It was Shelley. Shit. Normally she'd let it go to voicemail, but with Shelley off bring poked and roasted, and George waiting to be picked up, she heard herself say, 'Hey, Shell,' and then a man say, 'Hello? Who's this?'

'Who's this? Who are *you*?' Caroline responded, confused. She looked at the screen again. It definitely said Smelly Mob.

'Steven.'

'Steven? Steven who? Is everything okay? Where's Shelley? Where did you get this phone?'

'Ridley. Sort of. I'm at the RPA and my wife's having a baby. Well, not yet – but soon, we hope. It's our first. I just ducked out for a smoke while they give her an epidural and found this phone in the car park. I don't know any Shelleys.'

'Oh, my goodness!'

'I know – it's pretty rough in there. We've tried all the stuff we practised at home, but she just keeps screaming at me to fuck off – so here I am, in the car park, catching my breath, and I found this phone on the ground and your number showed up as the last call. So, I thought I'd ring and see if you knew who owned it.'

If someone wasn't beeping their horn at Caroline, anxious to know if she was leaving her parking spot, she'd think this Steven wasn't real, like Mary and her little lambs, but she could hear him inhaling and exhaling as clearly as she could hear the horn blasting behind her, her engine starting and herself saying, 'Okay. Steven, is it? And you're at RPA? There now? In the car park? And you've found this phone? All by itself? Not booby-trapped? No one tottering nearby, frantically looking for it?'

'Nope. Yep. Look, sorry – I've got to get back to my wife. So, do you know who –'

'Yeah. Yeah, of course. Sorry. I've just . . . I'm trying to . . . I'm just leaving a hospital myself . . . *Can you just give me a fucking second?!*' she screamed at the horn blower as she reversed, feeling the brake and accelerator beneath her feet and herself back inside of her body, shaking – intrigued. Trying to piece it together: a stranger, Steven – having a baby – a smoke in a car park – finding Shelley's phone at RPA – where she worked – but wasn't today, because she was over at Nepean Hospital – having treatment – which was exactly why Caroline was racing to pick up George, wearing fucking yellow – unless . . .

'Steven? Are you still there?'

'Yep. So, do you know who owns it?'

'I do. Look, it's my – her name's Shelley, and I've got a feeling she's not far from where you are. Could you do me a favour and take the phone to the social services department on your way back in? It's just opposite the chapel. You'll see all sorts of fat people. I mean sad people. Both probably. Sorry. I mean, I am, too. Fat and sad. I've got nothing against either. Anyway, it's on the third floor, right below maternity. You'll probably hear your wife from there . . . Steven?'

'Yeah?'

'That was a joke. Sorry. She'll be right when the epidural kicks in.'

'Sure. Okay. I hope so. I'm on my way.'

As she drove away from the hospital towards the M4, Caroline listened to Steven's breathing as he walked back towards RPA, a hospital she knew intimately, from lunching with Shelley and from a botched D&C that punctured Caroline's ovary, when the Mater didn't have a bed. Toby brought tissues and Aunt Martha dragged her outside into harsh daylight, to sit on a damp timber bench and eat rocky road overlooking the car park that Caroline now imagined Steven traversing.

'Have you got any names picked out for the baby?'

'Jessie,' Steven said.

'For a girl or a boy?'

'Either. My mother-in-law hates it, though. Says it reminds her of Jesse James. But we love it.'

'Good for you. Stick with it. And remember next time – don't tell a soul what name you've picked until the baby is born. This is *so* exciting, Steven!'

'I know. We're pretty excited. Nervous, though . . .'

'Me too!' Caroline meant the pursuit of Shelley was exciting, not the baby, but whatever. She wondered if it was better to pull over or just keep driving. She slowed down. Sped up. Then slowed again. 'Are you still there, Steven?'

'Yeah.'

Caroline braked heavily, thinking of a dopey boyfriend of Shelley's who used to do that. He'd almost sent her and her sisters through the windscreen, until they learned to shut up when he was driving. She moved into the left lane in case she needed the hard shoulder and to whack her hazards on. 'Okay.'

She listened hard as the sounds around Steven changed. She could tell he was now inside the hospital, heading towards the lifts. 'Here we go!'

The lift doors dinged open. She heard voices. Her heart pounded, and she wondered if this was how Obama felt watching his Seals storm Bin Laden's lair.

'When you get to social services, Steven, hold your fire. Don't go in. Just wait and I'll tell you what to say. Okay? . . . Steven?'

The line was dead. Caroline assumed – hoped – he'd lost reception in the lift.

'Hello, Steven? Steven? Are you there?' She pulled over and put the hazards on. People beeped and swerved around her, turning their heads to glare. She gave them the finger.

Steven said, 'Hi – I think you cut out for a minute. I can see the chapel ahead, and a sign – I think it says *Social Services*. Yeah. It does. So, what do I do now?'

'Okay, just keep walking along the corridor and look for a door that says *Squalor and Hoarding*. Can you see it?'

'Ah . . . yep.'

'Great. Don't open it. Just look through the fan light and tell me if you can see a woman sitting at a desk with –'

'Huge eyelashes?'

'Yes!' Caroline claps.

'She's at her computer.'

'Great. Now, go in there and tell her you found her phone; tell her it was ringing and you answered it.'

'Why?'

'I want to surprise her! Tell her you've got someone very important on the line – tell her it's her hairdresser! And then hand her the phone straight to her ear. Oh, and good luck with the baby. Let me know what you have. Thanks!'

Caroline listened as Steven entered Shelley's office and explained the situation, saying more or less what she'd told him to, and then Shelley prattled about rushing into work that morning and being flat out all day in her office – and RPA's wonderful maternity unit, how she'd had her George there too, and finally, 'Thank you, thank you, for finding my phone,' before gushing into it, 'Hello, darling!'

'Hello, Shelley,' Caroline said, and waited for a reply. There was none. Shelley hung up.

It was only later, when the shock had subsided a little, that Caroline realised she might have heard her sister mutter, 'Bitch,' right as the line went dead.

~

So Dette was right all along. Shelley didn't have cancer. Caroline had caught her red-handed, but the truth didn't bring relief; it brought disbelief, fury and fears for Shelley's mental health and an urgent desire to tell the other girls worrying themselves silly about whether or not they'd get it too. As Caroline pulled in to the kerb, she decided she'd call them after George had gone home.

'Hey, George,' she said as he climbed into the passenger seat. She didn't have a clue what to say to him. *April fool's, George – your mother made up cancer to get your attention!* Caroline wanted to spill the beans, tell George the truth. He was eighteen. He deserved to know. But why the hell shouldn't Shelley tell him herself? Caroline would confront her tonight, when she came to pick him up.

George looked as silly as she did wearing yellow. 'Hey, AC. What do you reckon?' George grabbed the droopy left pocket of his lemon polo shirt and stretched it out so she could read *Royal Prince Alfred Volunteer.*

'That's amazing! I didn't know you were a volunteer.'

'I'm not. Mum nicks them from work.'

Seeing her normally svelte, whip-smart nephew, who'd never be caught dead wearing yellow, let alone stolen goods to Daffodil Day to raise funds for a cancer he didn't know his mother didn't have, looking jaundiced and chubby after a month of Mi Goreng noodles and no uni; was the final straw for Caroline. She slapped the steering wheel and screamed, 'Fuck it, George, we're not going.' She untied her scarf, threw it out the window and sped off.

George was disappointed. He'd always hoped Aunty Caroline was an exception to the Birds' madness, but clearly, she was not.

Caroline drove like a maniac all the way home to wait for Shelley. She was pacing in the lounge room, waiting for the doorbell, when George's phone rang. It was Shelley, saying she was out the front and in a big hurry, so could George just come straight out to the car?

'Stay right where you are,' Caroline told George.

She opened the door and strode out to Shelley's car.

Shelley, catching sight of her, drove off.

'What the fuck? What the fucking fuck? Fuck off!' Caroline shouted as she stood on the road watching her sister's tail-lights recede.

'What happened?' George asked, when she was back inside, leaning heavily against the front door. 'You, okay?

'Sure. Yep. Fine.' *You know those people . . .*

'You look a bit weird.'

'Do I?' *I'm not one of them.* 'Hey, you should talk. Look at you in your old lady's shirt!' Caroline held both hands against her pounding chest. 'I guess your mum has to be somewhere in a hurry. Not to worry. The spare room's yours, if you want to stay? And if you want to get changed, you can borrow one of Toby's t-shirts. He'll be home in a sec, and be so happy to see you. You can watch the footy together. Play with Kurt. We'll order pizza.'

'Cool. Thanks.'

'Good. Look, I'm actually not feeling that great. I think I might just jump in the shower. The menu's in the busy drawer in the kitchen. I'll have a margherita with olives.'

Caroline went into her bathroom, locked the door, turned the shower taps on full, sat on the toilet and sobbed.

Later that night in bed, when Toby asked her how her day was and why George was really staying over, she pretended she was asleep, as she lay there worrying about how the hell she was going to face Shelley, or any of them for that matter, on Christmas day.

Everything all at Once

DECEMBER 2013

Frau Glint

25 DECEMBER 2013

'He's up.'

'You're telling me!' Toby reaches for Caroline's hand and rubs it between his legs. 'Morning!'

'Jesus. Are you kidding?' Caroline pulls away. 'Listen to him, the poor little guy.'

'You can't blame me for trying,' Toby says. He opens an eye and peers at the clock. 5.10 am. Fuck. Kurt's scratching the laundry door and whining. It's hot as hell. Christmas Day. The Birds are coming for lunch. So much for a boner.

Toby's horribly hungover and so's Caroline, after the closing night of her exhibition. 'Thank Christ that's over,' they'd both agreed, in the early hours, after too many reds, given all that had transpired the past few years – let alone in the past fucking week: from Leslie and Wallace's cross-country and hospital dramas to

Bernadette's fall to Shelley's disappearance after driving off, then reappearing at Dette's to look after her and the girls and rifle through her drawers and discover that back when Leslie and Wallace sold Batemans Bay it was to fund Dette's mortgage – half of which, Toby learned, was now floating in the Korean baths in Kings Cross (Amir's favourite spot, according to his partner Gavin, who invited Toby to join them for a soak).

Caroline thinks she must still be drunk, as the details of last night fade in and out. 'Wait,' she says, squeezing her eyes shut and reaching out to take hold of Toby's arm. She asks him to tell her it isn't true that Shelley had the audacity to show up and ignore her, then hide behind a column at the back of the gallery, batting her Tammy Faye's, screaming about Batemans Bay and bitches and talking to Michael's . . . shit. Caroline opens her eyes.

'One-armed girlfriend, correct,' Toby says, loosening her grip and giving her back her hand. 'Her name's Helen. Lovely girl.'

'Hardly a girl. Shame I didn't get to talk to her properly before Shelley cut in.'

'She's great. You'll love her. She's bookish, works at Lane Cove Library.'

'It's so weird seeing Michael with someone. Let alone someone taller and older.'

'A veritable Mrs Robinson. Who makes her own chutney. And loved your paintings. Follows your work. Had no idea you and Michael were related, though.'

'What? Wow. That's really weird. Why wouldn't he have just said, *We're going to my sister's exhibition*? He told me he was proud of me at the opening. Said my *Missings* were the truest paintings he'd ever seen.

'Which ones were they?'

'The ones of him and Shelley and Dette in various disguises. Remember he cried and hugged me?'

'I remember he cried and hugged your sisters, and said it was a complete invasion of privacy. *How could she. How dare she.* Et cetera.'

'So, what am I supposed to believe?'

'That both things are true? He feels proud and violated. Maybe that's the lot of an artist's family. You're the one who's always going on about people raging against feeling seen!'

'Do I? Yeah, I guess I do, don't I?' Caroline says. 'No one who's spent their lives feeling unseen, then pretending they're someone else, wants to be truly seen. Pretending's such an exhausting business.'

'Well, no one knows that better than you Birds.'

'True. You told her, though, right?' Caroline's eyes light up.

'Told who what?'

'Mrs Robinson – that we're related.'

'You and me?'

'No! Me and Michael.'

'I didn't actually. But who knows what Shelley told her?'

'Why didn't *you* tell her?'

'I didn't know what I was allowed to say. Remember the list you gave me?'

'It wasn't a list. Just a few suggestions.' Caroline shakes her head. 'Anyone with any' – she wants to say sense but instead says 'empathy would have known what not to say.'

'Jesus. Caro. It was hardly a Family Fun Night. Your brother's standing there faking an amputation with his scabby forehead and one-armed girlfriend, while one of your sister's scoffing all the canapes and the other one's hiding behind a column calling out, *Bitch*, and your parents are cowering at home, recovering from escaping what we're all surrounded by: these bloody giant paintings of you and your family, which we're all meant to believe are abstract. And if anyone dares to recognise themselves, you go mental and bang on about narcissism and metaphor. And if they don't understand the paintings, you say *they're* mental. Seriously, Caro. I did my best.'

'I know you did. Sorry. Sorry, darling.' Caroline needs Toby onside today, so she reaches over and rubs his thigh before saying, 'I wonder why Helen thought they were there, though?'

'And why you invited her for lunch.'

'Did I? Shit.'

Kurt yaps.

'You invited everyone, at the end of the night. I tried to grab the microphone from you . . .'

'Jesus.' Caroline reaches for the sheets and pulls them up over her head. The little breeze they make reminds her she's naked. 'Don't tell me we had sex pretending we were amputees?'

'Okay, I won't – Zsa Zsa Gabor.' Toby is interrupted by Kurt barking – his first big bark – and then whimpering as if he's scared himself.

'Oh, poor little guy.' Caroline lowers the sheets to beneath her chin. 'Can you just go and let him out, and then bring him back in for a cuddle? And what's with Zsa Zsa?'

'That's what you said I had to call you.' Toby moves closer and nuzzles her neck.

'Oh god. That's right. Mum told me that.'

'To have one-legged sex?'

'About Zsa Zsa Gabor. When I first talked to her about Michael's thing for amputees after Shelley showed her the video of him strapped up at the Intercontinental with a real one-armed woman – who I guess we now know is Helen – I told Mum I thought it might have started back when his weight blew out. Remember how his tummy got huge but his arms and legs stayed skinny? He probably found he had all this extra room in his sleeves.'

'Of course – so what else is there to do but strap yourself up and pretend to be an amputee?'

'Don't be mean. I showed Mum the dating site he used – Amputee Mate. It's great. She was speechless. I told her I don't think he necessarily set out looking for someone without limbs. He just wanted someone to believe him.'

'Believe what?'

'That he's damaged, stupid. Don't we all want someone to listen and buy our shit? Someone to understand us? I told Mum when Shelley saw him at high tea, she was so shocked she dropped her phone and Mum said she did remember seeing a flash of floor and ceiling in the video and heard Shelley swearing, which seemed to upset her more than Michael pretending he had a missing arm – which she said she couldn't see, what with all that light flooding in from the atrium – but then she agreed with me that he looked like quite the pro. Almost as if he was born disabled. Shelley said he looked straight at her, while he was pouring Helen's tea – looked straight at the camera and didn't recoil.'

'Fuck,' Toby said. 'Like one of those big cats in the Blue Mountains?'

'Yes! Anyway, Mum told me not to tell Dad. *As if*, I said, and she looked at me blankly, and I thought fair enough, the poor thing's probably in shock; who wouldn't be, finding that out about their son? But then she started waving her hands around in the air and stuttering, and I thought she was having a stroke until she said, *Greenacres. Dumb blonde. Darliiiing? Come on, you know exactly who I'm talking about!* I told her I had no idea, but then she shouted, *Zsa Zsa Gabor! Thank goodness, I thought I was going mad.* She'd read somewhere that Zsa Zsa had had her right leg amputated but didn't know for three years because her husband and nurse didn't tell her!'

'And you believed her?'

'I don't know. Who cares? That's not the point.'

'What's the point?' Toby is struggling to keep up.

'Amputee and Zsa Zsa go together. Like me and lesbians. That's my mother's mind right there, on full display – a moral thesaurus.'

'Remind me again why she thinks you're a lesbian?'

'I don't know. Maybe she's preparing herself for the worst, so I can't shock her anymore? Once, when I told her I had a secret to tell her – something really important – she got so excited, she shouted, *Don't tell me – let me guess. You're a lesbian!* just as I was telling her I was pregnant. I still don't know if she heard me. She didn't say anything. Neither did I. That was the last time I told her. Anyway, it doesn't matter. Let's get back to Michael. Do you reckon he chose which sleeve to empty before or after he met Helen?'

'Definitely after. He would have seen her profile, slipped the arm out, taken a selfie, then uploaded it. How else could they hold hands if their missing ones weren't opposing?'

'I guess. Were they really holding hands last night?' Caroline puts her fingers to her mouth.

'Yep. All night. They barely let go.'

'Jeez. We can't hold hands for a minute and we've got four to choose from.'

'I know,' says Toby. 'Whose fault is that? If you didn't have to lock my thumb, we'd be alright.'

'Whatever. I think it's fantastic for Michael. I know it's weird, but good on him. At least he picked the right arm. He's been so lonely for so long. Especially since Dad killed Trevor. Who are we to burst his bubble?'

Toby pinches his thumb and tall man together, as if he's holding a dart, about to throw it . . .

Caroline reaches over to stop him, just as he makes a popping sound.

'For god's sake, Caro, he's a forty-five-year-old man.'

'That's right – a forty-five-year-old man with sleep apnoea and hips who's never been kissed.'

Toby rolls his eyes. 'Does he still sleep with that machine?'

'I guess so, if the scabs on his forehead are anything to go by. But I did think it looked a bit better last night, didn't you? Not as angry. Maybe it's the Helen effect?'

'Let's hope his whiskers are next. What's with them?'

'I don't know. They just didn't grow, aside from the few wiry strands on his cheeks that sprouted in puberty and made him look menopausal.'

'Is that what you call it?' Toby looks offended. 'I'd say it's more Oliver Hardy slash weirdo.'

'Stop it.' Caroline slaps him. 'He's a beautiful sensitive weirdo, and for very good reasons.'

'Weirdo's an understatement. I didn't know where to look or what to say to him last night. At one point I just wanted to grab that stupid empty sleeve of his and strangle him with it.'

'But you didn't! Because even you, Christine Polon, knows he deserves a break.' Caroline leans over and kisses him.

Toby pushes her off. 'I didn't because it was top of your list. Don't say anything about Michael's arm. Don't stare at his head. And don't ever tell your dad. As if old Wal wouldn't notice his son's arm's missing. All he's got to do is look at him.'

'Exactly!' Caroline says, exasperated. No matter how many times she's explained to Toby that her father never ever looked at Michael, she knows he'll never understand, nor understand what it did to her brother. 'You still don't get it, do you?'

'No!' Toby says proudly. 'And the day I do, I'll be as mad as the rest of you. How long do you reckon before Helen figures out he's faking?'

'Maybe she doesn't care. Maybe she'll think it's sweet to have someone pretend they share your interests. Like we did when we were dating – me with the Sandinistas, you with your poetry. Hey, it worked for us! I know, it's probably different from what most people pretend, but everyone does it. Look at us pretending your parrot's the reason we haven't had kids, so our parents won't know about the miscarriages, and we won't have to suffer their pity.'

'Or lack of it?'

'Maybe.' Caroline shrugs. 'Maybe Michael's just a guy who wears his heart in his sleeve?' She props herself up on her elbows. 'Oh god – my head.' Kurt is still scratching the laundry door and yapping. She yells at him, 'Shut up!' and prods Toby to get out of bed.

'I think it's your turn.'

'Are you kidding? I've got twenty pavlovas to make.'

'*Twenty?* Jesus. How many are coming?' Toby yawns as he pulls himself slowly up to sit on the side of the bed.

'All of them . . . except Aunt Martha, of course. Poor darling. Did I tell you I inherited her Darrell Lea ribbon collection? And that I'm going to use them to tie up the serviettes today, so everyone can take one home as a keepsake. I still can't believe she's gone.' Caroline rubs her eyes.

'Or that your mother left her in an open coffin.'

'Sweet Jesus. Don't remind me.'

'Why do you reckon she did that?'

'I don't know. Anger? Revenge?'

'Revenge? For what?'

'Flying. Dying. For leaving her?'

Toby shakes his head. Stands up, stretches and slips into his Birkenstocks. 'How can it be twenty pavs? I thought you said you had the trifecta in hospital.'

From behind – if you ignore his bald patch – Toby still looks like an adolescent. The same muscular torso. Same beautiful bottom. That bum was the clincher, Caroline thinks. 'Yeah, they were all in hospital, but Mum got out Tuesday, the day after Dad sharted. And Dad only went in for tests. And Dette got sent home the same day she broke her leg – Thursday, I think it was. Remember? I told you all that!'

'Maybe? I don't know. It's pretty hard to keep up with all the crap in your family?'

Kurt barks.

'See? Even Kurt agrees!'

'Can you go and get him, please?'

Toby heads to the laundry and opens the door.

Kurt jumps up, quivering with excitement, and wees all over the floor. 'Don't forget to take him out and say, *Go toiley* – and wait until he's done his business,' Caroline calls out. 'And don't let him go on the aspidistras.'

'Sure thing,' Toby calls back.

After feeding Kurt and taking him outside, Toby returns to the bedroom cradling the puppy, whom he plops down on the bed. Kurt scampers up to Caroline's head and paws and mouths her hair. She untangles him and holds his velvety body close and breathes him in. As he wiggles and licks – he can't stop licking – she laces her fingers over his plump belly and practises holding him firmly against her body; his back to her tummy, saying, 'Settle . . . settle,' in the low growly voice the madwoman at puppy school taught them to use. Caroline wonders how they ever lived without this kind of love in their lives. Or ever would again.

'So you were saying it looks like old Wal will live to see another day?' Toby climbs back into bed and rubs a spot behind Kurt's ear that makes his head tilt and tail spin.

'So they say. For a man who claims he's been dying his whole life, he'll probably outlive us all. And kill poor Mum in the process. She had to leave her own hospital bed to shuttle him to that doctor of his that she hates. The tall one with the hair.'

'What's wrong with his hair?'

'Nothing. It's fabulous. It'd rival Mum's in the bouffy department. That's the problem.'

'She's jealous?'

'No. Not jealous. She's got a theory that any fella over fifty with a full head of hair is just stupid.'

'Stupid?'

'Because they haven't been humbled by baldness. She reckons hair's the only thing their bodies concede. And since they're not ravaged by child-bearing, they ought to lose something – their hair at least. She reckons an old bloke with hair is just a stupid spoiled boy.'

'Like your dad?'

'I guess. Yeah. He's got good hair, hasn't he?'

'Great hair. And your mother's a piece of –'

'Stop it – it's Christmas. Anyway, she took Dad to the stupid doctor and he sent them straight back to "my hospital", Mum said, where he had a whole lot of tests and got the all clear – of course. I had to drive them there, after Dad called me screaming from the car park of the doctor's surgery. Their car got stuck at the boom gate. Jesus, you should have seen them. Mum had got out of the car and left him. We found her half a kilometre away and I had to force her to get in. They fought the whole way to the hospital. When I dropped them off I had to sit in the car park for an hour just trying to compose myself. When I walked into emergency Mum was banging on about her chops defrosting and some blonde – she said Dad was groping.'

'Groping a blonde?'

'No – himself. He had both hands in his pockets, perving at the woman, rocking back and forth, shouting, *ShamWow*, like a complete Looney Tunes.'

'Atta boy, Wal! So, what do they reckon caused his bleeding?'

Caroline sighed. 'They diagnosed it as "idiopathic". Apparently, that's what you call someone with a Nu-Lax addiction who's lost half his blood, bleeding from his bum.'

'Oh, okay.'

'What do you mean *okay*? It's not okay!' Caroline roars.

Toby's hands fly up in surrender. 'Hey, I'm on your side. I'm not the enemy.'

'I know. It's just – it's far from okay. Sorry. It's insane. I just wish you knew for one day – not even a day, an *hour* – what it's like to be a Bird. When was the last time your dad fronted up to hospital in a bloody nappy, asking to see a little Asian doctor and quoting Julia Gillard's partner saying that a little Asian woman was what you needed if you were going to have a prostate exam?'

'He didn't!'

'He did! And it turned out the oncologist on duty was a little Asian woman, and when he told her that – with his pants off, mind you – she informed him that the ex-prime minister's partner was mistaken, and what you really need is someone with a very big finger. That shut him up – not. He changed the subject by saying, *I bet that husband of yours is happy he's got himself a nice little earner.*'

'He never!'

'He did. Word for word.'

'How do *you* know?'

'I was there, holding his hand. Looking the other way, of course.'

'Where was your mum?'

'Outside in the waiting room. She wouldn't go in, not in a million years. She reckons I'm perverted.

'You are. Whatever happened to privacy?'

Caroline gathers the sheets up under her chin. 'I've told you: I go to the doctor with Dad whenever I can to repeat what he can't hear and remind him where he's up to when he forgets what he's saying. Oh, and to sort out his parking. He thinks I'm a genius when the boom gate rises. It's nice. Nice to feel needed.'

'So, it's about you feeling needed, not him needing you.'

'Hardly. Maybe. Maybe it's both? Maybe that's love? I don't know.'

~

What Caroline does know, and Toby doesn't, is that after the prostate examination, when Wallace was getting himself sorted in the toilet, she joined Leslie in the waiting room and told her all about Shelley. About the hell she'd put them all through pretending she had cancer. Told her Shelley was the reason Bernadette strangled her at Sage's birthday party.

'Goodness,' Leslie said. 'That sounds unpleasant. I've no recollection of that. None at all. I thought it was a lovely party.

Except for you storming off before that awful cake was cut. And the singing falling flat. Not to worry.' Leslie stared down at the clenched hands in her lap as Caroline took a deep breath and launched into the story of her entrapment of Shelley and her sister's subsequent disappearance. 'Just two days ago, right after I was visiting you and Dad sharted.'

'Don't remind me,' Leslie said, rubbing her earlobe. 'I've never been so embarrassed.'

Caroline carried on, describing how she and her siblings had tried to spare Leslie and Wallace the grief of worrying about a daughter with maybe/maybe not cancer all the while wanting to say to her, *But now we know she doesn't have it, isn't it time* you *helped out, Leslie Bird? Because, at the end of the day, Shelley's all your fault. They all are. And if I hadn't spent my time mothering them, maybe I would have stood a chance of mothering one of my own? But I'll never know, will I, as I'm too terrified of what it would mean – the loss of hope for the mothers we both wanted to be – to say these things.*

A shrink had warned Caroline once not to confront her mother. 'At her age, a confrontation might kill her.' Caroline had shrugged. 'Okay,' she said. 'Why not make it a triple murder?' And then she explained that Leslie had already accused her of killing both her grandparents, and that Leslie's defence was always the same old, *If I believed you children were as affected* . . . blah blah blah. Except for the one time she added, *Because that would mean I was the worst mother in the world.* And Caroline had remained silent, letting the words hang in the air, as she thought, *Yes, you were, Leslie Bird, and I am a great mother*, before Leslie's bottom lip started trembling and Caroline reverted to consoling her – saying something silly about Wallace that made them both laugh and placed them back in the ring. Leslie in her corner as the good mother and Caroline in hers as the mad daughter.

Caroline implored her mother to drive down to Shelley's and check in on her. 'Tell her you know. Tell her she needs help. Don't you want to make sure she hasn't killed herself?'

Leslie shifted her gaze from side to side. Shrugged.

'Oh, and tell her George is fine. Not that she cares, apparently. She hasn't answered a single one of my calls. Are you listening, Mum? No one knows where the hell she is.'

Leslie sat biting her lip with her arms folded, counting the age spots on them where her hairs used to be. So many hairs. She remembered shaving them once, and that they grew back worse, consigning her to a life of long sleeves until she started moulting in her sixties. Better to just let things be, she thought, rubbing her smooth arms and saying nothing.

But what Caroline doesn't know is that, after she'd dropped her parents home from the hospital, Leslie fixed Wallace his dinner and told him she was popping out to the shops, but instead drove to Shelley's. She walked up to the front door and put her ear against the wood. Knocking seemed too intrusive, so she peered through the windows and concluded no one was home. What to do now, though, she wondered, given none of it was any of her business? She trawled through the garbage bins, looking for – what? Empty bottles? The reason Shelley was a liar – or Caroline? Who knew who really said what to whom? It was all so confusing. Never mind, Leslie sighed, and she sorted out Shelley's recycling before heading home. She didn't breathe a word of it to Wallace; there was no point dragging him into this.

~

With Kurt curled between her legs snoring, Caroline asks Toby if he remembers how, after Viktor died, Wallace went over to Lana's place to keep her company and patch the ceiling and got electrocuted and broke three vertebrae.

'Of course. He was almost the second person not to make it out of their toilet alive.'

'And while he was in hospital in agony, Bob Savage died. We told Mum not to tell him, but she did, and Dad fell first into the deepest depression and then fell in love – with the chronic pain specialist, who prescribed him morphine and eventually sent him home with two big bottles and a referral to a psychologist. Seventy-five years of age and Dad finally fesses up to feeling depressed for most of it, as opposed to always bullshitting in front of his doctors, telling them he was fine.'

'How many old blokes do you know who can talk about their feelings?'

'Exactly. They're too ashamed. Dad always says, *What's the point of whingeing about being sad?* As if being born in the Depression, inhaling it as temperament, living through a world war, seeing your old man go mad from your best mate bleeding to death on his knees, losing your first wife in childbirth and having your baby taken wasn't the point! Mum was furious that he was offered help, though. Said it was a waste of time and money.

'Anyway, he was so nervous about what he was going to say to the psychologist that he practised for weeks, and then asked Mum to go in with him. But she told him that whatever he had to say to some other woman was none of her business, so he asked me to go in with him instead. Of course, I said yes, but then Mum decided to come too, and she sat outside in the waiting room chatting and giggling with the receptionist while we met with this beautiful doctor – Julie was her name. Dr Julie. But she said just to call her Julie. Before we'd even sat down, Dad said to her, *Don't ask me, Jules – ask her, she knows me better than I know meself.* And he pointed at me.'

'And what did you say?'

'Nothing. I didn't need to. Dr Julie explained how she was just there to listen to whatever Dad felt like sharing, and he started talking about Sammy O'Sullivan and his dog and his dad and an uncle who jumped from the church tower into his schoolyard. He sat there rubbing his hands together, then blew in them as if they were cold and told her how Grenfell's winters were two dogs . . .'

'Two dogs?'

'Yeah, the number his mother threw on his bed. And then he went on about her dying of a broken heart and it being all his fault and my mum being the best woman in the whole wide world – and before you knew it his hour was up and Dr Julie reviewed his current meds, then went through a checklist with him. Stuff like: Do you ever have trouble getting out of bed? Thoughts of self-harm? Wish you weren't here? Feel nervous, worthless, hopeless, restless? I thought, *Of course. Who hasn't?*

You had to answer one for never and five for always. He scored all fives. She diagnosed him as having severe melancholic depression with narcissistic tendencies and prescribed him antidepressants and nine more sessions, and when we came out of her office it felt like we were floating. It was as if some enormous weight had been lifted off our shoulders. Well, off mine at least. Dad didn't say much. I asked Mum to check her diary so I could book his next appointment, and she tutted, *Is that really necessary? Hasn't he already given them his spiel?*'

'Maybe you go to protect him,' Toby suggests, folding his arms on top of the sheets.

'From what?'

'Your mum.'

Caroline shrugs. 'She refused to get his prescription filled. Called them happy pills.'

'Why doesn't she want him to be happy? It's not like he was a drunk or hit her or gambled or anything, was it?'

'No, it's just . . . I guess he just didn't amount to much. She told me once that she tried to leave him just after they were engaged, but couldn't because she didn't want him to see her from behind.'

'And then he goes and keeps quiet about being married before and having Lana.'

'I know. She thought she'd married a virgin! You can't imagine what a big deal that is for her. But I think there's something else – something I've never understood. Dad says it's the Maloney hatred thing, that they all have it, but I think there's something more, something worse that she's never forgiven him for. Anyway, I nicked his script, got it filled and then she threw them in the bin.'

'His antidepressants?'

'Yep. Chucked them in the bin but kept the morphine. *Just in case*, she said. *You never know* . . . And she was as cool as a cucumber when she said it. Not like when I asked why she threw his happy pills away, and she went ballistic; glinting and hissing, *Happy? Why should* he *be happy? He deserves to be miserable for all the dumb things he's done.*

'How big was the glint?' Toby's eyes widened.

'Huge. The biggest I've seen in ages.' Toby laughed remembering the first time he heard of the 'glint', not long after he and Caroline met, when she referred to Leslie as 'Frau Glint' and explained this thing Leslie did with her face, where she purses her lips and narrows her right eye that flashes a glint of something Caroline could only describe as absolutely terrifying. 'As if in that moment the rest of Mum is camouflage and the only truth is that glint.' Toby remembers too, when he saw it firsthand, at a family do, when someone accused Leslie of being insensitive and she exploded, 'Apparently, you're not allowed to say *golliwog* anymore either,' and pounded both fists on the dining table yelling, 'Golliwog, golliwog, golliwog.' Toby shook his head at the memory. 'So bigger than Golliwogs then?'

'Way bigger than Golliwogs,' Caroline said, 'I reckon her happy pill glint was about the same size as her UN Charter for Children's Rights glint. Come to think of it,' she said, 'her Shart glint was pretty big too the other day!'

'Speaking of sharts, what's going to happen to Dette's broken leg? I thought you said she was having surgery?'

'She was. She will. I mean as soon as the swelling goes down, they'll operate. That was the first thing Shelley told me when she called the other night. And when I asked what the hell she was on about, and told her to back up, that we really needed to talk, she told me to shut up. *This is serious, Caro*, she said. *Dette's in emergency*. And in the blink of an eye, it was just like old times, pre maybe/maybe not cancer – Shell and I saving the world.'

'One dope at a time.'

'Hear me out. Shell said she was dripping wet, just out of the shower, when Dette rang her screaming after falling at the beach.'

'The beach?'

'I know – weird, right? Anyway, Shell said she stayed on the line while Dette drifted in and out of consciousness and someone –'

'Someone at the beach?'

'I guess, I don't know – someone called an ambulance. Shell said it was hard to tell what was going on, with Dette groaning, throwing up and hyperventilating and the sound of seagulls and stupid people. She said she heard this guy saying, *Put your arm here. No here. Higher. You'll be right.* Then she heard Dette say that she was trying and then asking if her fringe was fuzzy, and a woman in the background yelling, *Just leave her – you'll break your back.*'

'Fair enough.'

'Poor thing. I'd rather die than have a fuzzy fringe. Shell said, *You can't imagine how awful it was, listening to all that*, and I said, *Hang on a minute*, but she went on talking right over the top of me, saying, *People who live in Balmain, with puppies and husbands who love them and without children – cruel children and ex-husbands with pregnant girlfriends – shouldn't throw stones, Caro. Don't you think it's amaaaaazing someone was compassionate enough to think of someone less fortunate than themselves for once, and make sure that Dette's phone stayed with her?*'

'Jeez, she's got form,' Toby said. 'I hope you told her what's amaaaazing is how she always makes herself the victim.'

'Shell said she listened to everything, from the ambos arriving – asking questions about allergies, giving Dette meds and calling ahead to St Vinnies, describing their patient as – get this – an ample semi-conscious middle-aged woman! Shell said she'd never heard a better description of Dette and yelled out, *Scallops! That's my sister!* but no one heard her. Then she started laughing. And I did too. Tentatively, at first, like – I was trying – I don't know? Remember at school when everyone skipped in a big line together and sang – *In came the doctor, in came the nurse, in came the lady with the alligator purse* – and you had to wait your turn to jump in under the big rope and if you went too early you got whipped and wrecked it for everyone?'

Toby said, 'Nope.'

'Well, it was like that.' Caroline continued, 'Waiting for the right moment to join in and then Shell and I just erupted. I could barely speak. I had tears rolling down my cheeks. It was weird. I was doubled over, saying, *It's not funny, Shell.* And she said, *You're right – it's not funny, Caro.* And the more we said it the more we laughed about how funny it wasn't – then Shell screamed, *Stop it, stop it – I've wet my pants!*'

'Well, there goes Lana's theory that she'd had her plumbing fixed,' Toby observed.

'So anyway, while Shell was looking for clean undies she said she'd heard Dette begging for morphine while in the background the ambos described her injuries – suspected multiple fractures and extensive soft tissue damage to the right leg after a two-metre fall from a rock ledge.'

'Shit!'

'I know. We stopped laughing.'

'Shell said the ambos placed bets on whether it was a spiral fracture and then discussed where to go for lunch at the end of their shift: Oporto or Mickey's.'

'Definitely Oporto. Why would anyone want to go to Mickey's?'

'That's what I said – unless it's taco night, right?'

Toby nodded. 'Correct.'

Shell said she blow-dried her hair and put a load of washing on, then drove to St Vincent's and found Dette sitting in emergency, with both hands pressing on her fringe and her swollen leg propped up on a chair. She was already triaged, MRI'd and off her rocker on Endone. Like she was two goldfish gone.'

'Two goldfish?'

'Remember when she used to swallow them at parties?'

'Swallow or gargle?'

'Probably both. The point is, she was off her head. Shell said she was calling herself Kathleen Turner, naming the movies she'd been in, while she was fitted for a moon boot then put in a wheel chair and told to return when the swelling goes down. Shell said it was so sweet, the way Dette introduced her to everyone, saying, *This is my big sister*, like she was proud of her or something. She said they held hands and it was the nicest time she'd ever had with Dette – even though she got a parking ticket and Dette made her stop and pick up a Thai green curry on their way home and it stunk out the car.'

'So, if she's in a wheelchair, how the hell's she going to get here? Should I go and pick her up?'

'God no. I don't want her here a second longer than necessary. I'm already shaking. Look at me.' Caroline holds out both hands. 'It'll be full-blown Parkinson's by the time they get here.'

'You'll be fine. You're just hungover.'

'I am not! I mean I am, but it's not that. It's them. I always start shaking when they're coming over. My body's a seismograph. Knows when things are going to blow. Amir and Gavin are bringing Dette and the girls in Gavin's seven-seater. Lana said she'd lend her the van but Dette said she'd rather die than ride in the Magic Pudding. Michael will make his own way here. Shell's gonna pick up Mum and Dad. So, fingers crossed she shuts the fuck up about Batemans Bay, or I'll have to spill the beans on Steven.'

'Steven?'

'Yeah. Look, things have been so insane, I haven't been able to tell you about him yet.'

'Tell me now.'

'I can't. It'll just stir things up. I'll tell you later. I'll tell you tonight. Let's just say that, for now, Steven's an alibi.'

'For who?'

'Take a guess. Let's just get through today and try to be gracious hosts. Believe me, you don't need Steven in your head – it's bad enough he's in mine, and I want to kill everyone. Not Steven, though. He hasn't done anything. On the contrary. Can you call Lana and see if she's got any Valium? Oh, and can you forget all the mean things I've ever said about my family and act like you love them, just for today – *pleeease*? I promise I'll get up with Kurt tonight.'

'Both times? And let me sleep in?'

'Yep.'

'Okay, deal. Hang on – just so I'm clear on who knows what today, Dette knows about Amir and Gavin, right?'

'Seriously? How could you forget? She met him the same night we did, after she came to my opening and walked around the gallery with her eyes closed telling everyone she couldn't see a single thing that she couldn't have painted herself – except for *Prickly*, that bloody piece of mine Gavin bought her. He introduced himself as Amir's partner and insisted she accept the painting as a peace offering. Even asked her if she'd posed for it. She called me the next day enraged. Told me how much she hated it and how disgusting I was for painting Mum's armpit.'

'Why'd you paint Leslie's armpit?'

'It wasn't an armpit. Or bloody Dette. It was a close-up of a cactus I saw in Arizona, when I took that trip there with my painting group a few years back.' She stretches. 'I bags the shower. Promise I'll be quick. Then I'll come down and start on the meringues. Remind me again why I decided to make twenty fucking pavlovas?'

'Because your mum loves them?'

'She does, doesn't she, the dear thing?' Caroline grabs Toby's hand from beneath the covers, holds it to her mouth and kisses it. 'Thanks, darling. Love you.'

'Love you too,' Toby says.

Caroline gets out of bed. Steadies herself and grabs her dressing-gown. 'Okay. Here we go.'

There You All Are

'But what am I going to say to them?'

'What about, *Hello, Mr and Mrs Bird*? Or, *Merry Christmas, Whoppy and Lanny*? Or, if you're feeling super chatty, you could try both.'

'I don't know.' Helen shrugs. 'What if they hate me?'

'Then we'll have that in common.' Michael winks. 'Are you okay? You look a bit red.'

'I'm fine.' Helen turns to look out the window thinking that she only has herself to blame for her rising anxiety. 'It's just so hot in here.'

Michael asks the driver to turn up the air.

Helen's only known Michael a few months. A bit longer, if you count back to when his big blushing face first popped up online and their copious communications began, the likes of which neither had ever experienced – Michael having never dated anyone real or cyber, and Helen with a long history of duds. So with that in common and so much more, from chihuahuas in dress-ups to finishing each other's sentences, Helen assumed – as you do when the alternative is loneliness – that meeting in the flesh would be a mere formality, not the shock it was when they did finally meet for high tea at the Intercontinental. Helen had never been or pictured herself going, let alone taking advantage of the valet parking and then nibbling scones and sipping Earl Grey while bathed in the lovely light of the soaring atrium. She wondered if there might be more to the bashful young man sitting opposite her than she'd imagined. And was that the problem? Had she imagined him as a naive oddball, a man of mystery and few words, and not the surly, cynical, evasive loafer he seemed to be, simply to suit her own needs? Or had he misled her? It was rather disturbing, the way he couldn't hold her gaze. And his gait, which appeared to be choreographed around concealment. Best to delay judgement and a second date and excuse herself to return to the comfort of her own home and unsullied impressions. Which worked a treat, Helen thought, when after an awkward start and a few short weeks, they resumed their old patter, chatting and messaging at all hours. Synchronising takeaways and TV programs. Even doing a little online shopping. Helen helping Michael with the purchase of a couple of shirts and some pressure pads to improve the fit of his CPAP mask so it didn't leak air in the night and give him crazy eyelid twitches during the day. And, after reading somewhere that a few drops on a cotton ball was a great way to sanitise and assist with skin irritation, she also bought him some witch-hazel. Embarrassed but grateful, Michael returned the favour by finally agreeing to accompany Helen to an art exhibition she'd been dying to see, which proved an evening full of surprises, from the way Michael stuck by her side and squeezed her hand, to who the artist turned out to be. Though to be honest, if she hadn't asked him on their way home last night how he knew Caroline Reid and the crazy women hiding and eating; Helen's not sure he would have told her that they were his sisters.

In much the same way, he never discussed the details of his amputation. From the bits she'd managed to piece together, Helen deduced it was quite recent and traumatic, and that Michael was still in the process of adjusting and would rather not talk about it. Of course, she'd thought, *Who am I to judge? I was only born with thalidomide and can't possibly imagine what it's like to lose something you've already had.* Just the thought of it made her want to squeeze his hand in return.

As their taxi crosses the Iron Cove Bridge at Drummoyne, Michael says, 'Don't worry. My parents will love you.' *Of course, they will*, he thinks. *You're skinny, single and white.* He takes a deep breath. 'We're nearly there.' Then, as if to reassure himself, he adds, 'The kids are great. Weird, but great. Lana's son Sage – Lana's the redhead you met last night – only walks in diagonals and is the sweetest kid. Whip-smart. And George, Shelley's son –'

'Is Shelley the doctor with the eyelashes who told me about her parents' hospitalisations?'

'Technically they're my parents too, and she's not a real doctor, but anyway, her son George is really cool. Sharp and funny as hell.'

'What do you mean technically?'

'Nothing. They're just . . . forget about it.' Michael vigorously rubs lint that's not there from his pant legs.

'Okay. Caroline and Toby seemed nice.'

'They're alright. Stuck-up. Selfish. My mother reckons that's why they haven't had kids and never invite anyone over.'

'But aren't we headed to their place now?'

'Yeah, but that's not what I meant. I mean they never invite family to stuff they invite their friends to. Christmas is just a chance to show off and make the rest of us feel like shit. That's why Dette arcs up. Dette's my youngest sister. She wasn't there last night.'

'So, you've got four sisters?'

'That's what they tell me. The minute Dette arrives, she starts picking on everyone, and it's only got worse since she divorced and moved to this flat on Parramatta Road that's got a giant neon sign flashing right outside and a twenty-four-hour kebab shop downstairs. When she can't sleep, my dad says, *She's a-doner.*'

Helen laughs. 'He sounds funny.'

'Does he? So, Christmas doesn't count. Anyone can do Christmas Day.'

'When was the last time you did it?'

'Are you kidding? I'd never have them at my place. Wait until you see Caroline and Shelley together.'

'Are they close? They seemed so different last night. Chalk and cheese.'

'Yeah, but thick as thieves. They shared a room growing up. They're like those old guys on *The Muppets*.'

'Statler and Waldorf?'

'Yeah! Always in cahoots, looking down on everyone, chuckling to themselves. Dette bought them matching Statler and Waldorf t-shirts last year for secret Santa. First they were furious, then they started fighting over who was Statler. The kids were too young to understand the irony but they laughed even more than the rest of us. It was good. Dette's girls are really funny. Kamelia only walks the perimeters of rooms, and her sisters copy her. It's messed up. Especially when they're in the same room as Sage doing his diagonals. You'll meet them all today.'

'Great,' Helen says.

But Michael's not sure if Helen means *great!* or *great*. He turns to looks at her and is surprised by a surge of anger – a feeling that's acute but so fleeting it's gone before he even has a chance to recognise that he's feeling defensive of his family. No matter how much we think we don't care, our bodies know otherwise.

'So why do you call her Dette?'

'Short for Bernadette. But also, as in debt collector.'

'Why?'

'Because she thinks the world owes her.'

'But you two are close?'

'God no. We shared a room too, that's all. Across the hall from Shelley and Caroline. But we barely spoke.'

'Why not?'

'I don't know. Didn't have much to say, I guess. She talked a bit. Used to go on about her dreams and stuff. But it was so boring, I'd fall asleep. There's only one I remember, because when she had it she used to scream and climb into my bed, and I had to kick her out. It was about our house being sawn in half, right down the middle of the hallway, then loaded onto the back of two flatbed trucks with big red flags reading CAUTION: WIDE, SENSITIVE LOAD.'

'I've seen trucks like that! It always seems amazing to me that you can cut a house in half and then put it back together somewhere else.'

'I suppose. The dream always ended with the trucks driving off in different directions. Pretty dumb, if you ask me.'

'Did you ever discuss what it might mean?'

'Sure. I told her it was stupid. That brick houses can't be cut in half and to go back to sleep. When you meet Dette, just say hello and then stay away from her and French potatoes and you'll be fine.'

'What's wrong with the French potatoes?'

'Nothing. They're my dad's favourite. Excuse me a sec.' Michael leans forwards to speak to the driver. 'It's just up here on the left.'

~

In the kitchen, Caroline's losing it big time.

'Don't tell me to calm down. It's thirty-seven fucking degrees – my whites won't meringue. Get off me!' She elbows Toby, standing beside her at the kitchen island and trying to console her as she whisks and frets. 'My wrists are killing me. Where the hell's Lana? Has she got any fucking Valium? Are you sure the air's on? Look at this!'

She holds up a shaking hand and foamy goo drips from the whisk onto the kitchen bench.

Toby places his hands over Sage's ears. 'Lana's out in the hallway, my love.'

'Oh, for fuck's sake – as if he's never heard the word *fuck* before. He probably knows it in German, too, don't you, Sage?'

'*Ja. Ficken*,' Sage says, laughing.

He is sitting next to George on the other side of the island, the cousins perched on rush stools that don't quite fit beneath the bench, so they sit back from it at an angle that permits Bernadette, parked behind them in her wheelchair, with her broken leg extended on a raised platform, an uninterrupted view of the action.

Tasked with keeping Caroline on schedule, Sage is the time-keeper and George the director. He reads aloud – '*Eleven am: potatoes in oven*' – from the to-do list she's prepared in advance of losing it and forgetting something as the family arrives. Last year it was three kilos of tiger prawns that Toby had bought and peeled after queuing at the fish markets at dawn; left in the back fridge after Wallace walked in and went on and on about how happy it made him and must make Toby, to see Caroline in the kitchen – where she belongs. The year before it was mint in the potato salad. The year before that, butter and jam in the bread-and-butter pudding. And the year before that, the year Viktor died, it was non-alcoholic beverages in the punch.

'*Eleven thirty: baste ham again*,' George reads.

Caroline puts down her whisk and bastes overzealously, in the process tearing the aluminium baking tray and causing sticky orange, clove and maple syrup marinade to leak all over the oven, wrecking its catalytic cleaning system and burning Kurt's tongue when he licks at the scalding mess oozing out of the oven door, down the kitchen cupboard and onto the floor.

Kurt yelps and runs out into the hallway. Caroline asks Toby to do something. 'Can't you help?' she pleads with him, but when he tries to, she yells at him to piss off and check on the air conditioning.

'*Eleven fifty: fix up mascara.*'

'That wasn't on the list.' Caroline licks her fingertips and dabs above and below her lash line, where tears have racoon-ed her eyes.

'I know, but you need to,' George says.

'Bitch!' Shelley calls out.

A twenty-minute car ride with her parents had been too much to bear, so after dropping them off out the front, she whipped around the back and parked illegally in the laneway, then tottered in through the back gate unannounced to lie down on Caroline's new sofa, calling out, 'Bitch!' every few minutes.

Caroline ignores her. 'What Lana's doing in the hallway?' she asks Sage.

'Paris is on the loo. Mum's waiting outside the bathroom, cheering her on.'

'That's great! Isn't that great, darling?' Toby says to Caroline, in a voice that makes her want to kill him. She swats him instead.

Even at nine, four years after Victor's death and after she christened her first cistern, news of Paris using the toilet for a number two was still cause for Bird celebrations. Toby raises his glass in readiness to toast.

'Shouldn't we wait for the flush?' Caroline says, then nods towards her glass on the bench. 'I'm empty.'

'Can I get you a top-up, my love?' Toby places his hands on her shoulders.

'Do you have to ask?' Caroline shrugs him off. 'And don't call me your love, *Christine*.'

Bernadette and Shelley are revelling in the tension. In the Bird family, Caroline and Toby's marriage, while barren and wanky, is still lauded by Leslie as the 'lone success'.

'It's not the heat, it's the humidity,' Dette sneers. 'Either use more elbow grease or throw out your whites and start again. I'll have a top-up too.' She waves her empty glass at Toby.

Whisking furiously, Caroline asks, 'Should you be drinking on meds?'

'Should you be cooking?' Dette quips then bellows, 'Shut up,' at her girls, who are chasing Kurt down the hallway, then she takes a swig and swivels in her chair.

Shelley shouts, 'Bitch!' just as Kurt unleashes the big bark he'd auditioned earlier that morning.

'Whoppy and Lanny are here,' Sage shouts, and he leaves the kitchen to join his cousins out in the hallway.

'Twelve pm: dress pavlovas.'

'Shit. Are you sure the air conditioning's on?' Caroline asks Toby.

'I'm empty too.' Shelley holds up her hand in the shape of a glass.

'Hey, Smell, Merry Christmas,' Toby says. He walks over, stoops to kiss her cheek, then hands her a drink.

'Is it?' she snarls.

'*Twelve oh five pm: take Valium*,' George says, deadpan

'Shut up.' Caroline is trembling.

'But it's on your list!'

'Then go and find Lana and get me some,' she whispers. Unable to look at Bernadette, she says to the ceiling, 'So throw out eighteen egg whites, just like that?'

'Refer to previous comment,' Dette says and moves her hands atop the wheels ever so slightly to reposition her moon boot, so that it's aimed directly at Caroline, who is flitting about the kitchen from the fridge to the stove to the bench, whisking and melting down. Bernadette swivels, trained on her target.

George returns with the Valium and Caroline swallows it. Puts down her whisk. Takes off her apron and begins to carefully set the table with a green-and-white tablecloth decorated with sprigs of holly on the table, then tops it with red gingham serviettes tied with Aunt Martha's Darrell Lea ribbons. then she heads upstairs for a 'Mary Had a Little – lie down', until the Valium kicks in.

'Bitch!' Shelley calls out. 'George, what about your mother? Give me one.'

'Well, I guess that's that,' Toby says. He opens the fridge, finds another carton of eggs and places it on the kitchen bench before removing the mixing bowl and tipping all of the whites down the sink.

~

'Just up here on the left,' Michael says.

'Where those old people are?' the taxi driver asks.

Michael looks and sees Leslie and Wallace, doddering along the footpath, peering into other people's gardens. 'Yep.' He motions with his head to Helen. 'That's them.'

Michael has never seen his parents look this old and vulnerable – as you tend to when you're pushing eighty and out and about in public, in broad daylight, without the camouflage of your own home's decor, geography and your daily choreography – and it baffles him. When had they got like this? One minute they seemed sixty and feisty forever, and now look at them, all stooped and feeble like real old people. He doesn't feel pity. He feels angry. Angry that they look nothing like the beasts that loom in his mind: Wallace the indifferent bully and Leslie, the Lubricator, wielding her feather duster and graphite powder. Who the hell are these little old fogies? And when did they shrink? He can just imagine Caroline saying: *What do you expect when you never see them?* When he last saw them – at Sage's party, four months ago – they seemed alright. Then he remembers that they were sitting down and he wishes they were sitting down now. When they get inside, he'll make sure they are.

'Oh, they look like such dears,' Helen says, breathing a big sigh of relief.

Michael's left knee nudges the centre console as he removes his wallet from his back pocket. He flips it open and Helen, who has the one-handed thing down pat, removes his cash to pay the driver.

When they come to a stop outside of Caroline's, Shelley's car is at the end of the street, turning left – off to find parking, no doubt. Michael supposes she's just dropped off these old imposters now standing inside of Caroline's front fence; Leslie bending over, pinching dead buds off gardenias, Wallace inspecting the watering system. To the right of them a van is hogging the driveway. How it secured the only spot is a mystery to Michael, until he remembers that Caroline said something last night about Dette and a wheelchair and Amir's new boyfriend.

It must be forty degrees, he thinks, wishing he'd worn short sleeves. His left arm, strapped down inside his shirt, sweating and chafing against his big belly, wants to do anything but pretend it doesn't exist. He picks up his empty sleeve and wipes his brow and behind his neck. 'Jesus, it's hot.'

'You're not wrong,' the driver says. 'I'll pop the boot.'

Michael climbs out, glad that he's worn thongs, at least. Over the roof of the cab he catches Wallace's eye and nods.

Wallace panics and, pretending he hasn't seen him, prods Leslie. 'Get a move on, will ya.'

'I *beg* your pardon?' Leslie stumbles, steadies herself, then straightens up to give Wallace a piece of her mind – but stops when she sees Michael standing by the cab. 'Look – Michael's here!'

'Jesus Christ,' Wallace shouts, seeing something – someone – move inside of the van behind Leslie. 'Christ al-bloody-mighty.' He grabs Leslie by both shoulders to save her from seeing what he'll wish to his dying day he didn't. He tells her to hurry up inside and prods her again. 'Get a move on, love.'

'I will not.' Leslie, refusing to budge, pushes him back.

Michael's not sure if Helen heard his father's *Jesus Christ*, but he expects nothing less from Wallace by way of a greeting, so accustomed is he to his father's revulsion he barely notices or even remembers the last time either of them looked at one another directly. Probably the day he killed Trevor, but whatever.

Michael has given up on painting, dogs and caring since the day Wallace accused him of strewing shit across his nature strip, when he was still living at home and selling his bark paintings out the front of Quarry Road, with tiny Trevor by his side. 'That's a rat not a dog,' Wallace had roared. 'And they're not paintings, they're humiliations.' And he had seized Michael in a headlock right there on his freshly mowed front lawn, while Trevor yapped and nipped at his ankles. Leslie, watching from the front window, was quite touched by the sight. She'd always hoped father and son might bond – not quite like this, but seeing them hold each other at all was nice, and it made her reflect on how short-lived her joy had been at the arrival of a living son, who grew too soon into a mirror for Wallace's worst traits. Michael's mere presence seemed a blasphemy in light of Anthony's absence.

Never mind, Leslie had thought. The sight of them wrestling – Michael's head nestled against Wallace's chest, his head tilted back and mouth open at an odd angle, reminded her of him as a baby at her breast, and this, she later claimed, as well as the fact that it was really none of her business, stopped her from intervening to prevent what happened next.

Wallace claimed he was moving – not booting – Michael's paintings out of the way of his sprinklers when his right foot hooked through a canvas and kicked Trevor, yelping, onto the road. Michael screamed. Brakes screeched. Trevor was hit by a Suzuki Jeep and died in Michael's arms.

Michael thanks the taxi driver and opens Helen's door, trying to distract her from his parents' pushing and shoving by telling her how lovely she looks.

'It could be worse,' Leslie whispers to Wallace. 'If it was a leg missing, he'd be hopping. Just ignore what's not there and focus on what is.'

Wallace nods, despite not having a clue what she's on about – he's too distracted by the van. Leslie waves and smiles at Michael and Helen through gritted teeth, gripping Wallace's elbow to stop him from escaping as, after only the briefest glimpse of one of her children (and not even her favourite), she feels herself slipping away from wife towards mother: the role she was born to play. And motherhood makes her feel extra special and teary today, what with Mary, all away in a manger, and her own nest filling. Leslie wipes a tear from her eye just as Helen looks over at her and smiles. Oh, how Leslie Bird loves Christmas Day. Especially when someone else does the cooking and cleaning. Picks you up and parks the car.

'Why the hell didn't he drive?' Wallace asks. He can count on one hand the number of taxis he's taken in his life. 'What's he playing at?'

Leslie tightens her grip. 'Keep your voice down. How do you think anyone can drive with one arm – let alone park around here? Shelley will be lucky if she makes it back by dessert. Pull yourself together and say a quick hello before you storm off . . . Merry Christmas!' Leslie says, beaming at Michael and Helen, who are walking towards them.

As odd as it is to see her only living son posing as an amputee, there's something about the symmetry of him with this slim, smiling woman, something about seeing him coupled and not sucking in his stomach for once, that's rather comforting to Leslie, despite Helen's age and flipper, and the fact that Michael is wearing thongs, displaying a disfigured big toe – the legacy of ignorance and an ingrown toenail, which Leslie thought epitomised her son. He's also wearing a shirt that he couldn't possibly have picked himself, and Leslie wonders if what this woman lacks in limbs and youth she might make up for in other ways. Leslie is suddenly so filled with gratitude for this one-armed woman, she feels she might burst before they even get inside the gate.

Wallace winces and, pulling his elbow from Leslie's grip, places his arm firmly around her waist, to ensure they both remain with their backs to the obscenity taking place in the van on the driveway. As he wonders how to distract the love birds in front of him and get them inside quick smart, he suddenly thinks, *My god, she's right – she's always right, this bride of mine; shoes do make the man and the sight of Michael hopping would have been too much for me to bear.* Though he still hasn't a clue why Michael might have been hopping, he's grateful he isn't and says, 'G'day, mate. Hello, love. Pleased to meet you. Bit of a looker, hey?' He winks at Helen then, noticing her arm, adds, 'Crikey. No one would even notice your little –'

Leslie jabs him and shouts, 'I hope you've brought your appetites?'

'Too right.' Wallace gestures towards the house. 'Shall we go in? CB's cookin' her ham!'

'Technically, it's Margaret Fulton's ham,' Leslie says, 'but let's not quibble. Hello, I'm Leslie – Michael's mother. Aren't you going to introduce us, Michael?'

Michael looks at Helen.

'Hello,' Helen says. 'Merry Christmas.'

Pretty face, Leslie thinks. Modest. Tall. Old enough to be his mother. Clearly besotted. Pity? Still. A second wave of gratitude overcomes her and she has to stop herself from grabbing on to this lovely slim woman. But how to hug someone like this and not bump into something unfathomable? She looks up at her instead, with her soft old face, and smiles.

Michael raises his eyebrows, shocked by his parents' geniality. 'Hey, Lesy. Merry Christmas. Hey, Dad.'

'Let's get inside.' Wallace waves them towards the stairs.

'Oh my goodness, who is this?' Helen squeals, as Kurt pounces down the front steps and jumps up on Michael's leg. She crouches to greet him.

'It's Caroline's new pup, Kurty', Wallace says. 'Weimaraner, isn't he, Les?'

Leslie shrugs.

'Bit of a looker too,' he says to Helen, 'if you don't mind me saying. Would you do me the honour of walking an old fella inside?' Wallace gets on the right side of Helen and holds out his arm. 'Come on in and meet the rest of the family.'

Up the front steps they walk, arm in arm, with Kurt, Michael and Leslie following.

Wallace is saying, 'Now tell me, love, how did you meet my boy?'

Your boy? Leslie shudders, shaking her head. She stops and lets the others proceed. Through the open front door, she can see a rowdy crowd gathered outside the bathroom down the end of the hallway led by Lana and thinks, *Now if you want to claim someone?* Lana is goofing around with Bernadette's girls;

conducting a chorus of, 'Go, Paris, go,' as if being the size of a house with lank cranberry hair, crowned by felt reindeer antlers and captaining a cheer squad to celebrate your nine-year-old defecating in porcelain and not outdoors were all perfectly normal. *Your daughter, Wallace. Your granddaughters.*

Seeing her father, Lana grins, shouts through the bathroom door to tell Paris to keep up the great work, then shuffles down the hallway to greet him, just as the girls spot him and romp towards him, shouting 'Whoppy!'

Wallace is almost levitating with all the female and puppy attention. Leslie listens as he tells Helen how much he loves dogs and that nothing makes him happier in the world than getting on like this with his son. *Like what?* Leslie wants to scream.

'That's lovely,' Helen says, wondering why Michael's said so little about these old dears.

Leslie needs a minute to calm down and forget about what lies ahead – the barrage of old baloney Wallace will bore her with tonight in bed, crowing about how well he and Michael are getting on. And she'll remind him that all they did was say hello to one another, then lie awake all night wanting to kill Wallace after he accuses her of always being so negative. Honestly, she's absolutely exhausted before she's even taken a step inside.

'Leave before your grace does,' Martha used to say.

Oh Martha. A great big lump swells in Leslie's throat at the shocking thought of facing her first Christmas without her beloved sister by her side. Enduring Lana's chafed apron of flesh, Bernadette's gaudy fingernails and snarling, Shelley's eyelashes and Caroline's showing off with no one there to share knowing sideways glances with, let alone leftovers, at their annual Boxing Day autopsy. Leslie clutches her chest and wonders if broken-hearted is a medical term – although 'broken' implies a thing can be fixed, and this grief feels more like a severing.

She has turned to walk down the stairs – to swallow and find a little air and privatey and shade in the stifling heat; to have a little weep and say a few Hail Marys – when she notices something moving in her peripheral vision. She looks more closely. Inside the van parked in the driveway people are . . . Good Lord, Amir is kissing another man.

Heat rises from Leslie's feet or descends from her head – she's not sure which – and gathers in her chest. She can't remember ever feeling this hot or claustrophobic before. Thinks she might faint, she grabs hold of the banister to steady herself, but her hands are so clammy she slips and stumbles a little and lands on the bottom step, jarring her back and hips but not her clotting device, thank goodness.

At least Caroline wasn't exaggerating for once, she thinks, when a gorgeous-looking man – Gavin, she presumes – steps out of the van with Amir and rushes over to help her up.

'Are you comin' in, Les?' Wallace calls to her from the house.

'In a minute,' Leslie calls back, determined to save him from seeing this.

'Suit yourself.' Wallace pats Helen's arm. 'Now, where were we, love?'

'Thank you,' Leslie says, taking hold of Gavin's hands and leaning forwards, trying to heave herself up off the step. But something isn't right and she sinks back down. 'I don't think I can.'

It's not just her hips – she feels queer all over. As if someone were tightening screws either side of her lungs and temples and had zapped her of all energy.

'This heat!' she says, fanning herself. 'I might just sit for a bit.'

'Of course.'

Gavin's hands are the softest Leslie has ever felt and his face – honestly, it's the most beautiful face she's ever seen in the flesh. As he crouches down in front of her, all Cary Grant with his glossy hair, straight white teeth and radiant skin, smelling of lemons and resin, urging her to take her time and catch her breath, she thinks, *Beauty like this must be a superpower and yes, Gavin, I'll do whatever you say (within reason), because you are just so handsome. So handsome.* Leslie thinks good-looking people are their own species.

Amir introduces them, and Gavin laughs and tells him not to be silly, that Leslie needs no introduction, for her reputation precedes her. 'I follow you on Instagram,' he tells her. 'But your pictures don't do you justice.'

'Oh, go on,' Leslie says, blushing, and Gavin does, telling Leslie she's a force of nature and that Amir would never have coped without her and Wallace's generosity and care when Bernadette left the girls. 'Amir told me your love saved them.'

Leslie looks to Amir.

Amir looks at the ground.

'Amir?' she says.

He shrugs.

Leslie is stunned. Speechless. Not a word has passed between them since the divorce was finalised. Her only news of Amir came via Caroline, who'd discreetly kept in touch. Leslie had felt as if she'd got divorced too, after Bernadette banned them all from contacting him, warning them they would not be allowed to see the girls if they did. Truth be told, Leslie had grown fond of him over the months she and Wallace were visiting. Amir was kind and gentle with his daughters. The place was tidier. But he never said a word. Ever. In fact, Leslie had wondered occasionally if Amir might even have blamed them – or, God forbid, blamed *her* – for Bernadette? Silly, she knew, to think such a thing, but in this day and age, with everyone blaming mothers for everything, she wanted to be sure, and so she had mentioned her concerns to Martha once, and Martha had laughed and said, *As if.* Silly, too, to miss Amir as much as she did. And Wallace even went so far as to say he didn't blame Amir one bit for divorcing his big dope of a daughter, who thought nothing of leaving them all high and dry. Which was nasty and unnecessary, but Leslie knew what he meant. She didn't really blame Amir either. In fact, she'd written him a letter saying so; trying to explain how she felt and how she was sorry things had come to this and how she hoped the money from the sale of the house would help him on his way. But he'd never replied, which really bothered her. 'What more do you want him to say?' Caroline had said. 'He couldn't make himself any clearer than not replying, destroying the flowerbeds, taking the money and dating Gavin, could he?' Which made Leslie wonder why Caroline always had to go and twist things.

'Why don't we just help you inside before we hit the road?' Amir suggests. 'Let's go around the back, to avoid the stairs.'

He and Gavin each offer Leslie an arm and she rises to her feet, dizzy, but feeling so much better for having cleared the air (if only in her head).

Gavin asks Leslie what Santa brought her for Christmas.

'Oh, I don't need anything,' she says, nodding towards the house. 'I have everything I need right here. Why don't you both come in and say hello?'

'I'm not sure Bernadette would appreciate that,' Amir says.

'Well, phooey to her – she can answer to me.' Leslie thinks it must be the heat, or Gavin's beauty, or both, making her lose her mind. 'Oh, come on, I insist,' she says, and they make their way down the driveway, around the side of the house, through the gate and beneath the lattice arch, where they stop to admire the pale pink Pierre de Ronsard roses climbing up and over it. And when Gavin asks Leslie about striking and staking, and listens intently to her propagating tips, she feels herself almost bursting with joy.

They take their time strolling arm in arm towards the glass back doors.

~

'You were telling me about your dog running away,' Helen says.

'Too right I was.' Wallace squeezes Helen's hand. 'He damn well broke me heart. Les's too. We had big plans on being a family of three after we married.'

'I'm so sorry to hear that.' Helen squeezes back.

'That's decent of ya. I mean, what more could any man want than the love of a dog, a son, a fine woman and –' A toilet flush interrupts him, then applause erupts in the hallway and moves like a Mexican wave through the house as the Birds cheer Paris's success.

'– and family,' Wallace concludes, nodding towards the ovation, as if it were for him.

He introduces Helen to Lana, and the two women greet one another with a kiss and inform him they met the night before at Caroline's exhibition.

'Well, I'll be damned,' Wallace says. 'I guess it's only a matter of time until we hear weddin' bells!'

Helen and Lana shrug at one another.

When the grandkids ask where Leslie is, Wallace launches into his usual, 'There isn't another woman in the world as wonderful as your grandmother.'

Helen is taken aback, having never experienced anything quite like this family before. Anything as noisy, tender and terrifying.

'There's no one who can keep a house as tidy or talk to anyone,' Wallace continues. 'I tell ya, that woman can even talk to pooftas. Talk to them like they're the same as you and me!'

The girls giggle at the sound of the funny word.

'Poofta!' they scream, and Kurt yaps.

'Don't – *ever* – say that again!' Lana shouts.

'Why not? It's true,' Wallace says, winking at Helen. 'Lesy thinks I don't know about her friend in the city. How she caught the bus to see him after he cut off his willy, poor bloke. I picked her up at the bus stop once or twice. Bob Savage told me all about it. His missus went to the same hairdresser. Mark my words, Leslie Bird is a saint!'

'Say it again, Whoppy!' The girls pull on his sleeve.

'Pooftas, pooftas, pooftas!' Wallace shouts, and shoos them down the hallway into the back room.

They scuttle away squealing, 'Pooftas!' as Leslie, Gavin and Amir arrive at the back door and watch, as squeals turn to screams, when Kamelia slips over in the raw sewage streaming across the floor.

Toby dashes to the door to distract them and welcome them and wish everyone a Merry Christmas. Amir and Gavin smile and excuse themselves, waving at the girls, saying they would see them later tonight as planned. They farewell Leslie, who has a hand over her mouth, gasping at the stench and the sight of Caroline, who appears dazed, sloshing through the muck and asking where her egg whites were.

'Twelve ten,' George announces. *'Toby threw egg whites down the sink, where they appear to have baked and blocked the drains.*

'Twelve twenty: Paris pooed in the loo.'

Another cheer erupts before George resumes.

'Twelve thirty: sewage floods the back room.

'Twelve thirty-four: Lanny arrives.'

'Watch your step,' Toby says, and he moves Caroline aside and holds her by both shaking shoulders. Looking directly into her eyes, he assures her he'll take care of the mess, if she takes care of her mother. 'Deal?'

She nods and draws a deep breath.

Toby grabs a mop and bucket from the laundry and starts mopping the floor.

George scribbles on the schedule: *12.38: Call plumber.*

Caroline aims prayer hands at them both, then takes Leslie by the elbow and starts explaining the meringue poo fiasco, but stops when she feels how hot and clammy Leslie is. She calls out to ask Toby to turn the air up, then steers her mother along a dry patch of floor by the back windows and deposits Leslie on the sofa next to Shelley, saying, 'I'll leave you two to get acquainted,' as Bernadette calls out, 'Don't anyone use the toilet and if you do –'

'Bitch!' Shelley calls out.

Leslie flinches as Shelley tells her how awful she looks. 'You look awful, Mum. Are you alright? You're all pasty and sweaty. Ew.'

'I am, aren't I?' Leslie whispers, then, 'Let it mellow.'

'What?'

'If it's yellow – your father and I do the same thing at home. Saves water. Honestly, it's this heat. I'm melting. My head's – throbbing. My chest . . .' Leslie pulls her top away from her body, inadvertently exposing her belly. She raises a finger to attract someone's attention and says, 'Cold drink?' but everyone's too busy sidestepping shit to notice.

Toby's squeezing his mop into the bucket next to Wallace, who helps himself to crackling straight from the pan before picking up Kurt and letting the dog lick his greasy face and hands. Michael introduces Helen to Bernadette, and Bernadette tells the girls not to pull on their uncle's empty sleeve, which they hadn't noticed, being too busy trying to get themselves to dry land. They shove Caroline's place settings aside and climb onto the dining table, where they huddle with Paris, swapping who-got-what-for-Christmas stories, as George whisks egg whites, Sage slices strawberries and Caroline whips cream.

Still shaking, but calmer now the Valium's kicked in, Caroline feels herself drifting somewhere up near the ceiling – looking around the room, thinking, *There you all are, my achingly wounded Birds! Not who I want you to be, but who you are – my big bonkers family. Jeez! I am one of them.*

She watches Leslie, holding her head, next to Shelley, who cannot abide the heat radiating from her mother a second longer and heaves herself up off the sofa to totter to the kitchen intending to fetch Leslie a Panadol and glass of water, but forgets when Caroline descends, holds out her arms and hugs her, until Shelley softens and hugs her back. Something wordless passes between the sisters, as Caroline peers over Shelley's shoulder at Leslie shooing Kurt away and lifting up her skirt, tucking it up behind her knees then sitting back against the sofa, beating at her chest with a small fist, like she does at mass during consecration. *Such creatures of habit*, Caroline thinks, slapping Wallace's hand away from the pan; suggesting that he make himself useful by stirring the gravy, she turns to find him a fork.

'Fair dinkum?' Wallace says, shocked to be asked to help.

Leslie shakes her head, not just at Wallace but at the lot of them and at the sight of sewage seeping beneath the sofa; her chest constricts violently – as if two continental shelves are colliding – she gasps, 'Look at all that pain,' and then closes her eyes, for the very last time. Without anyone noticing.

Sort of.

Caroline heard her and turns to say, 'Yes, Mother, look at all of us – look at all this pain' – but refrains when she sees how lovely Leslie looks, at rest on the couch. All the tension and anger in her jaw is gone. All the losses and privations endured, absent. And in their place, her cranky old face is relaxed, framed by a huge halo of hair (bless the humidity), her bare legs, belly and elegant organist's ankles are all exposed. In fact, Leslie Bird looks so lovely, so unbelievably unselfconscious, for the very first time ever, that when the others insist on waking her, Caroline tells them to let her be. 'Let's wake her later for dessert,' she says. 'I've made Mum's favourite.'

They shrug and dig in, shouting over the top of one another, passing platters across the table, as Caroline dings her glass with a spoon then twirls one of Aunt Martha's ribbons, explaining its significance, while trying to ignore the sight of most of them on the floor. She delivers a teary little speech about it being their first Christmas without their beloved aunt and raises her glass. 'To our dearest Aunt Martha,' she says, turning towards Leslie, who still appears to be resting. 'To friendship, food and family – oh, and health.' She winks at Shelley, who's mouthing 'wanker' at Bernadette, rolling her eyes at Michael and Helen synchronising good arms, feeding one another, as Wallace – feeling the warm glow of family, ham and gravy – holds his plate out to Caroline, who piles it high with tatties.

'More than his fair share,' Leslie would have said – herself.

Acknowledgements

What is a book? I keep asking myself this question. And what I mean is, not the printed pages that you hold in your hand, but rather what is *this* thing that exists *here* between us? Between writer and reader? This intimate conversation? This provocation? Vexation? Between veritable strangers?

'A book is half you and half me,' I once heard author Toni Jordan say. And it struck me to the core as one of the truest things I've ever heard said about what a book might possibly be. Half what I have given and half what you proffer, by way of your reading. So, wherever you are at this point of your engagement with this book – whether you want to bop me on the head or give me a nod – my first acknowledgement is to you, dear reader, to thank you for spending time with my Birds. I know how challenging they are – God knows they've challenged me – so, I thank you for entering their world and seeking alongside me to understand them and their messy lives. As trying to understand the lives of others, vastly different to our own, is still the best way I know to build empathy. To bring disparate halves together.

To my half then, there are so many parts. So many incredible people who have inspired and encouraged me over the more than a decade it took for my stories to find form. So many who have cheered me on relentlessly. None more so than Tony, my extraordinary husband of thirty-five years, and my beautiful children, Chris, Ben and Jessie, and their amazing partners, Morgan, Chiara and Adam. I am beyond blessed and inspired by the strength and depth of our unions and constant love and support. Tony, your unwavering faith, in what I don't know I'm doing; your cauliflower soup, generosity, and tender loving care of me, our pooches and home front, gave me greatest gift of time and space to write. Thank you so much, Scootch. And to you, dear Jessie, thank you for going above and beyond your already astonishing daughterdom, by being my first and most valued reader and insightful editor, engaging with all of your heart and luminous intelligence, for many long years. I am eternally grateful, Jubot. As I am to you, Mugs, Margy, Marvey; my other half. Bestower of jewels in the stars, faith, love and listening, for believing beyond reasonable doubt, from the very beginning. xx

Speaking of beginnings, there would be no book without my intrepid publisher and cherished friend, Vanessa Radnidge, whose constant unreasonable faith, patience and support has brought the book to life. It was you, dear V, that I was writing to all of these years.

To my mother and father, to whom I have dedicated the book, thank you for everything. For your love and poetry and for befriending my fictional world. Thank you dearly, Mum, for listening so endlessly. We lost my darling dad before this was published, but I had the great fortune to sit and spend many hours talking and reading to him. When I asked him what he thought when I finished reading, he sat very quietly, then said, 'Well, that's a lot of words and sentences and they all seem to go together, so I think you've got yourself a book, CT.'

I think Dad may have felt proud and bewildered. By both the book and me. Coming from a generation who suffered in silence, my need to name things always baffled him. Yet he also understood deeply how naming things helps us to escape them. Helps us to change. As he did, so monumentally.

Whilst Leslie and Wallace have their own entirely fictional lives, pain and secrets, they were conceived by me as way to acknowledge my parents and others like them, who were born in the Depression and grew up in rural Australia. A hard-working generation who sacrificed so much and whose views and values were born of harsh times. A generation who are leaving us and taking their stories with them – forever. The book is a place to hold some of their essence. And my dear Dad's syntax, which courses through my veins.

I am indebted too and grateful far more than I can express here to my writing family. Alice Nelson, for your unflinching faith and love. For the way you entered my work. For gifting me the book *Marine Life*, and for daring me to answer our dear friend Leah Kaminsky's curly questions. Thank you for challenging me, Leah. For friendship, listening and reading: Amanda Skelton, David Carlin and Carol Major, your insights have been invaluable.

Thank you, too, Peter Bishop, Wendy Dunn, Roanna Gonsalves, Robin Hemley, Hayley Katzen, Cate Kennedy, Kathryn Millard, Favel Parrett, Ali Whitelock.

Then there are the friends who've barely read a word of the manuscript but care deeply for you whilst you're writing it. The poet I most admire, the one I keen to, my dearest Kylie Rose. And Tara Winkler, precious piglet. Thank you both for your beautiful generous hearts, for seeing ahead and believing me there. My incorrigible old 5.30 am swimming crew, Nonagenarian Wallace, Doug, Zela and Sam, my cheeky full moon buddy, who never stopped asking after the book. I've spent many years and laps pondering our conversations. Wallace bears no resemblance to my Wallace Bird but allowed me to borrow his name, which lodged in my heart one cold dark winter's morning as we huddled together in our dressing-gowns waiting for the pool to open and I asked him how he still managed to drag himself out of bed and he said that a dunking each day was a way of reminding himself that he was still alive.

To all at Varuna for your constant refuge and welcome. Vera for The Maid's Room. Sheila for nourishment and friendship. The Dark family for your extraordinary generosity and vision. Rod Dark for his banter and rum balls. I still owe you a mower!

My sincere thanks to the incredible publishing team at Hachette. From the aforementioned bobby-dazzler Vanessa Radnidge, to my meticulous editors, Ali Lavau, Deonie Fiford and Emma Rafferty. Goodness only knows how we made it through Covid and my manuscript, but we bloody did it! Caitlin Murphy, Isabel Staas, Heather Lewis, Georgie Carroll, Fiona Hazard, Louise Stark,

Lillian Kovats, Chris Sims, Kelly Gaudry and cover designer Christa Moffitt. And to Pippa Masson for believing, encouraging and helping me to understand 'the through line'.

Lastly, the following books have been by my side and some have found their way into the text, as an ode to their extraordinary authors. *When I was King and Other Verses* by Henry Lawson. *Olive Kitteridge* by Elizabeth Strout. *On Chesil Beach* by Ian McEwan. *The Wig My Father Wore* by Anne Enright. *The Maples Stories* and the entire Rabbit Series by John Updike and everything else he's ever written. Linda Svendsen's *Marine Life*, which is the most potent poetic book. Linda's line, 'In the family's crumbling domestic empire, Irene and Peter's union, has been quietly, and despite tragedy, what our mother calls the lone success' set me thinking for years, about the relativity and contrary perspectives of suffering within families. As did Lawson's line, '. . . But the best men die of a broken heart for the things they cannot tell', which I read and re-read as a child until it became an earwig and to which I added, 'and women and anyone else who has suffered'. Anyone who doesn't have the language or impetus to express their pain or even an awareness that it exists, let alone how it has shaped their lives and the lives of those who came before and will come after them. I see you. I hear you. I understand.

And I wonder in conclusion if perhaps a book might simply be a place for us all to lean in closely and listen to one another, with open minds and hearts, despite our differences?

I can't read maps,
but I know the way forwards is back
here in our arteries,
where our blood accrues the best of us, the worst of us
and begets our stories.

Catherine Therese is an award-winning Australian writer, designer and educator with a lifelong passion for articulating the interior lives of people and places. She has lived and worked widely across the arts in Europe and Australia. Her memoir, *The Weight of Silence*, was a *The Age* and *Sydney Morning Herald* Book of The Year, a Varuna Fellowship recipient and finalist in the National Biography and ABIA Awards. *Things She Would Have Said Herself*, a keening portrait of a world and a woman, Leslie Bird, coming of age and to the boil, is her first novel.